THE SOUL OF
C. S. LEWIS

THE SOUL OF
C. S. LEWIS

A Meditative Journey through Twenty-Six of His Best-Loved Writings

Written and edited by

WAYNE MARTINDALE,
JERRY ROOT, AND
LINDA WASHINGTON

TYNDALE HOUSE PUBLISHERS, INC., CAROL STREAM, ILLINOIS

Visit Tyndale's exciting Web site at www.tyndale.com.

TYNDALE, Tyndale's quill logo, *New Living Translation, NLT,* and the New Living Translation logo are registered trademarks of Tyndale House Publishers, Inc.

The Soul of C. S. Lewis: A Meditative Journey through Twenty-Six of His Best-Loved Writings

Copyright © 2010 by The Livingstone Corporation. All rights reserved.

Extracts by C. S. Lewis copyright © C. S. Lewis Pte. Ltd. Reprinted by permission.

Other contributors: Andrew Apel, Debby Edwards, Karen Erkel, Robert L. Gallagher, Lori Miranda, Rachel Linden Tinon, and Colleen Yang

Livingstone staff: Betsy Schmitt, project manager; Bruce Barton and Dave Veerman, partners

Cover photo used by permission of The Marion E. Wade Center, Wheaton College, Wheaton, Illinois. All rights reserved.

Designed by Erik M. Peterson

Unless otherwise indicated, all Scripture quotations are taken from the *Holy Bible*, New Living Translation, copyright © 1996, 2004, 2007 by Tyndale House Foundation. Used by permission of Tyndale House Publishers, Inc., Carol Stream, Illinois 60188. All rights reserved.

Scripture quotations marked NIV are taken from the Holy Bible, *New International Version,*® NIV.® Copyright © 1973, 1978, 1984 by Biblica, Inc.™ Used by permission of Zondervan. All rights reserved worldwide.

Scripture quotations marked NKJV are taken from the New King James Version.® Copyright © 1982 by Thomas Nelson, Inc. Used by permission. All rights reserved. *NKJV* is a trademark of Thomas Nelson, Inc.

Library of Congress Cataloging-in-Publication Data

Martindale, Wayne.
  The soul of C.S. Lewis : a meditative journey through twenty-six of his best-loved writings / by Wayne Martindale, Jerry Root, and Linda Washington.
    p. cm.
  Includes bibliographical references (p.   ).
  ISBN 978-1-4143-2566-8 (hc)
  1. Lewis, C. S. (Clive Staples), 1898-1963—Meditations. 2. Meditations. I. Root, Jerry. II. Washington, Linda M. III. Title.
BX5199.L53.M35 2010
242—dc22   2010012678

Printed in the United States of America

16 15 14 13 12 11 10
7   6   5   4   3   2   1

Acknowledgments

WAYNE MARTINDALE

This has been a team effort, and I am grateful to have been a part of it. The captain of this team has been Jerry Root, without doubt. He has been the chief conceptualizer and motivator and has done the biggest chunk of writing. For me, encouragement has come mainly, as usual, from my wife, Nita, and daughter, Heather. Nita is my best reader, and Heather, though living with her family in Korea at this time, has continued to inquire into my progress. Of course, both have prayed for me, along with my son-in-law, David, and his and Heather's children, Joshua, Claire, and Jonathan. Who could be more blessed? Linda Washington is a professional writer and editor, and it shows. In addition to writing some of the meditations, she has edited the entire manuscript. Thank you, Linda, for your keen eye and sharp mind. Betsy Schmitt, as project manager, has kept us all encouraged and on track. Cara Peterson, at Tyndale, could hardly have been a more patient and careful editor. And, of course, all of us in the project stand on the shoulders of many contributors to Lewis studies. I have referred mostly for this project to Walter Hooper's *C. S. Lewis: A Companion and Guide* (1988), Jeffrey Schultz and John West's *C. S. Lewis Readers' Encyclopedia*, and Colin Duriez's *The C. S. Lewis Encyclopedia*. Among the many other related books I have dipped into is Bruce Edward's collection of writers in *C. S. Lewis: Life, Works, and Legacy*. Janine Goffar's *The C. S. Lewis Index* was, as ever, a reliable search tool.

JERRY ROOT

I would like to thank Betsy Schmitt of Livingstone for her tireless work in encouraging, guiding, and nurturing the effort to produce this book from start to finish. Linda Washington, Wayne Martindale, and the other contributors were a delight to work with at every stage of this process. I am also grateful to Tyndale House Publishers for its support of this project throughout its development. I owe a great debt to my family—my wife, Claudia, and my children and their spouses: Jeremy and Michelle, Alicia and Zach, Grady and Leanne, and Jeff and Jori. They always freely sacrifice time whenever I set my mind to some endeavor; furthermore, so many of my ideas have been shaped by conversations with them. I am grateful to my sister Kathy, who first told me about C. S. Lewis. Thanks also go to Jean Bilang for her administrative assistance, to my friend Tim Tremblay, and to the Mead Men (Lon, Rick, Chris, Brian, and Dave) for their encouragement and feedback during the process. The general editors would also like to thank Rachel Churchill and the C. S. Lewis estate for their kind permission to use excerpts from Lewis's published work.

LINDA WASHINGTON

As Wayne said, this has been a team effort. I want to thank the Lord, first of all, for his inspiration and help. All of the gilding in this volume comes from him. I also want to thank Jerry and Wayne. What a privilege to work on a book with these two! The world is indeed better because they are in it. (And that's not just hyperbole.) Betsy, as usual, has been long-suffering. You couldn't ask for a better project manager. And the rest of the contributors— Andy, Debby, Karen, Rob, Lori, Rachel, and Colleen—deserve a round of applause for penning their God-inspired insights into Lewis's great works. Thank you, Cara Peterson, for your hard work in editing this manuscript. I also have a great church (Wheaton Agape Fellowship) and many great friends who prayed for this project to be completed. Thank you, all!

Contributors

ANDREW APEL is a freelance writer who makes his home in Illinois. He has worn various hats, including that of a climbing instructor for individuals with special needs, a teacher, a youth pastor, an assistant minister, and a first lieutenant in the Army Reserves Chaplain Corps. He is one of the coauthors of *The Amazing Bible Factbook* (Time Inc. Home Entertainment).

DEBBY EDWARDS credits more than thirty years of reading C. S. Lewis's works as a key influence in her career and her love for literature, as well as in her belief in Christianity's undiminished integrity and relevance. Debby is a California-credentialed teacher of English whose undergraduate and graduate work was done at the University of California, Irvine. She and her husband, Robby, run a private tutoring business, specializing in language arts for high school and college students.

KAREN ERKEL discovered the writings of C. S. Lewis through The Chronicles of Narnia while in high school. She has attended various Lewis conferences and classes, including a weeklong seminar at The Kilns, Lewis's home, near Oxford, England. Karen, a freelance writer and speech/language pathologist and educator, graduated from California State University–Long Beach with a master's degree in communication disorders. She lives with her husband and daughter in Laguna Hills, California.

ROBERT L. GALLAGHER is an associate professor of Intercultural Studies at Wheaton College Graduate School, in Wheaton, Illinois. He holds master's degrees in education, theology, and missiology and a doctorate in intercultural studies from Fuller Theological Seminary, in Pasadena, California. He has worked as an executive pastor in Australia and a theological educator in Papua New Guinea and Oceania.

WAYNE MARTINDALE is a professor of English at Wheaton College, Illinois, where he regularly teaches courses on C. S. Lewis. He has authored the recently published *Beyond the Shadowlands: C. S. Lewis on Heaven and Hell*, coedited with Jerry Root *The Quotable Lewis*, edited *Journey to the Celestial City: Glimpses of Heaven from Great Literary Classics*, and written numerous other chapters and articles on Lewis. He and his wife, Nita, have taken students to many Lewis sites in England and Ireland. They have also lived and taught in China.

LORI MIRANDA is a native of New York and has studied literature, writing, and intercultural studies. She has traveled to numerous countries and is currently preparing for career missionary service in Colombia with Latin America Mission.

JERRY ROOT wrote both his M.Div. thesis and Ph.D. dissertation on Lewis. He has taught college and graduate courses on Lewis every year since 1980, as well as lecturing on Lewis throughout America and many other countries. He is coeditor of *The Quotable Lewis* and is the author of *C. S. Lewis and a Problem of Evil: An Investigation of a Pervasive Theme*. He teaches at Wheaton College in Illinois and at Biola University in Southern California.

RACHEL LINDEN TINON loves adventures, travel, wandering in nature, cooking, and learning new things. She is a graduate of Huntington University and Wheaton College. The author of the novel *Circle of Shadows*, she lives with her husband in Seattle, where she is working on her next book.

LINDA WASHINGTON is an author and editor living in Carol Stream, Illinois. She has written several books, including *Just Plain Mel* and *It's Me, Leslie* (Tyndale House); *Inside The Lion, the Witch and the Wardrobe* (St. Martin's Press/Griffin, coauthored with James Bell and Carrie Pyykkonen); and *Secrets of the Wee Free Men* (St. Martin's Press/Griffin, coauthored with Carrie Pyykkonen). She is currently working on a fantasy series for teens.

COLLEEN YANG is a freelance writer, musician, and graphic artist living in Carol Stream, Illinois. She is one of the coauthors of *Along the Way*, a book of inspirational stories (Jordan House), and *The Amazing Bible Factbook* (Time Inc. Home Entertainment).

Table of Contents

WORDS OF GRACE

Introduction

JOHN GODFREY SAXE WROTE A POEM about six blind men who encounter an elephant. They have heard of elephants, but their blindness has kept them from ever seeing one.

The first man grabs a leg and says, "An elephant is like a tree trunk."

The next feels the side of the elephant and says, "No, an elephant is like a wall."

Another, holding onto the tail, exclaims, "An elephant is like a rope."

Another still, holding the ear, says the elephant is like a very large fan; the fifth, grasping the tusk, says the elephant's like a spear. The last man, holding onto the trunk, declares the elephant's like a giant snake.

Of course, each has an accurate experience of the elephant, but no one has a complete experience of the elephant. To enlarge their individual understanding, each of the men must trust that the others are neither liars nor imbeciles, even though his own experience seems to contradict those of the others. An attempt to enter into the wider experience of the others with empathy and a teachable heart will reveal complexities that increase perspective and add to a larger and growing understanding.

The Soul of C. S. Lewis: A Meditative Journey through Twenty-Six of His Best-Loved Writings is an attempt to gain a wider grasp of the world and life experience. It is primarily a book of reflections building on quotations from C. S. Lewis and connecting each to Scripture passages.

What value does such a book have?

ENCOURAGING REFLECTION ON C. S. LEWIS'S THOUGHTS

Lewis's literary output has benefited readers all over the world. His clarity of expression and power of depiction have allowed him to speak to deep human needs and bring understanding to life's complexities. This book encourages a closer read of his ideas. The quotations within have been chosen from a wide range of his books, and a select group of writers have added their own reflections on them. These are not last words but rather models, helpful stimulants nudging readers to explore more deeply and apply more widely the wisdom and insight within each quotation. The writers are very familiar with Lewis's work, and their voices are united by a singular devotion to God and a passionate love for him that they desired to express in words. Their reflections give a vocabulary for quests of the mind as well as feelings of the heart.

C. S. Lewis wrote that "reality is iconoclastic"—that is, it is idol-breaking. At any given time, we may acquire a good image of God from a book, a sermon, or a conversation with friends. Yet the once-helpful image of a moment, if clutched too tenaciously, will begin to compete against the possibility of our having a healthy, growing understanding of God. In order to develop vitality in our faith and to gain a better grasp of who God is, we would be wise to reflect on our current conceptions lest we become idolaters, worshiping a notion of God rather than God himself.

Theology is not God; it is simply—and hopefully—the best idea we can have of him at any given moment. Vital faith is growing faith, full of thought and meditation. Challenges to any belief we hold will reveal the resiliency of true faith, which stands up to scrutiny. Of course, some challenges will require us to jettison prejudices once held as truth. That is part of growth. On the other hand, appropriate defense or modification of beliefs we hold will lead to a more robust and dynamic knowledge of God. We each have biases influenced by our age, culture, language, fears, and insecurities. To break out of the dungeon of a narrow perspective, we would do well to listen to the voices of others, relax our suspicions, and truly hear what they are saying.

In *The Soul of C. S. Lewis*—whether in the quotations of Lewis or the reflections on what he wrote—you will see the good intentions of flawed human beings whose meditations reveal a primary desire to love and serve God, following him as best as each is able. Hopefully, this will encourage the reader to increase his or her devotion to God and reading of his Word in a way that is honest and dynamic.

HIGHLIGHTING THE INTERCONNECTEDNESS OF SCRIPTURE AND LIFE

The Bible is a book for all time, the ultimate book for every age. The wisdom that inspired it anticipated the unique questions and challenges of each generation. God gave a book that would potentially equip all individuals and cultures to successfully navigate any rough waters they might experience; in fact, tragedies often come from neglecting its wisdom. No human interpreter of Scripture could ever fully mine its riches; nevertheless, there are some whose gifts of observation and clarification can be a source of great benefit. C. S. Lewis was such a person, and for a variety of reasons he makes a good guide for others.

First, Lewis's vision of life does much to encourage a worldview that is integrated and harmonized, reflecting life as it is truly lived, with all its complexity and rich texture.

Second, Lewis's insights help to widen the horizons of his readers. He would not allow his readers to cram human experience into the cramped space of compartmentalized or formulaic thinking. His God and the universe made by God are too big for such arrogance. Consequently, Lewis prodded his readers to look at the world with a sense of continual wonder, awe, and worship. Again, though there are no last words, this does not mean there are no *sure* words. Lewis was no relativist; he realized that truth can be discovered and known even though no one will ever explore it fully. God's truth never changes, but like his mercies—which are new every morning (see Lamentations 3:23)—something new of the height and depth and width of his truth can also be experienced in a fresh way.

We can think of faith as a tree, which does not give up its interior rings as it adds new ones; so, too, a vibrant faith will be a growing, dynamic faith. Core beliefs do not have to be abandoned while one assimilates a more robust understanding. Or we can think of growth in the knowledge of God like emerging concentric circles: if one looks inward at the knowledge acquired at any given moment, the increases could result in unhealthy pride. But if one looks out from the growing perimeter of what is known, this will always reveal—in greater and greater proportion—how much there is beyond our present knowledge that we know virtually nothing about. This should encourage us to live lives of reflection and produce in each of us a sense of wonder and awe.

Third, Lewis is a good guide because he was aware of his own fallenness and need for grace and mercy. The idea of human dignity was never far from his mind, nor was the idea of human depravity. Consequently, there was in Lewis a profound sense of his weakness and need. This, too, is a good model for anyone who wants realistic benefit from a life of contemplation.

KNOWING MORE OF GOD: TAKING ADVANTAGE OF LEWIS'S VARIETY

The Soul of C. S. Lewis: A Meditative Journey through Twenty-Six of His Best-Loved Writings draws inspiration from both Lewis's fiction and his nonfiction. Lewis was always the rhetorician: he wrote to persuade. He had a vision of life that was very God-centered. This being so, he recognized that the presence as well as the purpose of God were embedded in the very fiber of the universe. Consequently, the world as one encounters it day after day is far more complex than any explanation. The best descriptions would seek understanding from a variety of perspectives, and Lewis's richly diverse fictional and nonfictional forms provide different ways of seeing the world.

Lewis's descriptions and definitions are clear. His vocabulary and background with languages enabled him to be precise, minimizing ambiguity. Nevertheless, some things cannot be reduced to mere definition or be fully grasped by a propositional statement. In fact, the word *definition* literally means, "of the finite." We define things by virtue of their limitation and their function. It is finitude that makes definitions possible; a thing must be small enough to wrap words around it so as to distinguish it from other things if it is to be defined.

The question then arises, How do we define God? If he is infinite, then he defies simplistic and limited description. Even Jesus, speaking of the Kingdom of Heaven, proclaimed that "the Kingdom of Heaven is *like* . . ." (Matthew 13:24, italics added). He resorted to the use of similes and other figures of speech, parables, and stories. In other words, the most robust attempts to understand the character and nature of God will use a variety of modes of expression. Lewis wrote in over a dozen genres, employing both fiction and nonfiction to make his point. The reflections in this book seek to draw on the kind of breadth used by Lewis in the hopes that it will aid the reader's growth in the knowledge of God.

But there is another reason for including Lewis's fiction, in particular, in these reflections: Lewis himself was well aware that reason has its own weaknesses. If someone makes a bad decision or a questionable moral choice, reason is not so quick to challenge the choice and call the individual to repentance. It is more likely that reason will be marshaled by the will to make a host of rationalizations and excuses for the bad choice. Consequently, bad moral choices can lead to intellectual blindness; cleverness is no synonym for ethical clarity. The apostle Paul wrote in Romans 1:18 that "wicked people . . . suppress the truth by their wickedness." Lewis recognized that reason, having been employed to justify a bad choice, will stand like a dragon guarding access to the heart, thus keeping one's understanding darkened. Sometimes story alone makes it possible to get past a watchful dragon. The Scriptures themselves bear witness to this truth, for when Nathan the prophet had to confront King David about his sin (see 2 Samuel 12), he used story to do it. He knew the king was likely to resist an outright declaration of his wrongdoing. But the prophetic word, recast in a story, hit the target.

Each of us has certain blind spots we are likely to guard with rationalizations. Hopefully these reflections, using Lewis's nonfiction as well as his fiction, will penetrate deep into the soul of the reader.

THE IMPORTANCE OF REFLECTION

Why is reflection so important? Because the nonreflective person is at risk and will likely prove troublesome to those around him. This cannot be too heavily underscored. Each of us has embedded weaknesses that, without reflection, can remain hidden from us until life's circumstances squeeze them out like toothpaste from the tube. Undoubtedly, awareness of human weakness led Socrates to remark in the *Apology* that the unexamined life is not worth living. Perhaps a cautionary tale will highlight the dangers of a nonreflective life.

Herodotus, a Greek historian, tells a particularly applicable story, later retold in Plato's *Republic*. It is the story of Gyges, a Greek shepherd in the ancient city-state of Lydia. One day while tending his flock, Gyges endured an earthquake that opened a fissure in the ground before him. Curiosity drove him to investigate, and to his surprise, he found a body in a cavern below. Noticing a gold ring on the hand of the corpse, Gyges took the ring and fled. Another earthquake occurred and closed up the fissure. That night, gathered with other shepherds, Gyges ate his dinner around an open fire. Looking at the ring, he gave it a nervous twist, after which he heard the other shepherds exclaim, "What happened to Gyges? He was here among us only a moment ago and now he is gone!" Quickly, Gyges gave the ring another twist only to hear the shepherds declare, "Oh, Gyges, there you are! How is it that you were able to depart from us and return to our midst so quickly and without detection?" From this Gyges realized the ring was magic and gave its wearer the power of invisibility. With this power Gyges seduced the queen, killed the king, and set himself up as the ruler of Lydia.

American philosopher Mortimer Adler used this story while teaching. After telling the story, he would ask his students to reflect on it. If they had the opportunity to buy this ring, would they do it? And if they bought it, how would they use it? Reflection reveals that such power in the hands of mere mortals will inevitably corrupt. Of course, elements of the idea that unbridled power is likely to corrupt is a common theme. Its conveyance through a ring of invisibility is masterfully woven into the narrative of J. R. R. Tolkien's *The Lord of the Rings*, a story Tolkien read to his friend C. S. Lewis as he wrote it. Elements of the story of Gyges also appear in Shakespeare's *Hamlet* and in many other stories as well—including Lewis's own magic rings concept within the Narnian Chronicles. Writers throughout history have reflected on man's corruptibility. Very little imagination needs to be employed before realizing that each of us will possess many "rings of Gyges" throughout the course of a lifetime.

Every act of will, every choice we make carries an expression of the power to assert ourselves in ways that can move us one step, in a lifetime of steps, toward the corruption of our character or the positive development of it. Every decision carries in it a ring of Gyges.

THE SCHEME OF THE BOOK

The Soul of C. S. Lewis: A Meditative Journey through Twenty-Six of His Best-Loved Writings draws quotations from Lewis's writing. Limits of space as well as the authors' and editors' predilections narrowed the scope of these readings. Nevertheless, each of the twenty-four chapters of this book highlights a particular Lewis source (or two, in a few cases). Each chapter is introduced with a one-page summary; this is followed by ten Lewis quotations and ten reflections. Each reflection ends with a Scripture verse that affirms the concept from Lewis. The chapters are bundled in groups of six within a topic that loosely generalizes a theme running through each book in that part. The four parts of the book are Pilgrimage, Temptation and Triumph, Going Deeper, and Words of Grace. Each of these has an introduction explaining its general theme.

The purpose of *The Soul of C. S. Lewis* is to encourage reflection and thought. The selections are short; nevertheless, they are designed for the reader's personal growth. Lewis opened up more than just wardrobe doors. To read and reflect upon his work biblically is to take a journey of discovery. He opens a door into the liberal arts—those liberating arts that allow people to think well in order to live well. He leads them into new worlds of ideas and imaginative discoveries. Furthermore, Lewis integrates his faith into the learning process, and this, too, provides a significant model for a reader's own reflection.

PILGRIMAGE

O ne of the great themes in literature is that of pilgrimage, or quest. The great books of classical tradition reverberate with this theme— books such as Homer's *Odyssey*, Virgil's *Aeneid*, and Dante's *Divine Comedy*, to name a few. Such works often feature people who are aware that they are on a journey through time and are moving toward a significant end, though that end may be unarticulated or unclear. The commonality of these sorts of books indicates that the human heart pulses with longing for a secret place: Christians believe that this is ultimately a longing for heaven and that our lives are a quest to find that which will satisfy the deepest longings of our souls. It seems as if men and women throughout time, and in whatever region of the globe, have sensed deeply that something is missing—and each one longs to find it. The pilgrim impulse causes some to leave the familiar to find satisfaction in the unknown. For others, long estranged from things familiar, this desire manifests itself in the pain of homesickness and the desire to look for missing pieces in places all but forgotten. Still others never leave the regions of their birth; nevertheless, they know the desperate ache of longing to be fulfilled.

C. S. Lewis seldom put pen to paper without hinting at this perpetual tug at his heart, if not writing about it explicitly. Perhaps one of the reasons for his lasting appeal and his wide reading audience is that his words "scratch where we itch" the most. We all know longing at some level, and we are all on a kind of quest to find our hearts' deepest desires.

Like Lewis, French physicist and philosopher Blaise Pascal famously identified this longing as ultimately being a thirst for God. Pascal once wrote that there are only two kinds of reasonable people: those who seek for God because they do not know him and those who seek to know him better because they do. In the quotes and reflections found here under the topic Pilgrimage, it is the goal of the contributors to highlight this dominant theme in Lewis's writing. These meditations, taking their inspiration from Lewis, underscore the longing that ultimately nudges us toward fulfillment in Christ.

It is God who awakens desire in us, that through it he might woo us to himself. But as George MacDonald, a man Lewis regarded as an unofficial teacher of his, once noted, sometimes desire awakens us just enough to feel a woe. We are aware that we want to satisfy our hearts' desires, and we set out on our quest. We may find ourselves wandering many years before we begin to read the clues properly. It may be that we sense a longing like that of Abraham of old: we are on a quest for the City with foundations and whose architect and builder is God. This is the quest, or pilgrimage, for *place—in fact, for a particular place*. It is the longing for heaven. Another author who heavily influenced Lewis, his contemporary G. K. Chesterton, wrote that we are "homesick in our own homes." Every time we lay our heads down on our pillows, we lay them down in a foreign land. St. Augustine said we are pilgrims in our own land; Peter wrote in the Bible that we are aliens and sojourners while in our earthly existence. And as the old gospel song declares, "This world is not our home; we're just a-passing through."

But C. S. Lewis reminds his readers that there are other kinds of longings as well. There is a longing that sets those who experience it on a pilgrimage for the *perfect relationship*. We all know what it is like to feel lonely; we long for community as much as the thirsty long for water, as much as the hungry long for food. Loneliness confirms the fact that we are sociological beings made for relationship. But isn't it also possible to feel lonely while living under the same roof with others we know and care for, others whom we know love and care for us? The fact that we can feel this kind of loneliness, too, does not prove anything; yet it may strongly suggest we were made for relationship no mere human can satisfy. This kind of longing also sets us on a pilgrimage to find our perfect mate; that is, to find ultimate, relational satisfaction in Christ.

Another kind of longing mentioned by Lewis is the longing to have fixed what is broken inside us. None of us live to the level of our own convictions. Each of us, when honest, must be aware of some level of deficiency. We might work hard to right an injustice in one quarter and yet rationalize that same injustice when doing it ourselves. This reveals that there is something not quite right within us, and in our best moments, we do so long to have all the broken bits mended once and for all. This longing also sets our hearts on pilgrimage as we begin looking for someone to mend us and make us whole.

Lewis's books speak to his readers because they address something as common and yet profound as longing and the spiritual pilgrimage each finds himself or herself on. The readings in this section of the book speak generally to pilgrim longings and in this way address the pilgrim in each of us.

CHAPTER I

The Pilgrim's Regress

THE FIRST BOOK LEWIS WROTE after his conversion to Christianity was *The Pilgrim's Regress: An Allegorical Apology for Christianity, Reason, and Romanticism.* Lewis believed that the first problem in life is trying to fit reason and romantic longing together; that is, to fit the deepest aspirations of the heart with intellectual rigor. As a young man, Lewis believed that Christianity could not reconcile these competing parts of his life. In 1926 he published *Dymer*, a narrative poem featuring a young man questing for the Real. His pilgrimage ends in tragedy. Even so, the questions that permeate this earlier work are also present in *The Pilgrim's Regress*, but in the latter Lewis was able to supply the answers he was beginning to find in his newly acquired Christian faith.

The Pilgrim's Regress is the story of a young boy named John, who is raised in a city called Puritania. The religion of his world is dominated by pretenses, superstitions, inconsistencies, and legalisms. One day John has a vision of an island far, far away. This vision awakens in his heart a deep sense of longing, which he thinks is for the island. In time John will learn that the object of this desire, though awakened by the island, is actually for something much greater. So he sets out on a quest to find his heart's desire.

The route he takes on his quest has mountains to the north: these mountains represent reason. To the south are swamps representing romanticism. John finds himself continually off track, drifting toward a rationalism that denies his heart's longing or else a romanticism that slips into swamps of subjectivism and sentimentality. It is not until he encounters a hermit who represents history that he is able to sort out his longings. And it is not until he encounters Mother Kirk, who represents the church, that he is finally able to reconcile his reason with his longing. In seeking the object of his desire, John works through what Lewis called the dialectic of desire. This refers to a process of tethering the heart to some object expecting fulfillment from it only to be disappointed, then moving on to some other object and further disappointment. So, too, John tethers his heart to objects that only disappoint in the end. He longs for something greater than these objects, which can do little more than merely awaken his desire.

After his own conversion, Lewis noted that if we sense a desire that no earthly object can satisfy, that does not prove the world a fraud. Perhaps the things in this life only awaken the desire and set us on a pilgrimage till the true object of our deepest longing, which is God, is finally found. Lewis called this longing *joy*.

This book, Lewis's only allegory, is his first explicitly Christian book. It is also his first attempt at Christian apologetics, and it's worth noting that he uses fiction to make his point. Fiction was always part of Lewis's rhetoric when it came to apologetics. He knew that some things are more likely to be grasped with the imagination, and he wrote with this kind of appeal. Finally, it is important to remember that much, though not all, of *The Pilgrim's Regress* is autobiographical.

1 *It seemed to him that a mist which hung at the far end of the wood had parted for a moment, and through the rift he had seen a calm sea, and in the sea an island.* BOOK ONE, SEC. II, P. 8

The protagonist of *The Pilgrim's Regress* is a young man named John, who finds himself on a pilgrim quest. He has seen a vision of an island, and it set his heart to longing. But as we go on to learn, he only thinks it is the island that is the object of his desire, when in fact he longs for something far more important. Because the island became the occasion of his heart's awakening, it takes on special significance for him.

Longing is one of the most important of Lewis's themes. Its importance is not acknowledged merely because of the frequency with which Lewis writes about it but also because it speaks of something deep inside every man, woman, and child. Augustine observed that God made us for himself, and our hearts are restless until they find their rest in him.

John's island stands for countless other possibilities. Lewis's reference to mists parting and to the revelation of the island is significant. Things may often go unnoticed until an almost mystical moment when they appear to us with utmost clarity. And with the clarity comes an awareness of realities beyond our reach. Anything might awaken longing in us, and it is easy to deceive ourselves that the thing that awakens desire is actually the thing desired. In fact, the things that teach our hearts to ache with longing are, by virtue of their mutability—their temporariness—unable to sustain the longing they awaken. These things are given to woo us *to* God, not to serve as replacements *for* God. They are things that moth and rust destroy and thieves break in and steal (see Matthew 6:19-20). Only God, the great lover of our souls, can satisfy us forever. Only God can awaken our hearts to long for him, and only in him will we not be disappointed. First loves, distant lands, dreams of the future—earthly objects will often raise expectations that they cannot satisfy. Only God has the capacity to satisfy forever.

You will show me the way of life, granting me the joy of your presence and the pleasures of living with you forever. PSALM 16:11

You say that because you are a Puritanian. . . . You say that because you are a sensualist. . . . You say that because you are a mathematician.

BOOK THREE, SEC. VIII, P. 50

There is a common manner of speaking that should be characteristic of any sincere Christian: refusing to take the ideas of others seriously, choosing to dismiss others and calling them names rather than considering the content of their speech or the substance of their ideas. Lewis was particularly attuned to this problem and refuted it wherever he encountered it.

Who, after all, can really claim to know very much? Considering the number of books available in any given bookstore and the magnitude of information stored in those books, who could ever claim to be familiar with even a very small amount of this material? And considering how little any of us know, it is irresponsible to dismiss other people and relegate their ideas to mere categorization by names such as Puritan, Sensualist, Liberal, or Conservative. We must first hear someone's point of view and understand it. Then, if we disagree, we should use well-crafted arguments to show exactly why we disagree. If we cannot do this, we should simply remain quiet until we've learned enough to speak intelligently.

We are often too quick to dismiss those whose ideas are different from our own. Perhaps we lack the life skills necessary to listen patiently to the ideas of others. Perhaps we have not yet learned to treat all who are made in the image of God with the dignity that is due them. Perhaps we neglect to cultivate the kind of rigorous thinking necessary to engage in a fair-minded, lively debate. Nevertheless, an inability to hear and engage well with dissenting voices will guarantee that we stay stuck in our prejudices.

All Christians should be quick to acknowledge that we are pilgrims on this earth together—and nothing is more stifling to pilgrim longing than holding fast to one's prejudices. If we are sojourners, it is good for us to discover a world wider than our own experiences. If our views do not stand up to scrutiny, our position is not strengthened by simply calling those we disagree with unkind names. If our point of view is capable of standing up to those of others, we must begin by listening to what others say and then answer them with both reason and patience.

It is in honest debate, rather than name-calling, that we can measure the strength of our beliefs. Paul wisely warned Timothy to avoid contentiousness, through gentleness and consideration for everyone. Rather than prejudice and unfair judgment of others, let us embrace honest engagement with others and so allow the confidence of our own faith to grow.

They must not slander anyone and must avoid quarreling. Instead, they should be gentle and show true humility to everyone. TITUS 3:2

3   *"I would strongly advise you to take this turn. . . ."*
"Where does it go to?" asked John suspiciously.
"It takes you back to the main road," said Reason.

BOOK FOUR, SEC. IV, P. 65

John's quest to find the island he has seen in a vision will actually turn out to be a pilgrimage to God, for the island has awakened in him a desire that cannot be fulfilled by any earthly object. Such objects can awaken this unquenchable desire; only God can satisfy it.

The journey takes John along a path with mountains to the north, which represent Reason, and swamps to the south, which represent Romanticism—a symbolic polarization reflecting Lewis's belief that the first problem in life is to find concord between the head and the heart. Often, John gets off track. If he vectors toward the mountains, he finds Reason rigid and lacking heart, and he drifts toward legalism. If he vectors toward the swamps, his heart drifts to sentimentalism and sensuality. He must stick to the main road in order to satisfy his deepest desire.

Lewis is making the point that John's story is the story of every man and woman. As the old hymn observes, each of us is "prone to wander." Our reason may fail us and our hearts lead us astray. Each of us can drift toward one of those forms of rationalization that become self-referential—a tendency to interpret all life from one's own perspective.

But to create one's own sense of reality, to spin justifications from ourselves, is to live like a spider within its web, using others and justifying our bad behavior. On the other hand, drifting toward heartfelt impulses that are unresponsive to good sense can also lead to self-referential behaviors that, in the end, hurt us or those around us.

When we vector away from God and lose our pilgrim way, we must find our way back. Confession of wrongdoing and a cry for mercy are always appropriate at such times to put us back on track. God loves us and wants us to come to him, to follow him with constancy. He knows the tendencies of our hearts to drift and our reason to rationalize. Even so, he seeks to woo us back to him.

If we confess our sins to him, he is faithful and just to forgive us our sins
and to cleanse us from all wickedness.   1 JOHN 1:9

4   *There has been this gorge, which the country people call the Grand*
Canyon. But in my language its name is Peccatum Adae.

BOOK FIVE, SEC. II, P. 74

While John is on his pilgrimage, he learns of a great chasm that separates man from God. He is told that this chasm is called *Peccatum Adae*, which means "Sin of Adam." This is a reference to the first sin—in other words, what some call the doctrine of original sin, which asserts that somehow, by virtue of the first sin ever committed, the whole human race is infected.

Some have wrongly assumed that the doctrine is an attempt to blame all men and women for the act of someone who lived a long, long time ago. Nothing can be further from the truth. If you are struggling with this idea, simply try to live a perfect life. Therein lies the problem: no one *can* live a perfect life. We all make mistakes; we all live inconsistently with our own convictions. The doctrine of original sin is one established not so much to project universal blame as to explain a universal phenomenon: that each of us tends to live in a manner that is inconsistent and troubling.

As G. K. Chesterton observed in his book *Orthodoxy*, this is the only theological doctrine that is empirically verifiable. In other words, history is full of examples. Perennial wars, genocides, human slave trafficking, corporate greediness, political abuse, and powermongering all testify to the unsavory truth that something has gone wrong with the species called humankind. But, though the pages of history are useful in showing examples of sin and regrettable acts, looking there may keep the idea of sin remote. In fact, an honest appraisal of our own hearts should be enough to supply plenty of evidence.

The doctrine of original sin is only man's errant brushstroke across a wider canvas of God's goodness and grace. Furthermore, God did not leave humanity marooned in its predicament. After all, awareness of one's deep need to have mended what is broken inside is also an incentive for a pilgrimage. In Lewis's allegory, John ultimately finds grace. So, too, we can find grace in Christ.

Just as everyone dies because we all belong to Adam, everyone who belongs
to Christ will be given new life.   I CORINTHIANS 15:22

5   *All prayers always, taken at their word, blaspheme,*
        Invoking with frail imageries a folk-lore dream. . . .
        Take not, oh Lord, our literal sense, but in thy great,
        Unbroken speech our halting metaphor translate.

BOOK EIGHT, SEC. IV, P. 139

No matter what we think about God, he is bigger and better than our biggest and best thoughts about him. This is a constant theme in Lewis's writings, and it is an important one for the Christian pilgrim to keep in mind. After hearing a sermon or reading a book or after deep conversations with friends, we may understand something about God we did not understand before. Pieces of the puzzle come together and our vision of God may expand significantly. Nevertheless, if we hold on to this vision of God too tightly, it will compete against a growing understanding: the image once helpful becomes an idol because God is far bigger than our best thoughts about him.

This idea of pursuing God as he is rather than how one might want him to be is one that appears often in literary history. Baron von Hügel, a philosopher of religion, wrote about levels of clarity, warning, "Beware of the first clarity; press on to the second clarity."[1] Similarly, Robert Browning wrote, "Then welcome each rebuff that turns earth's smoothness rough."[2] When we think we have everything figured out, our conception of the world is nice and smooth and round. But the world is not smooth; it has texture and complexity, peaks and valleys. As Augustine wrote, "The house of my soul is too small. Enlarge it, Lord, that you might enter in."[3] And Stephen, accused of speaking against the Jerusalem Temple, told his accusers they could never contain God in a box.[4] Like Stephen, Lewis also understood that God is big; he is always kicking out the walls of temples we build for him because he wants to give us more of himself.

God is greater than our best thoughts of him, than our best prayers. Lewis recognizes in this fact a source of encouragement to the spiritual pilgrim: no matter how far beneath God our best thoughts of him, no matter how feeble our prayers, he still accepts us and receives to himself those very thoughts and prayers, accepting us as we are.

"Heaven is my throne, and the earth is my footstool. Could you build me a temple as good as that?" asks the LORD. "Could you build me such a resting place? Didn't my hands make both heaven and earth?" ACTS 7:49-50

6

[T]here sat a hermit whose name was history.

BOOK EIGHT, SEC. VII, P. 143

The word *allegory* comes from two Greek words: *allos*, which means "another of a same kind," and *agora*, which means "marketplace." This is where, for example, we get the word *agoraphobia*: fear of the marketplace. The book of Acts makes it clear that the apostle Paul's pattern when coming to a city was to preach first in the synagogue and then in the *agora*. So, taking the two words together, an *allegory* is a story configured in such a way that one thing is told in a different "marketplace." It provides a fresh way of looking at something and permits some things to be seen that might be missed if seen only from an old, familiar way.

In this particular allegory, Lewis's pilgrim, John, comes to a hermit who represents history. This hermit, as history, is a person less likely to get riled and easily upset about the current commotion. He takes the long view of things and seeks to understand them in their proper context. He seeks to understand the complexities that feed into any given moment rather than rushing to ill-informed conclusions. The hermit also shows that history is the source of tradition and speaks with an authoritative voice.

G. K. Chesterton observed that two mistakes can be made about tradition. The first is to simply accept all things traditional as if they were a last word on what should be thought, said, or done. This view allows the past to trump the present and hinders any kind of real development. It is the view that says, "We've always done it this way." The second mistake we can make about tradition is to flat out reject the voice of history and its traditions simply because its word is old and weary with the dust of the past. This particular mistake prevents accessibility to the benefits of the past. On the contrary, Chesterton says, "tradition is only democracy extended through time." Every time someone sits down to consider a matter, there is wisdom in many counselors; but it is equally wise to give a vote to those who have gone on before.[5]

These things happened to them as examples for us. They were written down to warn us who live at the end of the age. I CORINTHIANS 10:11

7

That is always the way it is with stay-at-homes. If they like something in their own village they take it for a thing universal and eternal, though perhaps it was never heard of five miles away.

BOOK EIGHT, SEC. VII, P. 146

How easy it is to think one's current understanding is fully accurate. How easy it is to think that one's social set—church, school, friends, community, political party, associates—have a fairly full grasp of matters and that those who are outsiders are simply ignorant all the way through. How easily we are given to such violent overstatements that quickly categorize others and rapidly dismiss them. One thing is for sure: each of us tends toward our own provincialism; we must break out of it in order to gain a wider view of the world.

Ever wonder what keeps a person so stuck in a rut and so unwilling to listen to other possibilities? No mere mortal gets a last word about anything. This does not mean one cannot have a sure word about some things. The fact that we can have a sure word keeps us from becoming a relativist; the fact that there are no last words preserves us from the pretense of supposing we have a complete and utter grasp of any particular matter. We may believe in the existence of absolutes, but we must never say, "I understand this particular matter absolutely; there is nothing about it I fail to understand. All applications that might ever occur concerning this thing I have fully grasped."

Nobody has achieved an intelligence to rival that of the Divine Omniscience. Human limits should keep all from such arrogance. Every truth known can still be plumbed more deeply and applied to challenges not yet considered. Furthermore, human fallenness should act as a reminder that anyone can twist the truth. Consequently, it is all too easy to imagine that those who fail to see things as we do are necessarily flawed or deficient. But the way of honesty—which can be taken as a synonym for humility—should keep us from such provincialism.

Some people have missed this whole point. They have turned away from these things and spend their time in meaningless discussions. They want to be known as teachers of the law of Moses, but they don't know what they are talking about, even though they speak so confidently. I TIMOTHY 1:6-7

8   *What is universal is . . . the arrival of some message, not perfectly intelligible, which wakes this desire and sets men longing for something East or West of the world.*   BOOK EIGHT, SEC. IX, P. 151

Many, like C. S. Lewis, have suggested that humans are in a sense amphibious beings—both physical and spiritual. We live our lives straddling two worlds. We have something in common with the animals—being creatures of flesh—and with the angels—as spiritual beings. Consequently, the mere life of the flesh cannot fully satisfy. These characteristics of our humanity often lead us to pursue the desires of the spirit against the desires of the flesh. Most often, however, we pursue things of the flesh at the expense of our deepest aspirations, which are spiritual and nonmaterial. Some people seem to live their whole lives in quest of earthly interests. But others, perhaps out of frustration, realize that earthly things cannot fully satisfy the cravings of the heart. Lewis understood this; he experienced it in his own pilgrimage to faith and wrote about it in nearly all his books.

In *The Pilgrim's Regress* the central figure of the narrative is awakened to desire spiritual things. This awakening of desire sends him on a spiritual quest, which he discovers can be satisfied only in Christ. Perhaps all of us long for something or, better, someone apparently beyond our grasp. Perhaps all of life is lived in the presence of one seeking to break through to us; and yet, in the midst of our earthly pursuits, our senses remain dull to experiences alerting us to tether our desire to Christ. Many things in the world God has made call us to attend to him. Nevertheless, the things in our world and in our lives that might awaken desire can also become objects we pursue to fulfill our longing. God gives gifts to woo us to him; he does not give these gifts as replacements for him.

There is wisdom in being sensitive to the wooing of God in our lives. His dawn is always breaking everywhere, all around. Let him illumine the paths that may be followed to him.

Awake, O sleeper, rise up from the dead, and Christ will give you light.
EPHESIANS 5:14

9 *[E]vil is fissiparous. . . . The walls of the black hole are the tourniquet. . . . It is the Landlord's last service to those who will let him do nothing better for them.* BOOK TEN, SEC. IV, P. 180

Writing about evil in this way, Lewis is drawing on the language of nuclear physics. What he means is that evil's tendency, in the manner of atoms splitting apart into fragments, is toward widespread rippling effects; left unchecked, evil will continue on ad infinitum. How can such a force be stopped if it is fissiparous? Lewis believed that hell is the tourniquet God placed on evil saying, "You can go this far and no further." Thus, he believed that even hell is a testimony to the grace of God.

Divine punishment is seldom something like natural disaster—God could use nature to fulfill his purposes, but he tends to act in a different way. We look at natural calamity and call it tragedy, but the tragedy is not in the act of nature; nature is doing only what nature does. Human ignorance or indifference to nature is what makes natural events appear to be tragic. In fact, the tragedy rests in human folly.

It is a timeworn truth that God's way of punishing is to give people what they want. Augustine, for example, develops this idea in Book I of his *Confessions*. God's laws are fences that define playgrounds where God reveals his intentions for his children as fair and good, because his design is for our ultimate happiness to be found in him. He gives gifts to be used in ways that ensure our fulfillment and prevent our abuse of them. It is only after having stepped outside God's intentions for us that we begin to feel the pain and loss that accompany our foolishness, the realization that we could have avoided that loss by obedience. Yet there is grace to be found even then, for in that moment we can turn to him for forgiveness, grace, comfort, and healing. But what if someone refuses to turn to God, preferring instead to control his or her own destiny? God in his justice does not contradict the gift of free will by removing its consequences. He allows the errant pilgrim to follow his or her own way throughout eternity.

Lewis believed that evil will one day be permanently encapsulated and that hell will be its immovable boundary. Hell is the tourniquet on evil, a prison for the eternally incorrigible. It is an asylum for those who say, "Better to reign in hell than serve in heaven." God gives them what they want.

Evil people don't understand justice, but those who follow the LORD understand completely. PROVERBS 28:5

10 *[I]t is fools they say who learn by experience. But since they do at least learn, let a fool bring his experience into the common stock that wiser men might profit by it.* AFTERWORD, P. 203

Anyone who has been inclined to pray, "Lord, discipline me," need pray it only once. Should God answer such a prayer, the consequences would certainly result in some hard lessons. In his *Devotions*, poet John Donne observed, "No man hath affliction enough that is not matured and ripened by it, and made fit for God by that affliction."[6] Much can be learned by suffering the consequences of our own poor choices. But of course there is another, far less painful, way to learn. It may be best to pray that God would keep us from hard hearts and stiff necks so that, wherever possible, we might learn vicariously from the mistakes of others.

Lewis's Afterword to *The Pilgrim's Regress* speaks of this vicarious learning. His humility is evident as he offers up his own experience—which may or may not have been born out of foolishness—so his readers might learn and grow from it. Perhaps what he writes here has more application than is noticed at first.

In fact, it may be that all literature provides material fruitful for vicarious learning. It is possible to benefit from the life's lessons of hundreds of literary characters on display in untold numbers of books. Anyone's spiritual pilgrimage will be benefited by careful attention to these characters. The same could be said of historical examples and also of the stories set forth in the Scriptures. Those who are most attentive to texts of any kind can hope to avoid the traumas of others by learning from these texts and applying such wisdom to their own lives.

The suffering of some of these characters recorded in literary texts, such as Miss Havisham in Charles Dickens's *Great Expectations*, reveals the consequence of long-nurtured bitterness. It may be possible for us, observing this outcome, to turn our own suffering into kindness and empathy. So, too, a Scrooge-like character who has grown miserly and stingy from what a good life has given him may be the occasion for us to learn, by contrast, magnanimity and kindness. Secondhand lessons can protect us from enduring unnecessary emotional heartache, but we must all learn some lessons the hard way. And God's guidance—and grace—are there so all sorrows may be turned to joy and so hope may be accessible to all.

Such things were written in the Scriptures long ago to teach us. And the Scriptures give us hope and encouragement as we wait patiently for God's promises to be fulfilled. ROMANS 15:4

CHAPTER 2

Surprised by Joy

C. S. LEWIS OFTEN DEALT with a particular theme in a variety of literary genres. If a thing is worth saying, it may well be worth saying more than once and in many different ways. This is certainly true when it comes to Lewis's own pilgrimage to faith. After *The Pilgrim's Regress*, Lewis wrote a second autobiographical book, *Surprised by Joy*. This one followed the first by more than two decades, and it takes a propositional rather than an allegorical approach. Yet its story has many of the same elements as the earlier work. Like John, the pilgrim in *The Pilgrim's Regress*, Lewis highlights his own journey to faith in *Surprised by Joy*. For example, he notes the awakening of his desire when, as a child living in Belfast, Northern Ireland, he watched his brother bring into the nursery a toy garden on the lid of a cookie tin. On its surface the event seemed so arbitrary, and yet something of the transcendent broke through and set the young boy on a quest in search of the object of this undefined desire. Lewis subtitled this autobiography *The Shape of My Early Life*. One could say that it refers to the shape he seeks to bring to his life as he selects out of the numerous details of his early days those events that helped him make the most sense of his experience.

Not all he experienced was good. Though raised in a Christian home—he was baptized by his maternal grandfather shortly after his birth—Lewis rejected his childhood faith due in part to his mother's untimely death when Lewis was only nine years old. He also had a deformity of his thumbs that made him awkward and, one can imagine, subject to ridicule at school; this awkwardness and his sense of personal struggle led to an early pessimism. He was not comforted by his childhood faith in light of life's complexities and sadness, and in time, he entertained grave doubts about God's existence. So it was that early in his life Lewis became an atheist. *Surprised by Joy* chronicles his pilgrimage from there to faith, offering us a firsthand look at how he was able to resolve his doubts and find substantive answers to his questions in a way that led him to embrace Christianity. Coupled with his quest for intellectual answers, his spiritual journey was driven by a deep sense of longing for some object the likes of which always seemed to elude him until he came to Christ.

Surprised by Joy, though uniquely Lewis's story, allows the reader to discover bits and pieces of his or her own story. As Lewis chronicled the events that shaped his life, we are free to revisit and reflect on our own life-shaping events. Each of us has a context into which we were born, a family history that becomes our own. The region or city in which we were brought up feeds into a sense of self and marks our understanding. The schools we attend, the friendships we form, the books we read all contribute to the life of the soul. Lewis would not let his readers forget that this is so. As we read Lewis, we are reminded of another idea as well: these events that shape us also send us on a spiritual quest; they mark our discovery of a world that, properly understood, reveals that God has been present and guiding us all along.

1

Any kind of academic growth begins with curiosity. In *The Theaetetus*, Socrates observed that all philosophy (that is, "love of wisdom") begins with wonder, another word for that trait. Even personal growth is dependent on curiosity. Our capacity to understand others is so contingent on our being curious about them—seeking to understand their loves and disappointments, their joys and sorrows—that there is a certain tragedy about the life of one who has never cultivated curiosity. If we are to truly know others, we must seek to see them as different from ourselves. And certainly an interest to grow and learn from the host of mistakes any human being is bound to make during a lifetime is enhanced by a sense of curiosity, as well as the desire that the same mistakes and their painful consequences can be avoided in the future. When Lewis wrote of his own spiritual pilgrimage in *Surprised by Joy*, he was aware of a host of benefits that can come from reflecting back over his life, and he thought this reflection could benefit his readers as well.

But in what way did Lewis indicate that objective curiosity can have a cleansing effect?

There is a kind of curiosity that may not be helpful. This is a curiosity that seeks to see things only in light of their utilitarian value; that is, to see things and value them only if we find them useful to advance our own personal interest, rather than seeking to know and understand things as they are in themselves. This is especially true on the personal level. If we are self-referential in our understanding of life, we will tend to be utilitarian in our relationships—spinning our sense of reality out from ourselves as a spider spins, only to catch others in our web and feed on them for personal interest.

But awareness of oneself and one's weaknesses can, when properly followed, lead to empathy and understanding of others. We need to cultivate an objective curiosity, an ability to see something outside ourselves and seek to understand others as they are. This kind of curiosity can become cathartic, for it cleanses us of our self-referential ways and allows us to see and value others as they are—creatures made in the image of God.

God blesses those whose hearts are pure, for they will see God. MATTHEW 5:8

2

With my mother's death all settled happiness . . . disappeared from my life. . . . [N]o more of the old security. It was sea and islands now; the great continent had sunk like Atlantis. CHAP. 1, P. 21

Seas and islands are common images in C. S. Lewis's work; he wrote about them perhaps most famously in *Perelandra* and in *The Voyage of the* Dawn Treader. Nevertheless, in *Surprised by Joy*, in which Lewis writes of his pilgrimage to faith, the image takes on special significance.

Lewis's mother died when he was only nine years old. Naturally, it was a defining moment in his life, and in *Surprised by Joy* his description of that event is telling. His mother had been the source of stability in his early childhood. She was like a continent for him, solid ground on which he could depend. And then she died. His imaginative description—as if he were on the legendary lost continent of Atlantis when it sank—reveals the truth that he discovered as a boy: in a world full of mutability, even what appears most stable can be taken from us. If we put our trust utterly in these things, we are giving up our hopes and aspirations to what Lewis called "false infinites." These things can tempt us to believe that they will always be there for us, that to have them is to be fulfilled. In reality, life looked at this way is destined to disappoint. Stability can be found only in Christ.

When Lewis wrote *Perelandra*, the second book in his science fiction trilogy, he made this point through the story. Perelandra (Venus) is a planet whose Eve has not fallen. Its great temptation is not the same as in the Garden of Eden—eating a forbidden fruit. Instead, the planet full of seas and floating islands has as its command that no one must remain overnight on the continent. Night must be spent on the floating islands. One cannot help but think Lewis is saying to his readers that the pseudostabilities of our "fixed ground" are merely "false infinites." We should enjoy whatever it is we find in our world—but not expect from anything the permanence and stability that only God can bring to life.

Whatever is good and perfect comes down to us from God our Father, who created all the lights in the heavens. He never changes or casts a shifting shadow.

JAMES 1:17

3 *Divine punishments are also mercies, and particular good is worked out of particular evil, and the penal blindness made more sanative.*

CHAP. 5, P. 77

Can God bring good out of the bad we suffer and endure? Lewis thought so. This may be true if the suffering is the consequence of our own bad choices or the consequence of the choices of others. Think of the worst thing that ever happened to you. Now, think of the next worst thing. And the next. And the next still. How far can you go before the well of your memory runs dry? Now begin to recollect positive things you've experienced: the times you've had great conversations with friends or the times you've laughed, read a great book, been given a gift, taken joy in giving a gift to another, noticed a sunset or a field of wildflowers in the spring. This second list can go on and on. The bad experiences we endure are relatively infrequent compared to the abundance of good ones that surround us on every side. It is certainly evident that over a lifetime even those who are the worst off experience far more good than bad. And in the hour of death, for most people the pain, significant as it may be, will remain relatively brief compared to a lifetime in which joys abounded. Nevertheless, we do endure painful experiences. Yet, could Lewis be right: can it be possible that good could be made from the bad?

Think back again to that list of bad things you have endured. The question is, have you seen any of them work out for good? Perhaps there was no resolution to the circumstances themselves, but have you learned valuable lessons through the pain? If, given time, you have seen good come from some of the bad you have experienced, then you have reason to believe that, given eternity, all the bad could result in some kind of good. If, arguably, the worst thing that ever happened in human history was the Cross, and if God turned that event on itself and through it brought about the greatest demonstration of his love and grace to us, then we have even more reason to believe he can take all the pain we endure and bring some good out of it.

Everyone is bound to suffer during life's pilgrimage. Yet everyone is invited to take hope in the fact that good can come from the bad we experience.

O LORD, do good to those who are good, whose hearts are in tune with you.
PSALM 125:4

4 *All joy reminds. It is never a possession, always a desire for something longer ago or further away or still "about to be."* CHAP. 5, P. 78

Lewis used a certain word as a kind of shorthand to describe the deepest longings of the soul; that word is *Joy*. He used it in reference to the awakening of desire for some object that is never fully given, yet the longing leaves in one an insatiable desire. Ultimately, that longing is for God, and it can be awakened by anything one experiences in a world made by him, a world that has evidence of his presence all around. There is much to suggest that faith pilgrimages begin when this longing sets out to look for its proper object.

God woos us to himself by giving us gifts, but he does not want us to attach our hearts' desire to the gift rather than the Giver of the gift. We encounter beauty and look for its Creator, even if initially our quest is only that we might offer deep thanks for the glory we have seen; beauty sets us on a pilgrimage that ultimately leads to God. We have our heart awakened by a first love, and we think it is the beloved we long for most. Though human relationships can be fulfilling, only God ultimately satisfies. Properly understood, relational loves acquaint us with the Joy that sets us on a pilgrimage to find our ultimate first love.

An awareness of our own moral shortcomings and the longing to have fixed what is broken in us also awaken a quest that can be satisfied only in God. The desire to make sense out of our experiences and discover purpose in our lives hints at ultimate truth. So, too, the desire to be safe awakens in us the desire for heaven—our ultimate safe place. Even the love of nature may reveal a longing to draw near the God of nature and be aware of his nearness.

All these common human experiences that awaken in us a sense of longing, an awareness that a deeper desire beckons, Lewis called Joy. No one will ever find the heart's true desire until he or she finds it in Christ. He is the object of that deepest desire. Our lives will not be fulfilled until they are fulfilled in him.

The LORD is my strength and shield. I trust him with all my heart. He helps me, and my heart is filled with joy. I burst out in songs of thanksgiving. PSALM 28:7

5 *He cares only for temples building and not at all for temples built.*
CHAP. II, P. 167

Another major idea in C. S. Lewis's writing is this: "Reality is iconoclastic." In virtually every book he wrote, this idea appears in one form or another. What does it mean? An iconoclast is a person who breaks idols. The idea as Lewis presents it is that any idea of God formed after hearing a good sermon, reading a book, or having an eye-opening conversation with friends, though a helpful image in the moment, can become problematic over time.

Images we have of God if held onto too tightly compete against our having a growing, expanding understanding of God. Such an image, over time, becomes an idol. God is in the business of kicking out walls of any temple we build for him, because he wants to give us more of himself. He cares nothing "for temples *built*; only for temples *building*." God is big—bigger than any of our best thoughts of him. Therefore, our ideas of God must be dynamic, not static; our ideas of him must be constantly on the stretch in order to better approximate a true understanding of him. This concept is not new with Lewis; he stands in a long tradition. As has been mentioned earlier, Augustine wrote of the house of his soul being too small, and he prayed that the Lord might expand it and enter into it. Welcome those experiences in life that help you see things as they are, rather than how you would have them be.

Again, Baron von Hügel, philosopher of religion, wrote that we must beware of what seems clear at first, pressing on to the "second clarity," and, we could add, to the third and fourth clarities as well.[1] God is bigger than our best thoughts about him. If our estimation of him does not grow, it will not be long before we will be worshiping a God of our own making and severing fellowship with all who fail to see things our way. Furthermore, we will paint "Thus saith the Lord" across all our own opinions as we drift toward idolatry. Lewis would have none of it—and neither should we.

Job replied to the LORD: "I know that you can do anything, and no one can stop you. You asked, 'Who is this that questions my wisdom with such ignorance?' It is I—and I was talking about things I knew nothing about, things far too wonderful for me." JOB 42:1-3

6 *My imagination was in a certain sense, baptized.*

CHAP. 11, P. 181

Like curiosity, the imagination is a valuable asset for one's spiritual pilgrimage. But, as with all other gifts, the imagination can be used for good or ill. It can be used to engage in creative enterprises that improve the lot of humanity, or it can be used in ways that make for destruction and havoc, causing harm to us and to others. Lewis recognized that his own imagination needed to be "baptized"—that is, redeemed for good purposes. In his book *The Discarded Image*, Lewis distinguished three kinds of imagination.

First, there is what he called the transforming imagination. Lewis cites English poet William Wordsworth as an example. This is not a positive kind of imagination, for it transfers onto people and circumstances those things that we want to see, for good or for ill, and usually for ill. This transference—which is engaged in what psychologists call projection—is the most damaging form of the imagination because it isolates us from others and keeps us from connecting with the world as it is. In time, we find ourselves living in a delusion from which we need to be awakened.

Next, there is the penetrating imagination. In various essays, Lewis notes that Shakespeare and Dante are examples of this; no matter what lies before them, they seek to understand it more deeply than first glance will allow. Penetrating imagination seeks to plumb the depths of a thing and grasp its intricacies and complexities.

Last, Lewis speaks of the realizing imagination, which he says is characteristic of medieval literature. Medievalists tended to look outward, using their imagination to realize their place in a wider world. This form of imagination opens up to the world around it with wonder and awe.

In Lewis's own pilgrimage and in the midst of his reading, he came across George MacDonald's *Phantastes: A Faerie Romance*—and he said his imagination was baptized by the reading of it. In other words, Lewis suggests that his imagination was employed in a kind of sacramental activity whereby he was having a first awareness of the presence and grace of God in his life. He would not have described it this way at the time, but in looking back, he knew this was so. Imaginative literature, perhaps more than meditative nonfiction, enabled him to grasp some ideas that could hardly be thought of in any other way. All true pilgrims would do well to cultivate the disciplines of the imagination in a way that breeds spiritual life and health. In its various ways, the imagination allows us to penetrate spiritual realities more deeply, as well as to realize more widely that we live always in the presence of God.

Fix your thoughts on what is true, and honorable, and right, and pure, and lovely, and admirable. Think about things that are excellent and worthy of praise.

PHILIPPIANS 4:8

7   *I thought [God] projected us as a dramatist projects his characters, and*
I could no more "meet" Him, than Hamlet could meet Shakespeare.

CHAP. 14, P. 223

Before Lewis became a Christian, he did not really think it was possible to have an encounter with God. He had reasoned his way to theism but, as he reports in his autobiography, he believed he could not meet God personally any more than Hamlet could have met Shakespeare. When Lewis became a Christian, he realized his Hamlet-Shakespeare analogy was still a good one. In fact, Hamlet as a character in the play could never climb out of the play to meet the author. But, it might be possible for Shakespeare to write himself into the play and make sure Hamlet had the opportunity to meet him. Lewis says this analogy does express something like what happened at the Incarnation, when God the Son wrote himself into the play of human experience and made possible the introduction between the Creator and the created.

As good as this analogy is, it will still not convince some. One can imagine a situation in Elsinore, where things have been very strange of late. The king has died at the height of his strength. The crown does not fall to the crown prince as it should have, but to the dead king's brother. Furthermore, the queen spends no time in grief for her fallen husband but immediately marries her brother-in-law—the new king. Hamlet has been acting strange (though some say there is a method to his madness); and Ophelia is a basket case. Suddenly a little man with a pointy beard shows up in court wearing Elizabethan tights and a ring in his ear. Everyone asks, "Who are you, and how did you get past the guards so as to show up in the king's court?" He answers, "Oh, I am Shakespeare, your creator. You are all living in a play I have brought into existence. I know things have been difficult lately, but I can assure you, given a bit more time, all the wrongs will be redressed and set right." And hearing this, the whole court dismisses Shakespeare as a madman.

The Word became human and made his home among us. He was full of unfailing love and faithfulness. And we have seen his glory, the glory of the Father's one and only Son. JOHN 1:14

8   *I examined myself with a seriously practical purpose. . . . I found what appalled me; a zoo of lusts, a bedlam of ambitions, a nursery of fears, a harem of fondled hatreds.*   CHAP. 14, P. 226

An honest pilgrimage is one full of self-discovery. Unfortunately, not all we might discover about ourselves is pleasant to know. Let's face it: to be human is to be a mixed bag of that which is dignified and that which is depraved.

A Christian view of what it means to be human must account for possibilities of both goodness and badness. Surely we are good by nature; we are made in the image of God, and that is good. For this reason, even the worst of criminals in Christian societies are given a fair trial and assumed innocent until proven guilty. But no Christian view of human nature is complete without the realization that we are also bad in our nature. The badness is an encroachment on a nature that was made good by God but in which something has obviously gone awry.

Christians can, by virtue of their creed, account for both the dignity and the depravity of humanity. The Christian doctrine of God recognizes that God could not make anything essentially bad. The Christian doctrine of Christ recognizes that, while fully God, he was also fully human and that sin was not found in his humanity. So sin is not essential to what it means to be human.

Furthermore, the Christian view of anthropology sees four categories of people in Scripture: Adam and Eve before the Fall, Adam and Eve and their progeny after the Fall, Christ in his humanity, and people in their glorified state in heaven. Sin is present in only one of these categories, so sin cannot be the essentially defining characteristic of what it means to be human. Nevertheless, a prerequisite to the restoration of dignity to our lives requires an honest assessment of what sin and self-will operating without respect to God's right to rule and reign in our lives will do to us. Before Lewis's conversion to Christ, he saw the true condition of his life and his desperate need for the grace of Christ. Honest self-examination is an important part of any pilgrimage that leads to God.

Examine yourselves to see if your faith is genuine. Test yourselves. Surely you know that Jesus Christ is among you; if not, you have failed the test of genuine faith.

2 CORINTHIANS 13:5

9

God is to be obeyed because of what He is in Himself.

Spiritual pilgrims are quick to discover, as Lewis did, that there is much they do not know or understand. But if these pilgrims come to believe in an omniscient God and accept his revelation in Scripture, then obedience by God's grace becomes an essential part of their lives. No amount of human knowledge, even when it approximates full capacity, is complete. Nevertheless, if the commands of God are given by virtue of his infinite knowledge, then every act of obedience accesses for the faithful the benefits of God's omniscience. Obedience makes it possible to live life better than we could live it on our own.

God is to be obeyed because he is God and sovereign over all. And yet, according to the teachings of Jesus, obedience is ultimately predicated on a realization that this one and only sovereign God loves his creatures. He said to his followers, "If you love me, obey my commandments" (John 14:15). Love comes first; obedience follows. Those who think obedience is the means to gain God's love live in spiritual impoverishment all their lives. But those who obey in response to God's love gain great benefit.

Lewis also noted that obedience is one way in which God enables his true followers to mend their brokenness. Obedience is a splint God places on a broken life so that it might mend. To put it another way, obedience is the way of rehabilitation that God has chosen for us so that we might mature into Christlikeness. The splint is not something to be seen as permanent, but it is necessary until we choose to do naturally what a Christlike person would want to do.

Blaise Pascal wrote in *Pensées*, "Two laws suffice to rule the whole Christian Republic better than all the laws of statecraft": love God, and love your neighbor as yourself.[2] People who love God do not need to be commanded to worship him. People who love their neighbors do not need to be told to avoid lying, cheating, and stealing for they would naturally be honest and generous. But until that love dominates our choices, it is obedience that moves us in the direction that best resembles what loving (that is, Christlike) acts look like.

If you love me, obey my commandments. JOHN 14:15

10

*I was driven to Whipsnade one . . . morning. When we set out
I did not believe Jesus Christ was the Son of God . . . when we
reached the zoo I did.* CHAP. 15, P. 237

Not everyone can remember the exact moment when he or she could say,
"Before this I was not a Christian, and after that moment I was." Lewis
could remember such a moment in his life. For years he had wrestled with
questions surrounding belief in Christ. He had many doubts; but in time
he came to the very threshold of belief. It was after a late-night talk with
his friends Hugo Dyson and J. R. R. Tolkien that Lewis put aside his last
objections to faith. A few days later on September 28, 1931, while riding
to the Whipsnade Zoo in the sidecar of his brother's motorcycle, Lewis
became a Christian.

Lewis's moment of conversion was unique to him; fortunately, it is not
necessary to come to faith while driving to a zoo. But there are many common things that can be observed about Lewis's experience. First, his faith
came at the conclusion of a well-reasoned process that took many years.
Faith and reason are not the same things; one can be convinced by the
reasonableness of Christianity and still not make a commitment. Still, it is
wise to be reasonable in matters of faith. Second, though Lewis wrestled
with spiritual matters for years, it was still due to the faithful testimony of
two friends whereby he finally made a commitment. The importance of the
personal witness of others cannot be neglected. Lewis would eventually do
what he saw modeled by Dyson and Tolkien, for he would also tell others
of Christ. Third, Lewis was willing to make a decision to follow Christ.
As some have described, it was not a single decision but more like a decision to make every decision for Christ from that time on. In other words,
Lewis made a lifelong commitment to Christ. Finally, the place where he
made his commitment was not significant to the decision. Commitments
can be made to Christ at church, at home, while alone, or in conversation
with friends. Lewis was, of all places, in the sidecar of a motorcycle. The
omnipresent God can be found anywhere.

*If you confess with your mouth that Jesus is Lord and believe in your heart that
God raised him from the dead, you will be saved.* ROMANS 10:9

CHAPTER 3

Till We Have Faces

TILL WE HAVE FACES is perhaps Lewis's most haunting book, and it has by far the most complex themes of any book he wrote. It is the retelling of the myth of Cupid and Psyche.

Lewis believed that good stories often draw from the wealth of stories that have preceded them. In the retelling, an author has the benefit of an old and beloved motif as well as the liberty of embellishment in order to feature some particular rhetorical interest of his or her own. Lewis wrote a few essays explaining the medieval practice of this form of embellishment. It can be seen in something like the story of Troilus and Cressida— Chaucer told his story drawing from Homer's *Iliad* for source material and from Italian poet Giovanni Boccaccio's *Il Filostrato* for character sources; eventually, Shakespeare would also embellish the story further for the theater. This is a practice still used today. *Romeo and Juliet* becomes *West Side Story*; *Pride and Prejudice* becomes *Bridget Jones's Diary* by Helen Fielding; *Oliver Twist* becomes the 2007 film *August Rush*. With a true embellishment, it is not that the author of the new story lacks creativity and must therefore plagiarize; rather, the new author, recognizing the power of the old story, makes it the vehicle for the new embellishment. There is a rhetorical point to make.

So it is with Lewis's employing the old myth of Cupid and Psyche as a vehicle for some freshly developed insights. His embellishment gave occasion for him to write of two things in particular. First, he wanted to explore how the relationship between two people is affected when one has a spiritual transformation and the other does not. To what lengths will one go to make the other see from his or her point of view; to what degree will the one with the unshared experience project delusion on the other? Second, Lewis explored the way even such an exalted theme as love could become tyranny in the hands of well-meaning men and women.

True love seeks to enter into the world of another and to give according to the real need of that other. But if our selfishness is unchecked, our love can morph itself into a controlling self-interest, justifying its tyrannies as concern for the beloved when in fact it is utilitarian in its designs. Perversions of love are not empathetic; they seldom care for another beyond temporary value and interest. So it is in this haunting book, as Lewis holds a mirror to his readers' faces and makes us notice what might otherwise go uncorrected.

1   *I will accuse the gods. I will tell all as if I were making my complaint of him before a judge.*   BOOK I, CHAP. I, P. 3

Till We Have Faces begins as Orual, the queen of Glome, lodges a complaint against the gods. The story is set in the time of the Grecian empire; Glome is a barbarian kingdom on the outskirts of Greece. Orual's life has had its privileges as well as its liabilities. But Orual is angry at the gods. The reader will learn that it is because her beloved sister, Psyche, has been taken from her by Cupid. Orual is convinced Psyche's circumstances could not possibly be improved by this arrangement, for the queen doubts the intentions all others have for Psyche except her own. She is even blind to what Psyche herself might prefer. Orual's love is poisoned by self-interest masked as love, when in fact it is tyranny. Rather than see the truth of her own misguided view of things, she sees anything that counts against her will as an injustice and an outrage. Orual is convinced that she understands how the universe ought best to run. Her point of view is self-referential. She even thinks she knows better than the gods how things ought to be. So the book begins with her complaint against them.

Through Queen Orual's complaint, Lewis connects *Till We Have Faces* to the hearts of all who have ever suffered and blamed God for it. In the Bible there are many who shook their fists heavenward: Job, that man most maligned among mortals; David, in many of the psalms; and Habakkuk the prophet. It is worthy of note that the God of the Bible does not seem to be offended by people's doubts, fears, and complaints. In fact, it appears he actually supplies templates for complaining against him. God permits—perhaps encourages—those who are heavyhearted to speak honestly and frankly to him so that sorrows might be purged from their souls. He makes it possible for people not to live in denial about the deep heartaches that often occur in a fallen world. An error of judgment is not found in complaint against God but rather in turning one's back on God. To turn away from God is to move in a direction where no resolutions may be found. But to turn to God in honest anguish is to move in a direction in which both comfort and meaning are most likely—given time—to be discovered.

God might kill me, but I have no other hope. I am going to argue my case with him.   JOB 13:15

2

I think that was the first time I clearly understood that I am ugly.

BOOK I, CHAP. I, P. II

Orual is ugly. It is not a fault, but it is a fact. She had not been aware of the fact until someone pointed it out. Unfortunately, when people point these things out to us—things we can do little about—they usually do so while registering their displeasure. Orual cannot live her life now without feeling devalued because of her appearance. In time she embraces the habit of wearing a veil. Hiding ourselves from others who have hurt us is not uncommon.

We tend to gain our sense of self based on how we perceive others to see us, and not all forms of peer pressure are necessarily bad. For instance, each of us has abandoned behaviors once tolerated in childhood that are now considered—for good reason—objectionable in polite company. Nevertheless, bad impressions of ourselves we've picked up from others may brand us and leave us devastated for years. Furthermore, though we look to others for a sense of self, so often those others to whom we look are as insecure as we are. What must be noted, however, is that we were made with a capacity to gain a sense of self from another. In fact, our very souls may be hardwired for this. But rather than looking ultimately to other humans, who are as weak as we are, we are ultimately to gain our sense of self from God. And when we look to him in the hopes of his defining us, we discover that he loves us.

The book of Revelation says there will come a day when those in heaven receive a white stone with a new name written on it. In Scripture a name often speaks of an individual's identity; this white stone will be the identity God has assigned to an individual. It is new, and yet somehow known to us. Perhaps all our lives we are, in one way or another, receiving down payments on the identity indicated by the white stone. Like Orual, we may have difficulty embracing our current identity, but when that future day comes, our true identity will finally be perfected in the presence of God. Even now, if we base our self-esteem on God's assessment, that true identity will not be an utter mystery—we will have had hints of it all along.

To everyone who is victorious I will give . . . a white stone, and on the stone will be engraved a new name that no one understands except the one who receives it.

REVELATION 2:17

3

"Don't you think the things people are most ashamed of are the things they cannot help?"

I thought of my ugliness and said nothing. BOOK I, CHAP. 10, P. 111

Queen Orual, flawed as she is both without and within, nevertheless reveals over her lifetime remarkable capacities to accomplish glorious feats. Yet she seems to be hardly aware of her various victories and leadership gifts as queen of Glome. She is driven by other things. Her perpetual complaint against the gods marks her earthly pilgrimage; she is a woman obsessed.

As many of us are prone to do, Orual has gained her sense of self from her relationship with another; that is, with her sister, Psyche. Now Psyche has been claimed as the bride of Cupid. But Orual does not believe Psyche is truly the bride of the god, choosing instead to believe that her sister's failure to view life as she does must mean that Psyche is delusional. Ironically, it is Orual who cannot see things clearly, or at least she refuses to do so. She lacks any kind of self-doubt that could help her understand the actions of others when they conflict with the habits she has developed to cope with her deep brokenness. For her to see things otherwise would require a significant re-evaluation of her choices. Instead of accepting reality as it is, Orual chooses to project onto it what she wants it to be. She wants to reclaim Psyche for her own. She wants others to see the world as she sees it, and she will employ very manipulative means in order to make that happen.

Orual is painfully aware of her outward ugliness; she covers it up, hiding behind a veil. But she is unaware of the ugliness that dominates her inward self—her controlling self-interest. In a moment, Orual recognizes that the things most people are ashamed of are things they cannot help. Though she tries to hide her appearance from others, she can do nothing about it. On the other hand, she could do something about the ugliness of her character, but she denies any such problem. How sad it is when we, like Orual, fail to accept the things we cannot change and fail to make the changes we can. Failure to change may begin innocently enough, but in time it can have disastrous consequences.

God shows his anger from heaven against all sinful, wicked people who suppress the truth by their wickedness. ROMANS 1:18

4   *If they [the gods] had an honest intention to guide us, why is their guidance not plain?*   BOOK I, CHAP. 12, P. 134

Queen Orual asks a question that most understand intuitively even if they have never asked it explicitly or have been afraid to ask. Christians know they ought to seek and also obey God's will. But if God wants everyone to obey his will, why is it often so hard to know what that is? What is one to make of the fact that the God of the universe expects something of his creatures and then seems to withhold the necessary components to make that happen? Furthermore, if he promises to be with us and to guide us, what does it mean if we do not feel his presence?

In his anthology of George MacDonald, the Scottish author who had such a lasting influence over him, C. S. Lewis quotes MacDonald as saying, "Obedience is the opener of eyes."[1] The comment does not clear up all the mysteries surrounding this topic, but it does provide some potentially helpful advice: do the little bit that is clear to do in any given moment, and wait for greater clarity to follow. When the psalmist wrote about "a lamp to guide my feet and a light for my path" (Psalm 119:105), the lamp he had in mind, like the light of a candle, illumined only the next step. To see what follows requires the faith to move into the lighted space.

Orual's problem occurs partly because she chooses not to do what she knows she ought to do and then complains that guidance has not been given. In fact, she has already made up her mind what kind of guidance she is willing to follow. She rejects what does not suit her inclinations. Certainly there are times when we are mystified, longing to know and do the right thing. But if we are honest with ourselves, we must admit there are also times when enough of the right thing is clear, yet we refuse. Worse still, we blame God for hiding his will when it is really our refusal to do his will that is the core problem. Our own pilgrimage, like Orual's, may become more problematic when the obvious is ignored.

Your word is a lamp to guide my feet and a light for my path.   PSALM 119:105

5

Orual is angry at the gods. Her sister, Psyche, has been given in marriage to Cupid on condition that she does not see his face. In the retelling of the old story of Cupid and Psyche, Lewis gives his readers opportunity to revisit the story with a greater appreciation for complexity and wonder. It was Lewis's belief that any present understanding of God will always be incomplete, for how can finite minds ever fully grasp the infinite? Our best, and truest, theologies are still man-made approximations, and we should always be seeking better and better approximations.

Orual is not only concerned that Psyche cannot see Cupid; she is also angry that she herself cannot see the gods. And she is not alone in that complaint. "I'll believe in God if you can prove his existence to me" is a common perspective. Yet there is something irrational about the expectation that the omnipresent God could reveal himself empirically. If, for example, lead were melted down and poured into a mold, it could in a sense be considered omnipresent in the space of that mold. Lead is something that can be seen and touched. It has mass and substance. If lead were made omnipresent in the space you are occupying at this moment, there would be room for nothing else of material substance because the lead would push everything else out of the way. If God, omnipresent, existed in a way compatible with empirical perception, he would leave no room in the universe for the existence of other material objects. So if God exists as an omnipresent being in a manner compatible with that which is material, then he must be an immaterial omnipresence.

God does reveal himself in time and space. As Protestant reformer John Calvin put it, God donned the garment of Creation that he might be seen in what he has made.[2] He also reveals himself in his Word, which he gave through inspiring the biblical writers. Best of all, he revealed himself to us through his Son, Jesus Christ. We are wise to at least begin the search for God in the way in which he can truly be found.

By faith we understand that the entire universe was formed at God's command, that what we now see did not come from anything that can be seen.

HEBREWS 11:3

6 *You are indeed teaching me about kinds of love I did not know. It is like looking into a deep pit. I am not sure whether I like your kind better than hatred.* BOOK I, CHAP. 14, P. 165

Orual refuses to accept Psyche's experience because it would negate her own vision of reality. Rather than availing herself of an opportunity to change, she presses her vision of life upon her sister. Orual seeks to force Psyche's hand, coercing her to act contrary to her own conscience and will. Orual's motives are no longer masked by pretension and sophistication. She is unequivocally controlling, seeking to manipulate Psyche in the name of love. How often the words "I am only doing this for your own good" have been employed by those who have no interests in mind but their own. They assert their will as if it should be the equally shared opinion of everyone.

Enough of Orual's story is given in *Till We Have Faces* that the reader realizes Orual's pilgrimage has been one full of pain and suffering. And perhaps all controlling self-interest may have its root in some deep-seated pain. Hurt begets hurt. Often, controlling people have endured great sorrow and want never to go through such circumstances again. But rather than allowing grief and forgiveness to untether their emotional lives from the past, controlling people vow to control the environment no matter what.

Controlling people are a force to be reckoned with. Often masking their own deep-seated pain, they fail to notice the pain they may be causing others to endure. Controlling and coercive bad acts are often justified as being for the good of others, but as Psyche says to her sister, some kinds of hatred may be better than the kind of control that masks itself as love. Souls deeply hurt are at risk of hurting others, of sucking the life out of them. They must draw on God's strength to grieve and to forgive those who hurt them, so they can instead offer life to others.

If we love each other, God lives in us, and his love is brought to full expression in us. I JOHN 4:12

7

Go. You have saved your life; go and live as you can.

BOOK I, CHAP. 14, P. 167

Though she claims to love Psyche, when Orual asserts her will over Psyche's—coercing her sister to do something she would never have done on her own—she is seeking to save herself at Psyche's expense. This idea of protecting oneself at the expense of others has been a regrettable theme throughout history. If we know that certain behaviors cause us pain, then we are without excuse when we inflict such pain on others whose natures are similar to our own. Such a self-serving attitude contrasts with what has been called the "high courtesy of heaven"—most dramatically expressed in Christ's death on the cross when he said, in essence, "I offer my life for you." To bear the inconvenience of others is a Christlike practice.

Those at the foot of the cross that day, like Queen Orual, knew the self-serving way and couldn't understand why Jesus didn't follow it. They derided him, saying, "If you are the Son of God, save yourself and come down from the cross!" They thought of matters in terms of self-interest. They had no category for Jesus, because Jesus didn't come to save himself. If the men who were taunting him had been omnipotent and on the cross, they would have employed their powers to save themselves; why wouldn't Jesus? Since he did not save himself, they concluded that he wasn't able to—he must have been a mere man like them.

In fact, Jesus was fully man—and far more. He did have powers, but he operated from a different set of values. The Scriptures are clear: he had legions of angels at his beck and call. He could have come down from the cross and saved himself. But he hadn't come to save himself; he came to save lost humanity. That is, he came to turn the world right-side up. It was self-centeredness that led to the conditions under which he was giving up his life. Self-centeredness expected the Savior to save his own life. But Jesus came to rescue lost humanity by giving his life. And in so doing, he set the standard, the high courtesy of heaven: "I offer my life for you."

If you are the Son of God, save yourself and come down from the cross!

MATTHEW 27:40

8

I now determined that I would always go veiled. . . . It is a sort of treaty made with my ugliness.   BOOK I, CHAP.16, PP. 180–81

Queen Orual cannot accept herself, nor is she willing to let others see her as she is. She has determined to remain veiled at all times. There is sadness in her choice, just as there is in the choices people make to hide themselves from others in any subculture. It is heartbreaking when members of a community feel such a lack of love and trust from others that hiding in some way is common. This is especially sad when it occurs in churches.

It begins innocently at first. Someone is marginalized and described by such words as *out of fellowship, backslider,* or *carnal.* While nobody would ever say it explicitly, the implication is that one must be perfect in that community; there is no room for failures or imperfections. Since no one reaches the implicit standard of perfection, pretense is born in the community. Everyone tries to make himself or herself look better than the reality, and certain struggles are quietly suppressed within. Thus the community embraces behaviors far removed from real life. But then the aberrant behaviors must be rationalized, and at that point a kind of pharisaical justification of the community's emerging pathology occurs. These rationalizations and self-justifications estrange people from one another; the only fruit they produce is isolation and loneliness. So it was for Orual, queen of Glome, on the day she pulled her veil across her face and began her diatribe against God and others around her.

Those who wish to grow, mend, and do better than they have in the past need to be as determined to cultivate transparency and honesty as Orual was to hide herself. True growth is encouraged by a healthy community. Nevertheless, staying connected in community takes effort. Pretense can be easier than honesty. But the love of God, which casts out fear and insecurity (see 1 John 4:18), is the means by which one might grow individually and contribute responsibly to the growth of a community. Orual took a way that compounded her sorrows and lengthened her recovery. She embraced unnecessary sorrow in isolation, rather than opening up to graces available to her. There is a better way.

Whenever someone turns to the Lord, the veil is taken away.

2 CORINTHIANS 3:16

9

How can they meet us face to face till we have faces?

BOOK II, CHAP. 4, P. 294

In this line, Lewis shows he's grasped the fact that meeting God demands self-awareness; one will meet God truthfully or not at all. A true meeting begins with awareness of one's weakness and woundedness. Everyone is wounded, but not all are broken.

Woundedness is merely a symptom of being fallen and living in a fallen world where generational sins are passed on through time. Nations experience the fallout as evil acts proliferate and compound over the ages. All things human—cultures, institutions, families, workplaces—have suffered the fallout of woundedness. The wounds lead people to withdraw into defensive postures and often lead to addictions of various sorts. But anesthetizing behaviors cannot heal; they merely deaden pain temporarily. Furthermore, habits of inordinate self-protection lead, in the end, to self-referential tendencies, which in turn lead to utilitarian behavior. Thus, what begins as protection from wounding can so easily be used to wound others.

On the other hand, brokenness characterizes people who are in touch with their wounds, who, in their pain, become sensitive to the fact that others sharing a similar nature also are prone to the same kinds of hurts and sorrows. They are self-aware—unlike those who are self-referential, they experience empathy, an Incarnation-like activity.

Just as the embodied Christ entered our world and identified with our infirmities, the empathetic person tries to understand the points of view of others. So the broken can become what priest and writer Henri Nouwen called "wounded healers." We have seen that there is a great chasm separating the wounded from the broken. There is an equally great chasm separating the wounded from God. God is God to all, willing to give grace to those in deep need. But, whereas the wounded are blind to their neediness, the broken are desperate for grace. And it is they—the self-aware—who are beginning to grow solid, to gain a "face." It is they who have an identity and can begin to meet God face-to-face.

Though our bodies are dying, our spirits are being renewed every day. For our present troubles are small and won't last very long. Yet they produce for us a glory that vastly outweighs them and will last forever! 2 CORINTHIANS 4:16-17

10

I know now, Lord, why you utter no answer. You are yourself the answer. Before your face questions die away. What other answer would suffice?

BOOK II, CHAP. 4, P. 309

At the end of her days, Queen Orual comes to a place of resolution. Her interior life has been characterized by a perennial complaint against God. Yet Orual, weary and perhaps even near the end of her life, finally gives in and accepts God's way. Even if her yielding is merely out of weariness, it gives witness to the grace of God, who accepts even spent lives that are truly yielded to him. It is a testimony to the fact that his love and grace are never earned. After all, what could any man or woman do to merit them?

In Jesus' day, after he had fed the crowd of five thousand, the multitude wanted to make him king (see John 6). But they were looking only for an economic savior, someone to feed their bellies and grant other material benefits. The very next day, the crowd came to Jesus again, reminding him that Moses had given their forefathers bread in the wilderness—the manna that had come down from heaven each day as sustenance for their journey. In essence, the people were simply asking Jesus for another meal. They had filled themselves on the food Jesus gave, but now they hungered again. But Jesus had a reminder too.

He reminded the people that it was his Father, not Moses, who had fed their fathers in the wilderness. Furthermore, Jesus told them the food they had eaten the day before could satisfy them only temporarily; ultimately, they needed the Bread of Life, which satisfies forever. Intrigued, they asked Jesus to give them this bread. They were shocked when Jesus offered himself to them: "I am the bread of life." In other words, Jesus was saying, "I give myself to you; find your satisfaction in me." Most of the people left him then. He had offered them the greatest gift he could give: the gift of himself. He had nothing greater to offer, for he alone could satisfy. And the people turned away to look for something else.

At the end of her pilgrimage, Orual finally finds what she has been looking for all her life—though it is not what she had thought. Her lifelong complaints reflected gross misunderstanding on her part. At last she discovers that her sorrows were due to misplaced expectations. When she sees God's true purposes and accepts them, she is at peace: "What other answer would suffice?"

I am the bread of life. Whoever comes to me will never be hungry again.

JOHN 6:35

CHAPTER 4

Dymer

THE NARRATIVE POEM *DYMER* is one of C. S. Lewis's most significant publications, though it was written years before his conversion to Christianity. One might wonder why such a work would be included in a book of Christian meditations, but there are at least two reasons. First, much of his later work can be found in seed form in this narrative poem. Second, the questions Lewis posits are perennial ones. He would find, later, in just what way Christ had provided answers to these gnawing intellectual matters and addressed the conditions of his heart.

Dymer is a young man who has been nurtured and raised in a city modeled after the ideal set forth in Plato's *Republic*. Lewis tells his readers that the shapers of the City had tortured "into stone each bubble the Academy had blown," that what had been mere theory was forced into rigid formulas having nothing to do with reality. By contrast, Dymer realizes that the programming and indoctrination he's had to endure are inaccurate, given the complexities of the real world. A spring morning is visible from the window of an indoctrination hall, and the poem asks, "Who ever learned to censor the spring days?" Dymer bolts from the City and sets off on a pilgrim's quest to discover what is real and substantive. Unfortunately, much of what he discovers is disquieting, for he has to face truths about himself as well as his world. He thinks himself brave, but caught in his own cowardice, he begins to discover his many weaknesses.

In one such lesson, Dymer comes upon a mortally wounded man, whose story makes him realize that his own flight from the City has caused anarchy. This wounded man curses the name Dymer. The pilgrim flees farther and so discovers the home of a vile magician, whose interest is in dream-fantasies and in suppressing realities. Dymer must escape the magician's house, just as he had escaped the City; neither would produce a true vision of reality. The temporary explanations of the Academy, calcified into unyielding formulas and subject to the dreams of the moment, fail to satisfy Dymer. And so, one imagines, they might have been unsatisfactory to Lewis even at this preconversion stage of his life.

Paul wrote that "no one is seeking God" (Romans 3:11). Anyone questing after God, therefore, could in fact stand as evidence that God has already been at work, wooing that one to himself. So it is that in a book such as *Dymer*, in which Lewis does not yet proclaim faith, we can discover material that points us toward God.

1

[T]hey laid
The strong foundations, torturing into stone
Each bubble the Academy had blown.

CANTO I.4

Dymer, the primary character in Lewis's narrative poem, was raised in a city modeled after Plato's *Republic*. Lewis wants his readers to grasp the idea that the Academy (the world of academics and the ivory tower), helpful as it may be, does not have all the answers.

Educational institutions should be a place where truth can be robustly pursued. Hopefully, some truths will actually be discovered; however, these can always be explored more deeply and applied more widely. We do not get last words about anything, but that does not mean we cannot have sure words about some things. It is the sure words that keep us from becoming relativists; it is the fact that we cannot discover a last word about anything that prevents us from becoming tyrants. We may rightly believe in some kind of transcendent absolute, but we would be fools to say we knew anything absolutely. We may believe conceptually in the infinity of numbers, but no one would take us seriously if we said we knew the infinity of numbers. There will always be depths still to plumb and applications yet to be made. Those who take the knowledge of the moment and make of it a last and tyrannizing word or formula are the kinds of people Lewis is criticizing in *Dymer*. They have taken the bubbles, the fragile assumptions of the Academy, and coerced them into the hard realities of their social engineering.

Lewis's book was published at the time totalitarian states were emerging in Europe. He saw the problems that occur when objective reality is surrendered to the subjective assumptions of some. He wrote long before the expectations raised by these utilitarian experiments exploded into horrendous disappointments. Lewis's perception on these matters is nearly prophetic. It is not that he was a prophet but that he was able to think imaginatively and reasonably to the natural conclusions of false assumptions. In this way, Lewis models for his readers the necessity of avoiding inflated justifications of even our best thoughts. No matter what we know, more can be understood. Even the truths we assert must be asserted with deep humility and honesty.

There is a path before each person that seems right, but it ends in death.
PROVERBS 14:12

2

Who ever learned to censor the spring days?

CANTO I, 7

Dymer, sitting in a lecture hall in the City, is being indoctrinated into the cultural expectations of social engineers. He looks out the window onto the real world. It is an April morning, the kind of morning that set the pilgrims in Chaucer's *Canterbury Tales* on their way. Spring reveals melting snow—the awakening of nature to life and vibrancy. The lecturer with his formulas and cant descriptions of reality is unable to compete with the complex realities of nature. Birds sing, flowers bloom, trees bud, and the sun shines; this world counts against that world described in the lecture hall. Lewis asks, "Who ever learned to censor the spring days?" The cycles of nature and their predictability make it possible for farmers to plow, plant, and harvest in season. The fixed nature of the stars allows navigators to find their way across the seas. Theories of astronomy come and go, but navigators still make their way. All nature declares the watchful care of Someone whose graces are commonly given and whose bounty is abundant. Dymer, glimpsing the real world, abandons the City to discover the world as it is, not as the lecturer would have it be.

Nevertheless, does this world testify to the existence of a good God? Surely good is observed in nature, but as Dymer learns, honesty demands that vicious things be acknowledged in nature as well. Yet one must ask, Where did the distinctions between good and bad arise? If the world is all that bad, how did the concept of good occur? If sense is to be made of the universe, it is most likely to be found in an explanation as complex as the reality described. What is it about the human pilgrimage that inspires one, like Dymer, to want to make sense of his or her experience? If there is no sense to be found, why is it continually sought? Why seek to understand or explain anything? The key is to look more deeply at the world as it is in spring days, or any day, in the hopes of making sense of one's pilgrimage.

Ever since the world was created, people have seen the earth and sky. Through everything God made, they can clearly see his invisible qualities—his eternal power and divine nature. So they have no excuse for not knowing God.

ROMANS 1:20

3 *And as I fled I wondered*
       Into whose alien story I had blundered.

CANTO I, 22

Dymer bursts from the City and feels more alive than ever before. He begins his pilgrimage while discovering a wide, wide world. His curiosities run unabated, giving rise to questions; questions awaken into wonder; wonder gives birth to awe and often to worship. Dymer realizes that he is living in the midst of a story but cannot help but wonder whose story it is. Like Lewis's character, G. K. Chesterton observes in *Orthodoxy* that he always felt he was living within a great story that was unfolding before him. It dawned on him: if life is a story, then there must be a storyteller. If there is a storyteller, then the story must be told for a purpose. There is an end in sight, a moral to be made, sense to be grasped. If there is a story, there must be a plot.

Considering that your life is a story with an author and an intention will affect your life's pilgrimage. For one thing, no story is satisfying without a cast of characters. The story each of us finds ourselves a part of is one in which self-definition can be achieved only by discovering our true identity in proper relationship with others. And—here the plot thickens—no one can fully understand himself or herself in isolation from others. As poet John Donne famously tells us in *Meditation XVII*, one of the works for which he is best known: "No man is an island."

We all find ourselves in our own stories, but they are not merely ours alone. They may be perceived from our particular point of view, but such is the complexity that every angle of vision has some validity. Our growth in the story is encouraged by trying to understand the points of view of others. Seen only from our own perspective, this story would become rather boring. It is necessary to break out of the dungeon of self to see with greater clarity. Dymer wonders into whose story he has stumbled. Certainly it was his, and certainly it was the story of other characters yet to be met in the narrative. But Dymer is also a part of Lewis's story and, it could be said, a part of everyone's story as well. Perhaps most books—certainly most good books—give readers an opportunity to discover something of their own personal narratives as they read.

All of you together are Christ's body, and each of you is a part of it.

I CORINTHIANS 12:27

4 *Out of the unscythed grass the nettle grew.*
CANTO III, 8

While his escape from the City opened up to Dymer a wider world full of its own mysteries and enchantments, it also brought him to the discovery that "there are snakes in Eden," that the world is full of both wonder and woe.

Lewis would eventually come to understand the problem of evil and suffering from a Christian point of view. Good is primary; evil is a perversion of good. One cannot think of a bad banana without thinking of it as a once-good banana gone bad, or spoiled. Put another way, evil compares to good as mold compares to bread. Like mold on bread, evil, having no independent existence, must feed on good. Yet even a person made in the image of God can take mold, which is bad for the bread, and make something good out of it: penicillin. We must at least entertain the possibility that God, being greater than humanity, can take the evils of this world and make something good of them. It could be argued that the crucifixion of Christ may have been the most heinous human act in history: the creatures turned against their Creator, who had sent his Son to communicate his love to them, and they crucified the Christ. Yet God took that evil act and turned it on itself and created a kind of divine penicillin. Supernaturally, God produced good even out of human evil: the life-changing work of Christ's resurrection.

Besides the redemptive grace God has brought into the world, there is also a kind of grace that occurs in spiritual discipline. Dymer's experience of leaving the City brings him into a world where nettles grow in the "unscythed"—uncut—grass. Lewis recognized that disorder can lead to compounding difficulties. Scythed grass keeps back nettles, just as tending a garden allows it to flourish. Leave it alone, and the weeds are bound to grow. What is true of gardens is also true of one's character: spiritual discipline and exercise allow us to mow the nettles of the soul and pull the weeds from our character. Sometimes painful experiences are a necessary part of the maturation process.

Train yourself to be godly. "Physical training is good, but training for godliness is much better, promising benefits in this life and in the life to come."
I TIMOTHY 4:7-8

5

Joy flickers on
The razor-edge of the present and is gone.

CANTO V, 10

Joy is available to all, in any given moment—but it must be chosen. This does not mean sorrows are to be suppressed or ignored. Certainly sorrows are best dealt with by emotionally processing our losses and forgiving, where necessary, those who have hurt us. Without allowing grief and forgiveness, we remain perpetually tethered to those who have inflicted heartache upon us. But processing sorrow by means of grieving and forgiving offers a way to choose joy, for it makes the acquisition of joy possible at some future time.

Joy gives one a trace of the flavor of eternity. Lewis observed that the eternal and unchanging, if eternity can be experienced at all this side of heaven, can be encountered only in the midst of the mutable. Eternity is met in mutability; that is, eternity can be encountered only in the transitoriness of time. For those who do not know God and his grace, every joy is a manifestation of his presence and an expression of his desire to break into their lives. He woos us to himself through joy. In fact, Lewis said that joy was the serious business of heaven. And for those who do know God, joy is a testimony of God's nearness and presence. Every moment, eternity with all its joys is breaking into our world; every bush is a burning bush, and the world is crowded with God. We choose in each moment to notice. The razor edge of time sets before each of us a choice. If this is true, then any decision to follow Christ is actually the decision to make *every* decision for Christ, each time he manifests himself and woos with his gifts. Where else can the eternal be met but in the moment? We must awaken to his presence and avail ourselves of his joys; even more, we must practice his presence so that we remain awake to him.

Momentary sorrows cannot steal these joys if we choose to go deeper in those moments and discover his presence more deeply. And true joy cannot be eclipsed by the shadows of any given moment, for the light of his grace cannot be so hidden for long.

I pray that God, the source of hope, will fill you completely with joy and peace because you trust in him. Then you will overflow with confident hope through the power of the Holy Spirit. ROMANS 15:13

6 *Great God, take back your world.*
CANTO V, 15

It is easy, in the midst of anguish, to register a complaint against God; in fact, it is quite common to do this. Ours is a world of hurt, suffering, and pain. This is bad enough in itself, but every night we can also turn on the TV and bring the world's pain into the living room. Anguish compounds. It is not long in anyone's pilgrimage before he or she comes to the place where Dymer was—crying out to God to take back his world. There is a psalm in which the psalmist cries out that someone would even be happy to bash the babies of his or her enemies against a rock, so great is the pain they have caused (see Psalm 137:9). I am convinced that God does not want us to bash anyone against a rock—yet aren't there times when in our pain and bewilderment we wish we could just shake someone? What do we do with those feelings? Should we assume that our faith is irrelevant when we fall into such anguished times? Or, is there something to be discovered even in the dregs of human sorrow and devastation?

The Scriptures are not dismissive of sorrows, nor do they deny the likelihood of their occurring. In fact, the Scriptures speak frankly about events that even cause existential despair. This is why there are the "imprecatory" psalms—such as the one quoted above—and books in the Bible such as Job. We have the option in our sadness to turn our backs on God and walk away from him. But to do so is to turn away from the only real viable source of rescue. Those Scriptures that Dymer's anguish seems to echo actually provide a template by which we can go to God in honesty and let him bring us to the place where deep sorrows can be processed. We can come to God and speak truth to him out of our frustrations and fears. At the end of the day, people of faith do not have to deny what they are likely to encounter in a fallen world. On the contrary, they can go to God with an honest prayer for him to make sense of the world, and it is likely that resolution will come. If a good God allows evil to exist, then it must be because he knows that he can bring greater good from its existence than he might have otherwise.

He makes these things happen either to punish people or to show his unfailing love.
JOB 37:13

7

[T]he unwearied joy that brings
Out of old fields the flowers of unborn springs.

CANTO V, 29

There is a kind of joy that sets a pilgrim on a search for more than sandy beaches with wide horizons and crashing waves, a search for more than glorious vistas of fertile fields or purple mountains' majesties. There is a kind of joy that longs for the landscapes of the soul to reveal an emerging fruitfulness of character. To engage in the cultivation of the interior life is to make a commitment to the future; it is to build now for what is yet to come at some later date.

The ancients knew virtue as a means to the good life. It was an integrated whole, comprised of courage, temperance, justice, and wisdom—the four cardinal virtues (as opposed to the three theological virtues of faith, hope, and love). Lewis writes propositionally of these attributes in *Mere Christianity*.

Courage is the habitual ability to suffer pain and hardship; it is manifest in endurance, fortitude, and staying power. Courage is the ability to say yes to right action even in the teeth of pain. Temperance is the habit of resisting the enticement of immediate pleasure in order to gain the greater though remote good. If courage is the ability to say yes to right action even in the midst of pain, temperance is the ability to say no to wrong action even with the prospect of pleasure; in this regard it is a mark of maturity. Justice, another characteristic of virtue, is the habit of being concerned for the common good—the general welfare of society. Justice recognizes its responsibility to others and knows that moral development cannot occur without concern for others. Moral development cultivates empathy by breaking out of the dungeon of self; it requires courage to redress wrongs and temperance to deny oneself those things that prevent one from standing up for the good of others. And lastly, there is wisdom, the habit of being careful about the decisions one makes. Wisdom seeks advice, recognizing that the world is complex and that an openness to understand this complexity will lead to a better life—or, as Dymer notes, the benefits of flowering fields and unborn springs.

The more you grow like this, the more productive and useful you will be in your knowledge of our Lord Jesus Christ. 2 PETER 1:8

8

"Have you heard
My gun? It was but now I killed a lark."
"What, Sir!" said Dymer; "shoot the singing bird?"
"Sir," said the man, "they sing from dawn till dark,
And interrupt my dreams."

CANTO VI, 10

While on his pilgrimage, Dymer finds himself in the presence of a magician. This man's way of relating to the real world is extremely utilitarian, and Dymer's association with him will grossly truncate Dymer's development and the discovery of his own way in the world.

The magician appears to have no capacity for genuine love. All his acts are a pretense. He portrays himself as concerned for others, but his real interest lasts only as long as those others will serve his interests. Dymer might have noticed this at the beginning of his encounter with the magician, but he does not, for he, too, is still in the process of discovering how to break free of self-serving interests and open himself up to a wider world. He first notices a bird singing to its heart's content, and a moment later, he hears a crack of gunfire that ends the bird's song. The bird falls dead to the ground, and when Dymer goes to investigate, he meets the magician. The magician proclaims that it was he who shot the bird, because its song interrupted his dreams. Here is a character in the poem who asserts himself against his world. That which he values he preserves, and that which counts against his vision of the world—his dreams—he destroys. Influences like the magician's can be found in the midst of anyone's personal spiritual pilgrimage. Flee from any such entanglement: it can lead only to delusion and heartache.

Certainly all reasonable people have dreams of one sort or another. How do you know when dreams are beneficial and when they are dangerous? Perhaps a clear indicator will be in answer to the question, "Do my dreams and aspirations allow me to see others and their hopes and fears more clearly, or do my dreams cause me to value others only if they serve my interests?" There is an eternity of difference between these two visions of life.

These people scoff at things they do not understand. Like unthinking animals,
they do whatever their instincts tell them, and so they bring about their own
destruction. JUDE 1:10

9

Human tears and pain
And hoping for the things that cannot be,
And blundering in the night where none can see.

CANTO VI, 77

Many of our biggest disappointments are the result of unfulfilled expectations. So it is for Dymer, who longs for things that were not to be. Perhaps his difficulties lie in his own weaknesses, as so many of ours do. He blunders "in the night where none can see." It is fair to believe that nobody is very life skilled. All are likely to blunder to one degree or another. Nobody is ever ready to get married, but if people wait for marriage until they are ready, they will miss out on so many of life's joys. Nobody is ever ready to have children, but if people waited until they were ready to have children, the human race would cease after this generation. Everyone is awkward in some way. A toddler learning to walk falls down and gets bruised. A five-year-old taking the training wheels off the two-wheeler will fall down and get scraped. An adolescent picking up a skateboard for the first time and attempting to take on a half-pipe will sprain an ankle or perhaps break a wrist. Everyone is awkward with some new endeavor; in fact, if you are not awkward somewhere in your life, you are just not growing.

Have you ever had a perfectly pure motive for anything you have ever done? If you think you have, you may be living a life of delusion. Furthermore, if you waited until your motives were perfect, you would never do anything. At some level, all human function is a kind of blundering. And it is at this point that the love of God becomes so significant, for it is not given by virtue of human merit, nor can it be diminished by human failure. God's love is always given in spite of our lack of skill, in light of our awkwardness. In fact, he loves us in spite of our sin (not because of it, but certainly in spite of it). And it is because of his love that those blundering on in life's pilgrimage find encouragement to get up after a tumble and get going again.

God showed his great love for us by sending Christ to die for us while we were still sinners. ROMANS 5:8

10
There was a Dymer once who worked and played
. . . there was a Dymer in the forest glade
. . . but I am none of those.

CANTO VIII, 81

From the time we are born until the day we die, we remain the same person. Then again, the person who dies is so very different from the child who was born. How do we make sense of all this? The Dymer at the beginning of Lewis's narrative poem is not the same Dymer at the end. He begins as a student indoctrinated and conditioned to believe whatever social engineers have told him. But that Dymer ceases to exist when he begins to see the wider world and leaves the small confines of the City for something bigger and less stifling. He gains richer understanding as he sees himself reflected in his treatment by others. And like Dymer, we are constantly transforming developmentally; yet amid this change, there is continuity. We discover that we are not who we were at birth. We are not who we were as adolescents. We are not who we were when we first became adults. We are none of these, for by God's design and grace, the believer is ever becoming like Christ. This continuity in change is often accompanied by some degree of pain.

John Donne observed, "No man hath affliction enough that is not matured and ripened by it, and made fit for God by that affliction."[1] The young Dymer is not the same man who started out on his pilgrimage—nor is he utterly different. Though there is continuity throughout his life, it could be suggested that the Dymer who finally dies is, in fact, a better version of himself. He has grown through his adventures. He has learned to let go of falsehood and embrace life as it is, not as he would have it be. He has adjusted the scoliosis of his soul to the plumb line of reality. Like Dymer, every man and every woman is in process. Decisions made and habits formed determine the kind of person we are becoming. Through joy and sorrow each must choose well.

Dear brothers and sisters, when troubles come your way, consider it an opportunity for great joy. For you know that when your faith is tested, your endurance has a chance to grow. So let it grow, for when your endurance is fully developed, you will be perfect and complete, needing nothing. JAMES 1:2-4

CHAPTER 5

The Voyage of the Dawn Treader

THE VOYAGE OF THE DAWN TREADER is the Narnian chronicle in which Lewis best approximates in children's literature the kinds of adventure one meets in Homer's *Odyssey* or Virgil's *Aeneid*. Both of these books include a sea voyage and feature heroes who just want to find their proper home. While King Caspian has set out on the *Dawn Treader* to discover what happened to the seven lost lords of Narnia and to check on distant Narnian islands, he, too, carries someone who simply wants to go home.

All who have ever read *The Voyage of the* Dawn Treader have fallen in love with Reepicheep, the most chivalrous of mice. Reepicheep's longing to go to Aslan's country speaks about something deep within each of us as well. None of us were made, ultimately, for this world. We will not be satisfied, as we were meant to be, until we find ourselves at home in heaven. But there are journeys still before us. While the *Dawn Treader* has as one of its missions to deliver Reepicheep to the shores of Aslan's country, other transformations must occur along the way.

In this book, the reader accompanies Edmund and Lucy back to Narnia for their third and final visit. By the will of the Lion, their cousin, Eustace Clarence Scrubb, also makes the voyage. Eustace has the heart of a dragon beating beneath the skin of a boy, and in the magic of that land, he is actually turned outwardly into that which he was inwardly all along. Eustace has been blind to the burden he is to everyone else around him; he has no sense of his horrible behavior and self-centered ways. But once he is turned into a dragon and sees his true self reflected in a pond, Eustace weeps to discover the truth about himself. In his repentant state, though still a dragon, he becomes quite useful in assisting the crew of the *Dawn Treader*. He is able to help repair the ruin of the ship's mast as well as revictual the ship for its return to sea. Still, helpful as he has become, he cannot un-dragon himself. It is in his dragon state that Eustace meets Aslan the Lion—the Christ figure of the Narnian books. The Lion tells him that he must undress. In that moment Eustace realizes that being reptilian, dragons must have the capacity to shed their skins, and Eustace assumes the Lion is instructing him to shed his skin to be a boy again. Yet try as he might, after each shedding of skin, Eustace remains a dragon. In frustration he looks to the Lion only to be told that he must be undressed. Eustace surrenders to the Lion's claw, which alone can cut through all that dragon flesh, going to the very core of his dragon heart to make him a boy again.

It is dawn when Eustace returns to the company of the ship. All are asleep but one—Edmund—and he is able to hear Eustace's confession. How insightful of Lewis to have Edmund play father confessor, for he was the one child who, in an earlier story—*The Lion, the Witch and the Wardrobe*—discovered his own dragonish ways and was also transformed by the Lion. Edmund would be empathetic and patient, tender and kind.

1

When she had finished dressing, she looked out of her window at the water rushing past and took a long deep breath. She felt quite sure they were in for a lovely time. CHAP. 1, P. 13

For Lucy, who had made a previous "surprise" trip to Narnia (in *Prince Caspian*), the transition from Eustace's guest room to the deck of the *Dawn Treader* is a welcome adventure! In fact, Edmund and Lucy are reminiscing about their favorite place, Narnia, when they are called back there. Unlike Eustace, Lucy is a pilgrim ready and eager to go! She lands in icy water and counts her blessings that she had swimming lessons in school last term. Her clothes are ruined, but she is content to have Caspian's old clothes, though they are too big for her. Lucy takes in her new surroundings and her new companions (some of them actually old friends), responding with an attitude of joy and eagerness to participate in whatever comes her way.

In *Prince Caspian*, Edmund tells us that Lucy sees Aslan more often than anyone else. As a result, it seems she has acquired many of his attributes: a caring and nurturing heart, an honest and brave spirit, and sometimes patience and wisdom beyond her years. This is evident in the excitement Lucy experiences in *The Voyage of the* Dawn Treader as she returns to Narnia. She looks forward to an adventure, especially one that hopefully involves Aslan.

How much more could we be like Jesus if we had the faith and focus of Lucy . . . if we could just look for him and his purposes in everything we do and be eager when adventures and trials come our way . . . if we could change our focus from the immediate discomfort and the anxiety of the unknown to being mindful and thankful for what preparation we have had, and so reveal what we truly treasure: Jesus. Living fully in the moment, looking for glimpses of God's hand in all things, rejoicing in his presence, we might find we struggle less, enjoy more, and become a bit more like him in the process. Are you willing, like Lucy, to be watchful for glimpses of God this week?

Wherever your treasure is, there the desires of your heart will also be.
MATTHEW 6:21

2

Why should we not come to the very eastern end of the world? And what might we find there? I expect to find Aslan's own country.

CHAP. II, P. 16

The valiant and noble mouse, Reepicheep, is on a pilgrimage to Aslan's own country aboard the *Dawn Treader*. He is on a quest, and he seals his legacy in a final and dramatic way by riding off into the horizon, into the unknown, with great courage and faith. He seeks Aslan's country as if to seek his final and forever home, the place his life in Narnia has prepared him for, the place he has always been familiar with in his heart of hearts. He has fulfilled his life's purpose through gallantry and courage in war and through peace in Narnia. He has served the kingdom and the highest of kings, Aslan, and he has served them well. Reepicheep has the confidence of knowing he has done his very best.

There is a lesson here for those of us who drag through our lives without confidence, those of us with wavering faith and little courage. If we live according to God's purpose with confidence in his strength and guidance, we can go courageously through any valley, including the valley of death. It is important that we have the perspective of Reepicheep: that the journey is not complete until we reach the other side. In this way, we remain on guard, instead of growing lax.

The Bible promises that Jesus is preparing a place for us (see John 14:2). We will go to "God's country," the place where God dwells, where we will experience God with all our new senses. We will be with him and know him fully. But until that day comes, we can take the advice of the apostle Paul and "stand firm in the faith." Steadfastness ensures that we will finish well, just like Reepicheep.

How can you encourage someone to be steadfast?

Be on guard. Stand firm in the faith. Be courageous. Be strong.

1 CORINTHIANS 16:13

3

I felt it my duty to point out that we didn't know there was any land ahead and tried to get them to see the dangers of wishful thinking.

CHAP. V, P. 59

Eustace considers himself superior to most in knowledge. He likes books of information. He knows about things that can be measured, counted, pinned onto cards—such as his beetle collection. Priding himself on knowing his rights, he demands that he be put off at the next port to get a hearing at the British consulate. So the prospect of being in another world, far from filling him with Lucy's excitement, makes him physically and emotionally ill. He cannot imagine such a possibility because he has neglected the life of the imagination and apparently doesn't read enough fiction. It is obvious that he does not like people much, either—and he is highly intolerant of other species, as is evident in his dealings with Reepicheep.

In fact, such a "noble" one as Eustace feels it his duty to warn the other pilgrims and adventurers of the inherent dangers of the "wishful thinking" they display in enjoying Narnia. Yet our dreams and desires, aspirations, high expectations for ourselves and our families—these are all the stuff of wishful thinking.

In his *Wishful Thinking,* Frederick Buechner said this about the matter: "Christianity is mainly wishful thinking. Even the part about Judgment and Hell reflects the wish that somewhere the score is being kept. . . . Children playing at being grown-up is wishful thinking. Interplanetary travel is wishful thinking. Sometimes wishing is the wings the truth comes true on. Sometimes the truth is what sets us wishing for it."[1]

If we perceive our lives as purposeful, if we perceive that God is directing our course, then we are actively involved in fine-tuning our abilities to imagine and determine what God would have us wish for and what direction he would have us go. As David, the psalmist and king, reminded us, the first step is to "take delight in the LORD." For in delighting in him, in imagining for ourselves lives worthy of a calling, we may just find our "wishful thinking" has come true.

Take delight in the LORD, and he will give you your heart's desires.

PSALM 37:4

4 *He had turned into a dragon while he was asleep. Sleeping on a dragon's hoard with greedy, dragonish thoughts in his heart, he had become a dragon himself.* CHAP. VI, P. 75

Eustace behaves wickedly. His journal during the voyage is rife with selfish perceptions, vicious criticisms, feelings of entitlement, and "victim" resentment. He manages to rationalize that everyone else on board the *Dawn Treader* is to blame—that they are foolish and selfish, and he is the smart and noble one. As we read of his actions and deeds, as well as his thoughts, the evidence reveals that Eustace is downright self-centered, twisted, and useless. He doesn't draw a bid on the slave market of the Lone Islands—he couldn't even be *given* away.

On Dragon Island, Eustace is neither noble nor smart as he sheepishly slips away from the others in order to avoid the hard work ahead. Coming upon a dying dragon, he takes shelter in its lair, having no idea what magic might befall him, because he has read the wrong books all his life. So Eustace's thoughts become his actions and then, ultimately, his outward appearance—he becomes the beast on the outside that he is on the inside.

Sin, like a cancer, can start as a small problem and quickly grow to monstrous and fatal proportions. It begins in our selfish nature and is easily fed by a negative thought life. Injustices and life's inevitable challenges can encourage feelings of blame, resentment, victimization, and entitlement. Without a daily diet of humility, confession, and spiritual nourishment, we may quickly find ourselves growing hard and cynical hearts with minds full of beastly thoughts. When every word out of our mouths becomes an expression of annoyance—or worse, a curse for others—and every action a tangled pursuit of our selfish desires, we are on a collision course for trouble. We must consider the state of our hearts today, lest we grow intolerable in relationships and find ourselves alone—alone in a self-made lair with our human skin stretched over the heart of a dragon.

What sorrow for those who drag their sins behind them with ropes made of lies, who drag wickedness behind them like a cart! ISAIAH 5:18

5

I was afraid of his claws, I can tell you, but I was pretty nearly desperate now. So I just lay flat down on my back to let him do it.

CHAP. VIII, P. 90

Eustace, now a dragon, is not delighted by his future prospects. In following Aslan, he takes a huge risk. He gives up his clever manipulations and plans, his will, and maybe his life—certainly life as he has known it. He has nothing left of value, not even a good idea that would help him change himself back into a human being. He is helpless, and he is sorry. Though he has no power to change himself, he has finally followed and submitted himself to the one who does. The great Lion, through the mysteries of deeper magic than Eustace could possibly know, can save him—but not without pain. In lying flat on his back, Eustace gives up any dragonish or human power and waits to endure the pain, the surgery without the anesthesia; yet he knows he is in the most excellent care of the Master Surgeon.

We, like Eustace, do not change easily. It may take a crisis of beastly proportions to make us willing to shed our layers of skin. It is only in God's "claws" that the real work is done—cutting deep through layers of wrongful attitudes and defensive behaviors to give birth to a changed life. It is painful to be changed. It is painful to put our wills aside and to give up the struggle. In the process, however, we will experience relief in finding the one whom we can finally trust. He has us in his hands, and whether we perish or not, we are at last right with him.

Spiritual rebirth is the process that "un-dragons" us. As Jesus promised Nicodemus, we are reborn with new eyes, new sensitivities, and a new reception to God's words of comfort and of grace. And as we lose ourselves in this process, so we gain ourselves—our real selves that God intended for us.

Are you helping or hindering the work of God's "claws" in your life?

Jesus replied, "I tell you the truth, unless you are born again, you cannot see the Kingdom of God." JOHN 3:3

6 *After a bit the lion took me out and dressed me. . . . [H]e did somehow or other: in new clothes—the same I've got on now.*   CHAP. VIII, P. 91

Eustace tells his story to Edmund, explaining how the great Lion Aslan called him, "un-dragoned" him, washed him, and finally put him in new clothes. Eustace is no longer an old dragon with tough skin and beastly ways: he is a new boy with a redeemed body and regenerated mind, and though human again, he is dramatically changed! Eustace finds it difficult to explain what has transpired, as even he does not understand fully what has happened to him. But Edmund—the one who betrayed the others in *The Lion, the Witch and the Wardrobe* and found himself in similar desperate need—understands exactly what Eustace is telling him. Edmund bears witness to Aslan's ability to forgive and to change people from the inside out. He participates in Eustace's healing process as he listens to his contrite confession.

Aslan has intervened to save Eustace, just as he did Edmund, through dramatic and unearthly means. Eustace is given his old body back, cleansed, with new skin and new clothes. He's also given a new perspective, a new attitude of humility, a new awareness of the truth and his place in the order of things.

It is beyond our ability to fully understand how or why God transforms us in the supernatural ways only he can. But it is well within our ability to acknowledge that we desperately need his transforming grace—and it's when we reach this point that God can begin the metamorphosis. We may have tried numerous ways to improve ourselves on our own but have fallen short. Whether we come immediately, gradually, or only as the result of a crisis, when we open our hearts and minds to God to do the work, recognizing it is beyond what we can do for ourselves, he will act on our behalf.

I am overwhelmed with joy in the LORD my God! For he has dressed me with the clothing of salvation and draped me in a robe of righteousness. I am like a bridegroom in his wedding suit or a bride with her jewels.   ISAIAH 61:10

7

*"Well—he knows me," said Edmund. "He is the great Lion, the son
of the Emperor-beyond-the-Sea, who saved me and saved Narnia."*

CHAP. VIII, P. 92

When Eustace asks Edmund if he knows Aslan, Edmund's response is
that *Aslan* knows *him*. Edmund knows who Aslan is; he states the truth
affirmatively, giving Aslan's proper title and the most important fact about
their relationship. But he hesitates to say that he knows Aslan. Although
Edmund recognizes Aslan and his actions, he also realizes that Aslan
is awesome and wonderful—and not well understood. He is far beyond
Edmund's ability to really comprehend him, to predict his thoughts,
reasoning, or behavior.

Likewise, many of us know Jesus as the Son of God, as the Savior of the
world, and as our personal Savior. We are familiar with Christ's story and
his words, and we can sense his presence. We may have become familiar
with his voice and are growing in our knowledge of him, but can we honestly say that we really know him? We are human and don't have the ability
to comprehend the mysteries of our omnipotent God.

Yet, *he* knows *us*. He has known us since before we were born, and he
knows our past, present, and future. He has plans and purposes for us. He
knows our every thought, move, and inclination. Though he knows our sin,
our shame, and our stubbornness, he loves us. He created us and is still in
the process of forming us. Our part in the process is to receive with humility the grace and love that always motivate God to act.

*O LORD, you have examined my heart and know everything about me. You know
when I sit down or stand up. You know my thoughts even when I'm far away.
You see me when I travel and when I rest at home. You know everything I do.*

PSALM 139:1-3

8   *To be strictly accurate, he [Eustace] began to be a different boy. He had*
relapses. There were still many days when he could be very tiresome.
But . . . the cure had begun.   CHAP. VIII, P. 93

Eustace is changed, not merely on the surface from being a physical dragon to being a human boy but on the inside as well. On the outside, Eustace has new clothes. Gone are the old clothes with pockets stuffed with treasure from the dragon's lair. Gone is the lovely but painful bracelet from the dragon's cave—a bracelet that no one wants any part of after the curse of Eustace's "dragoning." Just as Eustace casts aside his material treasures as useless or even dangerous, so he will cast aside those things that he once found important in his thought life and emotional life.

In describing his encounter with Aslan to Edmund, Eustace reveals he does not even know who Aslan is. Though he has submitted himself to Aslan as Savior and Lord and suffered through the process of shedding many layers of his dragon skin, he has much to learn of Aslan's ways. Eustace has a fresh start, with a new version of himself both on the inside and out, but his journey as a "new creature" has just begun.

It is easy to see the remarkable parallel C. S. Lewis draws between the "un-dragoning" of Eustace and our own "rebirthing" in Christ. Christ gives us a fresh start, and then he gives his Holy Spirit to live inside us. We are born again, but we are merely babes in the woods, still in the process of learning who Christ really is and how to walk in his ways of righteousness. Yes, we are different following our rebirth in Christ; the disease of sin and rebellion has been abated. Though we are yet imperfect, the cure has begun.

Anyone who belongs to Christ has become a new person. The old life is gone; a new life has begun!   2 CORINTHIANS 5:17

9

"Oh, Aslan," said she, "it was kind of you to come."
"I have been here all the time," said he, "but you have just
made me visible." CHAP. X, P. 135

Lucy is not aware that Aslan is present; she cannot see him with her eyes. She has accepted the task of finding a magician's book somewhere in a castle's upper floor. In so doing, she is fearful but brave. Searching through the book, Lucy inadvertently performs a spell to release the friendly Narnian Dufflepuds from the magician's curse. Suddenly, turning at the sound of heavy footfalls down the hallway, she finds the great Lion, Aslan, standing before her. She is surprised and overjoyed to see him. She has made him visible!

We do not see our invisible, but omnipresent, God. He is present even though our eyes cannot see him. He is present when we do what is right, present when we do what is wrong. He is present when we are fearful and when we are brave. It is his presence that prods us on, giving us confidence when we cannot find confidence within ourselves. He is the sufficient one and he is here and in him we find what we need, but most of the time we are unaware of his proximity. Some of the time, we do not trust that he can be found. Once in a while, we wonder if he even exists.

Though we may not have eyes to see a spiritual God, there are many other ways to sense that our God has touched us, that he has awakened us, that he has said something directly to us. And when we do not sense him, we can start on that path by an act of the will: by worshiping. It is then that we sense his great love and care, and we realize that he has been here all the time.

Happy are those who hear the joyful call to worship, for they will walk in the light of your presence, LORD. PSALM 89:15

10 *But there I have another name. . . . This was the very reason why you were brought to Narnia, that by knowing me here for a little, you may know me better there.* CHAP. XVI, P. 216

In the final chapter, Lucy and Edmund are told by Aslan that they can never come back to Narnia. They both cry out in horror, and Lucy verbalizes their greatest fear—of being separated from Aslan. In that same chapter, Aslan (in the image of a lamb) invites the children to breakfast and tells them that there is an alternate entrance to Aslan's country from their world. The Lamb changes from white to gold and turns into Aslan, and explains that he's the bridge between their world and his.

Lest there be any mistake, Aslan, the great Lion and Lamb, the son of the Emperor-beyond-the-Sea, is the Christ figure of Narnia. In this way, C. S. Lewis brings us all into Narnia and reminds us of the beauty of the gospel—Jesus' story. Like Lucy and Edmund, by meeting Aslan and getting to know him a little there, we, too, might desire to know more about Jesus. Lewis created a fictional story of a Christlike lion in another world as a way for readers to experience the gospel story outside of presumptions that might otherwise hinder them from contemplating thoughts of the supernatural or divine.

To those of us who know and love the gospel story, Aslan's story serves to remind us of its power and its truth. In the same way, Paul's letters reminded his readers—in this case, the Corinthians—of the Good News he preached to them. He wanted this news to be a firm part of their lives, informing their every decision and keeping them faithful to God. Through their knowledge of Jesus and by continuing to study the Scriptures, they would come to know him better. This is true for us as well.

Let me now remind you, dear brothers and sisters, of the Good News I preached to you before. You welcomed it then, and you still stand firm in it.
I CORINTHIANS 15:1

CHAPTER 6

The Silver Chair

THE SILVER CHAIR IS THE FOURTH VOLUME of the Narnian Chronicles as Lewis wrote them and is the sixth volume according to their linear chronology, as often occurs in modern editions. The story centers on the rescue of King Caspian's son, Prince Rilian, who has been taken captive by the Green Witch to live underground. The witch has devised a plan whereby she will mount an army to invade Narnia and set up Rilian, the true bloodline heir to the throne, as king—but only as her puppet. She has been holding Rilian under a spell that keeps him from knowing his true identity, except for one hour each day. During that hour he is strapped into a silver chair, with full consciousness of his true identity. He screams and raves for someone to release him, that he might conquer the Green Witch and return to Narnia. But he can be set free only if, in his ravings, someone breaks the silver chair.

It is under these circumstances that Aslan, the true Lion King and Christ figure of the books, beckons Eustace Scrubb and his school friend Jill Poole from England. And it is to Jill, who has never been to Narnia before, that Aslan gives the instructions for Rilian's rescue. He reveals his strategy to her, who shares it with Eustace, along with several accompanying signs that they must follow closely. They are fortunate to be joined on their adventure by a Marsh-wiggle named Puddleglum, one of the most endearing characters in all of the Narnian books. Puddleglum is very pessimistic and Eeyoresque, but he is loyal and true. With Aslan's signs and goodwill for their adventure, the party sent to rescue Prince Rilian manages to make what appears to be every possible mistake. But at the end of the day they release the prince, vanquish the witch, and restore their prince to Narnia in his right mind.

If *The Magician's Nephew* is the story of Narnia's creation and *The Lion, the Witch and the Wardrobe* is the story of Narnia's redemption, then *The Silver Chair* is Lewis's ecclesiology, or the story of the church. A band is called out of their world to go and restore the king's son to his rightful and true identity. They are sent on their great commission by the Lion's breath. The band sent into enemy territory to accomplish the rescue is full of flaws and fears and manages to make many, many mistakes, yet the will of Aslan is still, by grace, accomplished through them.

1 *Although she had been longing for something like this,*
Jill felt frightened. . . .
"Can we get back? Is it safe? . . ." asked Jill. CHAP. I, P. 9

Fleeing to avoid a thrashing at the hands of school bullies, Jill can only wish for some kind of miraculous escape. But when, unbelievably, another world opens up before her, she balks. Although her salvation has so conveniently materialized, she senses that to cross over into it entails a commitment that could prove irreversible.

Jill's escape wish is not unlike our temptation to casually flirt with religion as a safety net or some sort of life insurance, just in case there actually is an afterlife. But to follow Christ constitutes a change of heart that devalues much of what we once thought to be real and important before establishing a relationship with him. It is almost like stepping into another world without knowing whether or not we can get back.

What would Jill be leaving behind? Punishment from mean children because she will not cater to them? Injustice from school authorities, who tolerate bullying in the name of individual expression? A system in which values of naughty and nice are turned upside down? Yet she has no guarantee that the new world will be any better; she has only her friend's claim that he has seen it and it is real.

Narnia, the world Jill teeters on entering, is not a metaphoric vehicle for Christianity. At this moment in Jill's experience, however, its appearance represents a step of faith that, if taken, may separate her from life as she has known it. No promises for Jill—only a chance that something better might exist—so she enters Narnia more out of desperation than anything else. Yet in crossing that threshold, she encounters Aslan and from then on looks only forward, never back. Similarly, for those who have eyes to see Jesus, the reality of the Savior renders the call to forsake all else reasonable, compelling, and possible. What aspect of this call are you sensing? Will you, like Jill, answer the call?

Everyone who has given up house or wife or brothers or parents or children, for the sake of the Kingdom of God, will be repaid many times over in this life, and will have eternal life in the world to come. LUKE 18:29-30

2   *"Will you promise not to—do anything to me, if I do come?" said Jill.*

CHAP. II, P. 17

Jill's in a predicament. Having caused the loss of her only companion, she's alone in a world she knows nothing about, and she's frantically thirsty. She has found a stream, but there's a rub: a huge lion lies between her and it. Running away or walking toward the lion to get to the water seems an equally fatal choice. Skip the drink altogether? She can't!

Jill realizes that she needs this water. The Lion—whom readers recognize as the Christ figure in Narnia—refuses to promise that he will not consume her. And, he confirms, without this water she will certainly die. But death is exactly what Jill seeks to avoid by not moving toward him.

Jesus once spoke to a thirsty Samaritan woman of "living water" (John 4:10). This invitation to come and drink is repeated in the book of Revelation as the Holy Spirit and the bride of Christ—the church—bid all to come and drink of "the water of life." All who wish to quench their thirst at this spring must count everything else—even life itself—worthless by comparison. Everlasting life comes by accepting the offer: if you're thirsty, come and drink. It's a sweet deal: we trade everything we *think* we need for that which the Creator *knows* we need to live happily ever after. He promises not necessarily physical safety but complete satisfaction.

Jill is only a child who is weak and tired, lost and scared, hungry and thirsty. Spiritually, so are we, and we cannot save ourselves. Our common struggle is to acknowledge the lack of any other suitable option and to exchange the things we cling to for the "water of life," an illusory promise of safety for a taste of all that is eternally good.

Let anyone who is thirsty come. Let anyone who desires drink freely from the water of life. REVELATION 22:17

3 *"You would not have called to me unless I had been calling to you,"*
said the Lion. CHAP. II, P. 19

From folktales and myths to modern literature, stories speak of journeys. Whether or not a story's character actually goes anywhere, very often a transformational journey takes place within the character. Pilgrimages—journeys taken as a means to a spiritual end—are all similar in that some cover miles while others cover internal distances. Whether in reality or in fiction, a journey begins with the traveler's response to a draw upon the heart or mind.

In *The Silver Chair*, Jill and Eustace hear the call of Aslan upon their lives. The funny thing is they think it's their own idea. Eustace wishes for Aslan to allow them into Narnia as an escape from school bullies. Eustace, who has been there before, invents a pseudo-religious chant the children begin to perform, only to be interrupted by the thing actually happening. A gateway opens before them into the other world. So later, when Aslan alludes to his having called them, Jill wonders whether there could be some mistake, since their going had really been Eustace's idea. But Aslan assures them that he had enabled them to ask.

Jill and Eustace's progress (errors included), hardships, and lessons learned in Narnia parallel those of any Christian pilgrim who strives to stay focused on the task and the final destination. But there would be no progress, no lessons learned, without a call and a response. As Jesus explained to a group of complainers, no one comes to Jesus unless he or she is first drawn by God. Even our desire is not the initiator of our finding him but an affirmative answer to him who has already called us. He wants us even before we *want* to be wanted.

No one can come to me unless the Father who sent me draws them to me.
JOHN 6:44

4 *But, first, remember, remember, remember the Signs.*

CHAP. II, P. 21

Aslan gives Jill signs and instructions upon which the children's mission depends, as well as the destiny of not only the missing prince but all Narnia. So much rests upon Aslan's words—the knowing and following of them—that he has Jill repeat them several times until she gets them completely right and in the right order. He admonishes her to keep saying them to herself morning and night, and even when she wakes in the middle of the night.

Two salient points for us emerge from this instruction. First, get the words right. For the Christian, that means knowing what God has communicated to us in the Bible, because it contains the words of life. Read them; reread them; hear them; and remember, remember, remember them.

Second, get the sequence right. God's instructions often rely on a particular order, as do Aslan's to Jill. For example, "Seek the Kingdom of God above all else, and live righteously, and he will give you everything you need" (Matthew 6:33). Get the directions backward, and you simply won't end up at the right destination.

Even a child can remember and find guidance and protection in God's directing words. During Israel's time in the wilderness, God commanded the people through Moses to remember his instructions. Parents were to teach them to their children and perform other tasks to keep God's commandments in remembrance. In this way, they committed themselves "wholeheartedly" to God's instructions, just as Jill is reminded to commit to Aslan's. Talking about them at home or while traveling was the best way for the Israelites to keep them at the forefront. We, too, must keep God's words of guidance at the forefront of our lives.

Commit yourselves wholeheartedly to these commands that I am giving you today. . . . Talk about them when you are at home and when you are on the road, when you are going to bed and when you are getting up. DEUTERONOMY 6:6-7

5 *Both the children noticed that he said "we," not "you" and both exclaimed at the same moment, "Are you coming with us?"* CHAP. V, P. 61

With childlike acceptance, Jill and Eustace unquestioningly assume they will do as Aslan instructs, though they have no knowledge of the place or situation they are in and no resources other than their empty-handed selves. Yet everything falls into place as they find themselves clothed, sheltered, and feasted in a king's palace; transported and counseled by wise, talking owls; and delivered to Puddleglum, the Marsh-wiggle, who knows how to begin the journey. Better still, when Puddleglum includes himself in discussing their travel plans, the children realize with great joy that he is going with them as their companion and guide.

Aslan meets the children's needs entirely, reflecting the way God provides everything we need to accomplish his intents. Besides the Holy Spirit's subtle promptings from within, God gives us other helpers who, though imperfect humans like we are, may have just the spiritual resources and knowledge to complement our own. These helpers compose the church, the body of Christ, whose hands and feet and mouths do God's bidding throughout the world. They come alongside to guide and accompany.

In Narnia, the King's household gives out of its wealth. The owls provide flight and good advice. And though he possesses little—a mud hut, a hat, a fishing pole—Puddleglum himself (the person that he is) proves invaluable to them. It is in God's people that we will find the type of wealth most valuable to us in our own pilgrimages.

Equally important, we must realize that we, too, are a part of the body. And we must assume our responsibilities in contributing to the health, wealth, and well-being of our fellow members so that the body can respond effectively to the directives of its head, Jesus Christ.

What is your place in the body? How would you encourage someone who isn't sure of his or her place?

The human body has many parts, but the many parts make up one whole body. So it is with the body of Christ. I CORINTHIANS 12:12

6

There are no accidents. Our guide is Aslan.

CHAP. X, P. 134

In *The Silver Chair*, Lewis highlights God's amazing tendency to use all manner of human inadequacies, transforming them into tools for shaping his good purposes. Eustace, Jill, and Puddleglum prove weak vessels for Aslan's work; often confused, they fail to recognize their adversary and fall for her deception. They argue, lose interest in the signs, and choose to temporarily disregard their mission in exchange for the bodily comforts of food, warmth, and rest. In going off course, they almost become food for giants. However, their dalliance in a place they never should have been puts them in a position to see one of Aslan's signs that they had missed earlier. While trying to get back on track, they find themselves pursued by giants and hunting dogs. They duck into a hole in a rock, which deposits them exactly where they need to be: in the Underworld, where their mission awaits them. Would they have found the opening otherwise?

Jill and Eustace are slow to see that, despite their mistakes, Aslan conducts the events, bringing them face-to-face with the very person they seek, Prince Rilian. The prince, bewitched and unaware of his own identity, throws them into further doubt by using logic to undermine their interpretation of Aslan's sign. But Puddleglum has noticed the pattern of Aslan's "paw-print" upon their journey. He remembers what he has long known: Aslan is trustworthy in all things. Aslan's words test human logic, not the other way around.

Although as humans we make mistakes, with God there are no "accidents" and no "what-ifs." There is only the interweaving of all things as God determines each step we take and remains in control of every outcome.

We can make our plans, but the LORD determines our steps.

PROVERBS 16:9

7

There is nothing like a good shock of pain for dissolving certain kinds of magic. CHAP. XII, P. 158

Pain, a natural teacher with consequences that even babies and animals translate into learning experience, can fill us with useful knowledge. Pain comes both from harmful contacts and from the loss of good things. And it works as a wake-up call to teach us caution and attention.

In the story, Puddleglum does something that takes great maturity, something the children are incapable of doing. In an effort nearly too late already, knowing that in another moment he will be utterly lost to the mental stupor the witch's fatal enchantment is working upon him, he chooses pain to rouse himself. He stamps his foot into the fire, and his sizzling flesh clears his thinking fast!

Many Christians have discovered the principle Puddleglum employs here: that pain must sometimes be the friend with whom we journey. It takes maturity and strength of character to fight against the "magic" of enticements the enemy would use to lull us into complacency. Pain is always a warning signal, and sometimes embracing pain with its unpleasant consequences may be the only way to avoid even greater disaster. Washing up against rocks may be a better choice than going over a waterfall. Similarly, any amount of personal risk is preferable to the graver danger of sinful choices. Pain should not intimidate us. Rather, we should expect it as a consequence of being in the world but not of it.

Don't be afraid of those who want to kill your body; they cannot touch your soul. Fear only God, who can destroy both soul and body in hell. MATTHEW 10:28

8   *I'm on Aslan's side even if there isn't any Aslan to lead it. I'm going to live as like a Narnian as I can even if there isn't any Narnia.*

CHAP. XII, P. 159

Through her patronizing tone and banter, the Queen of the Underland suggests that a belief in Narnia (the Overland) and Aslan is beneath Eustace, Jill, and Puddleglum, who have gained knowledge through education, travel, and experience. And to these followers of Aslan, the idea that the objects of their love and loyalty are mere fictions is more than discouraging; it threatens them with despair. Yet, as his declaration shows, Puddleglum decides he prefers even a fruitless search for the good he senses must exist to remaining in the Underland with the alluring queen.

In some ways we, too, live in an underland, though our world is not so entirely glum as that in *The Silver Chair.* Unlike the inhabitants of the Underland, we see natural beauty so exquisite that even great artists have been frustrated in their attempts to capture it. Our history testifies to glorious acts of heroism, sacrifice, and love. Still, an underland-like dimness plagues our minds in insidious forms of greed and self-aggrandizement, leading to all types of injustices. Yet coexisting with this darker side of human nature is a longing for true justice that is tempered with mercy, for love that is guarded by discipline and discipline guarded by love, and for other ideals that have never been satisfactorily achieved in human history. And our intuition that such things *could be* reveals itself in our stories, which in turn inspire our aspirations and efforts toward these perceived ideals.

God's Word and Jesus' life provide the only models for thought and behavior that can produce the type of world we instinctively wish for. We show that we belong to Christ when we obey his commandments. And even if there were no Jesus or an eternity to be spent with him, so perfect are his teachings and example that following them would still be the worthiest of goals for a good life here in our Underland.

When you obey my commandments, you remain in my love, just as I obey my Father's commandments and remain in his love. JOHN 15:10

9

And she wanted to say "I'm sorry" but she could not speak.

CHAP. XVI, P. 210

Jill and Eustace have by now found the missing Prince Rilian and played a significant part in returning him to Narnia. Despite their success, they are mindful of the folly that nearly cost them the completion of their mission. All the reasons they might have failed—forgetfulness, tiredness, hunger, bad attitude, selfishness—show Jill the weaknesses inherent in her humanity as a "daughter of Eve." When she approaches Aslan, remorse precedes her joy in meeting him again.

As people, we cannot step outside our flawed nature any more than we can step outside our own skin. How mortified we will be at the sight of our shortcomings when we stand face-to-face with perfection! But Aslan comforts the children and congratulates them on completing the work for which he sent them.

God knows the frailty of human minds and hearts and bodies. And Aslan knew it when he chose Eustace and Jill for his agents. At the end of their journey, he is pleased. He meets them not with frowns and scolding but with love and forgiveness, and he says, "You did it!"

Our days are composed of similar journeys, with our sense of accomplishment compromised by an acute awareness of our personal failings. But the message of Matthew 25:21 is that God celebrates our obedience. He accepts our participation in his work, changing our shame and sin and toil into blessing and reward and rest.

Well done, my good and faithful servant. . . . Let's celebrate together!

MATTHEW 25:21

10

"I have come to bring you Home," said Aslan.

CHAP. XVI, P. 210

From Homer's Odysseus to Tolkien's Bilbo Baggins, warriors, thieves, adventurers, and sundry wanderers have ultimately sought the reward of homecoming. In *The Silver Chair,* as in the Christian's journey, once the task is done hearts yearn for the end of the road and for home at last.

If home is where the heart is, it is important that the heart arrives where it longs to abide. Eustace and Jill know the importance of their mission, but at the same time their hearts yearn for the presence of the Lion. Only Aslan can return them home to their own world and England, but more important, he *brings* them *Home* to himself. In *Planet Narnia*, Michael Ward notes, "The capital 'H' [in Home] and the verb 'bring,' rather than the expected 'take,' help make Lewis's point that home can be no other place than where the Christ-figure [Aslan] is."[1]

When our hearts are set upon Jesus, he brings us to himself. He is our home, no matter the circumstances, whether in sickness or in success, and no matter the place, whether in a palace or a prison. Paradoxically, in him we are home—we are already there—even while we journey, for his love and power surround us always; he has promised never to leave us nor forsake us (see Hebrews 13:5, NKJV). And, even greater, he promises to provide an eternal place of rest for us. When it's ready, he'll return for us.

As Aslan returns the children to their earthly home, Narnia dissolves before Eustace's and Jill's very eyes. They must, as we must, continue awhile longer in their native world. School and growing up and whatever else life holds for them still lie ahead, until this world, too, dissolves away and they have their eternal home in unobstructed view and they know Aslan without impediment. So may we all come home: as Jill and Eustace to the Lion of Narnia, so we to the Lion of Judah, both now and then.

When everything is ready, I will come and get you, so that you will always be with me where I am.   JOHN 14:3

TEMPTATION AND TRIUMPH

The world that God has made is good. Christians have always believed that evil is the perversion of good, that its existence is dependent upon the presence of good, which evil exploits and uses for bad. In fact, for purposes of analogy, one might say that evil compares to good as bread mold compares to bread. The mold is not good for the bread, but it still may have some significance to play. Man, made in the image of the Creator, has demonstrated the capacity to take the very bread mold that is so bad for the bread and make something with healing properties from it: penicillin.

Applying this principle, Christians believe that though this world was made good, tragedy occurred. The created beings sought to manage things themselves, without thought of God's purposes or intentions. The rebellion reached its zenith at Calvary: creatures crucifying their Creator, the Son of God. Nevertheless, God demonstrated, through the Cross of Christ and the Resurrection, his power to make a kind of divine penicillin to bring about forgiveness for sin, reconciliation to God for all who were estranged from him, and healing for the deep sorrows of the soul. And if his power to redeem and rescue lost humanity could be displayed in the macrocosm of Calvary, then certainly it can also be displayed in the microcosm of the particular events of every individual life.

This reading of temptation and triumph does not take lightly the facts of fallen humanity and our propensity to stumble. We live our lives as novices and often make mistakes. Yet despite this reality, we are infused with the hope of triumphant life in Christ. It is by the grace of God and our faith in that grace that we can have this hope. C. S. Lewis writes honestly about human failure, but he does so with optimism, confident in the triumph of the love of Christ and the hope found in him.

Because God knows all about us and loves us still, we also can be confident that he hears our honest words of repentance, forgives and comforts us, and encourages us to grow and do better. And it is love for him that increases our desire to follow him and makes temptations less attractive. In time, the things that distract us from God reveal their true nature, which is unable to satisfy, leaving us empty. After we have tethered our hearts to the things that moth and rust destroy, after our hearts break because we've sought fulfillment in the things that awaken desire but cannot fulfill it, in the moment of self-awareness when we awaken to our weakness and need—it is then that the love of God becomes even more precious to us, for we discover that he loves us even then. He comes to offer us his all; his love is not diminished by our poor performance. He will not cast out those who come to him. Lewis's writing is full of reminders of this triumph over temptation, this forgiveness for those who fail, this help and strength for all who call upon God.

CHAPTER 7

Perelandra

PERELANDRA IS THE SECOND BOOK in Lewis's science fiction trilogy. The main character in the books is an academic—a philologist, a lover of words, named Elwin Ransom. In fact, Ransom is a character Lewis patterned after his close friend J. R. R. Tolkien, who was a philologist at Oxford University. The intentionally selected name Elwin means "friend of elves."

In each of the science fiction novels Ransom has an important role to play to confront the devilry of wicked people. In each book the wicked characters use subjectivistic means to rationalize their malevolent intentions, and Ransom is called to thwart them as best as he is able. In *Out of the Silent Planet*, he finds himself on Mars, which Lewis calls Malacandra. It is an old, unfallen civilization. An evil man, Weston, must be stopped in his intent to colonize Mars and exploit its resources.

Ransom's conflict with Weston continues in the second book of the trilogy and achieves its zenith on Perelandra, or Venus. Perelandra, a young planet, has a young woman and a young man as its sole inhabitants. They are the Eve and Adam of that world. Eventually, Weston becomes so compromised by evil and subjectivism that he can no longer be called a man; Ransom refers to him as the *Un-man*. A battle between himself and the Un-man for the soul of this woman is the source of tension.

Perelandra is a planet made up of a continent and seas full of floating islands. And it has one inexorable law: no one is to remain overnight on the continent. The great temptation, then, is to seek an artificial permanence. How easy it would be to imagine that stability and security are found in life on the continent, rather than in Maleldil—the name by which God is called. In some ways, the Perelandrian temptation is one common to all—the desire to abandon God for a "false infinite" that can never fully satisfy. This temptation can be understood as making a permanent idol out of a temporary, merely present, understanding. No matter what one knows about anything, especially about God, it must eventually be abandoned for a more robust understanding. The Un-man thinks his way is the ultimate way; to linger long on the continent is to make permanent what ought to be held loosely. Ransom's role on Perelandra is to fight for true permanence in God and against artificialities. He fights for triumph in the midst of temptation.

1 *I suppose everyone knows this fear of getting "drawn in"... the sense that a door has just slammed and left him on the inside.*

CHAP. I, P. 10

As Lewis, the narrator of *Perelandra*, travels to the home of his friend, Ransom, he contemplates seeing one of the mysterious, angel-like eldila Ransom has previously talked about. While the thought of seeing an eldil terrifies him, being "drawn in"—deciding what he truly believes—is the only way to triumph over that fear.

Life is full of events that threaten to go beyond our control or cause us to think deeply about its true meaning. After being battered by temptation like a door breached and loosed at its hinges, we realize that the ability to triumph lies beyond another door, one we have yet to open because we've never turned the knob.

Saul, dutiful Pharisee and persecutor of Christians, was knocked to the ground by the reality of the risen Christ. Hearing his voice and seeing "a light from heaven" (Acts 9:3)—just as narrator Lewis would hear Ransom's name called and see a light—Saul could no longer linger in the belief that "He was just a good teacher" or "He was only a man." Consequently, Saul—later known as Paul—could no longer believe that Christians were the enemies of God. Instead, *he* had been in the wrong. And the loss of his physical sight for three days underscored the metaphor of his spiritual blindness.

We don't always have such vivid glimpses into the supernatural to help us walk through the door of belief. Yet every day, as we face temptation of some kind, it's up to us to walk through the door.

As he was approaching Damascus on this mission, a light from heaven suddenly shone down around him. He fell to the ground and heard a voice saying to him, "Saul! Saul! Why are you persecuting me?" ACTS 9:3-4

2   *As long as what you are afraid of is something evil, you may still hope that the good may come to your rescue. But suppose you struggle through to the good and find that it also is dreadful?*   CHAP. I, P. 17

Running the gauntlet of fears along the path to Ransom's home and having an eldil waiting to meet him is a rock-and-a-hard-place situation for the character, Lewis, in *Perelandra*. After struggling through this barrage of fear along the way, Lewis faces another struggle: deciding whether the eldil in Ransom's home fits his definition of good. It seems dreadful to him—almost on par with the horror he felt while walking along the path.

Sometimes we view God through the veil of fear or even horror. Such a view can stem from misconceptions with which we have yet to wrestle. Therefore, we find approaching such a God—the God of our imagination—difficult when we're feeling fearful or weak. Would you agree?

If you're wrestling with a fear-filled view of God in the nonreverential sense, consider the message of Psalm 136. The psalmist doesn't just tell you that God is good; he also explains *why* he is good. Not only was he the Creator (v. 5); he also acted for the good of his people. He rescued Israel from their enemies, provided food for them, and gave them Canaan, the land he had promised them.

Unlike a tyrant who tries to crush the will of the people, God was and still is ever mindful of the fears and weaknesses of his people. He knows when we wrestle with our beliefs about him. He just wants us to admit that we do. Best of all, he doesn't chide us for any misconceptions we have. Instead, he reminds us of his qualities and what he's done in the past.

Give thanks to the LORD, for he is good! His faithful love endures forever. . . . He remembered us in our weakness. His faithful love endures forever. He saved us from our enemies. His faithful love endures forever. He gives food to every living thing. His faithful love endures forever.   PSALM 136:1, 23-25

3   *This itch to have things over again, as if life were a film that could be unrolled twice or even made to work backwards . . . was it possibly the root of all evil?*   CHAP. 4, P. 43

As Ransom acclimates himself to Perelandra, he discovers the refreshing bubble trees and a tree with yellow fruit so succulent that it would be irresistible in our world. Having tried both, Ransom has a strong desire to indulge again. Yet to do so, knowing that he is full, seems wrong.

We might wonder what the harm is in reliving precious moments. Yet, as C. S. Lewis explains through his character, problems arise from the desire to continuously live in those moments—to hang on to them or hoard them, instead of moving on. Ransom considers whether overindulgence in any form—in the past, in self-pity, or in food—is "the root of all evil."

Perhaps this is the issue behind the apostle Paul's reminder to his spiritual son, Timothy, of how godliness and contentment work together. As a missionary striving to be Christlike, Paul knew the value of being content with what he had—whether he had a little or a lot. He kept his sights on gaining more of Christ, rather than gaining anything else.

What is the "itch" in your life? We sometimes clutch our children to us—wanting to keep them with us or dependent on us forever. Perhaps we try to keep other relationships unchanged, living in the past, thus keeping life in the present on permanent pause. Paul's admonition to be content and strive for godliness reminds us that life isn't always about hoarding or indulging. It also involves releasing and standing still. We can release our need to hoard by standing in the contentment God offers. As with Ransom, the key for Paul was remembering that he was full. Contentment in Christ makes us full.

True godliness with contentment is itself great wealth. After all, we brought nothing with us when we came into the world, and we can't take anything with us when we leave it.   I TIMOTHY 6:6-7

4   *"So that," he thought, "that is why I have been sent here. He failed on Malacandra and now he is coming here. And it's up to me to do something about it."*   CHAP. 6, P. 70

"It's up to me."

With dawning clarity and a sinking heart, Ransom realizes his awesome responsibility: he has to deal with the-thing-that-was-Weston before the Un-man's cancerous influence corrupts the heart of the Green Lady and thus all of Perelandra. On Malacandra, in *Out of the Silent Planet*, Ransom could do very little about Weston. But here on Perelandra, no one else will step in and do the work. The buck stops with Ransom.

One of the reasons the Old Testament book of Esther is so compel-ling is that the buck stopped with Esther, too. As her relative, Mordecai, explained to her in no uncertain terms, Esther and her people would die unless she acted to stop Haman's plan of extermination. Her ascension to the limelight of queenship made such a step possible.

During those rubber-meets-the-road experiences, we're sometimes tempted to shirk responsibility, or at least procrastinate, as Ransom does for a time—hoping that God will send someone else to do the job. Growing in maturity involves taking the responsibility God gives us. Sometimes he places us in positions or at just the right place to enable us to take a stand. But such a step is risky. Esther could have been killed for appear-ing before the king without being summoned. But she went anyway. As a result, Haman's plan was thwarted.

As Ransom contemplates the step he needs to take to save the Green Lady and Perelandra, he also considers the pain God sometimes allows. God doesn't always spare the lives of his risk takers. You have only to read any book of church history to know that. Are you willing to take a stand for the Kingdom even at the risk of life and limb . . . or the death of your reputation?

If you keep quiet at a time like this, deliverance and relief for the Jews will arise from some other place, but you and your relatives will die. Who knows if perhaps you were made queen for just such a time as this? ESTHER 4:14

5

Have you ever had an argument in which you felt totally bested? Such is the case for Ransom as he seeks to protect the Green Lady, while Weston, now the Un-man, tempts her to sin. Though it seems as if Ransom is on the losing side of the verbal spar, the pearl of his persuasive argument comes at last: why not obey simply because Maleldil—the God of the universe—asked?

This situation mirrors that of Adam and Eve in the Garden of Eden. The command to avoid eating from the tree of the knowledge of good and evil might have seemed strange. Yet it was a necessary first step on the long path of obedience. Sadly, this step was the one on which our foreparents stumbled after the snake's persuasive argument.

When temptation beckons, we, too, sometimes think about what we'd be missing if we resist it. Weston tries to convince the Green Lady of the "unfairness" of Maleldil's rule about not living on the Fixed Island. Likewise, the enemy of our souls tries to convince us of the unfairness or irrelevance of God's commands. Yet the Bible assures us that God never changes (see Hebrews 13:8; James 1:17).

A harried mother might tell her children, "Because I said so," when her directions are questioned, and in a way, God says those words to us. Sometimes he wants us to obey him simply because he asks. Of course, unlike a parent whose "Because I said so" might signal anger or a lack of patience, Father God always leads us lovingly and for our good.

The LORD God warned [the man], "You may freely eat the fruit of every tree in the garden—except the tree of the knowledge of good and evil. If you eat its fruit, you are sure to die." GENESIS 2:16-17

6

We cannot walk out of Maleldil's will: but He has given us a way to walk out of our will. CHAP. 9, PP. 101–102

The Green Lady on Perelandra fails to realize the danger of giving in to the temptation until Ransom explains the situation to her. Because her understanding is childlike, she doesn't recognize the subtleties of Weston's evil. With Ransom's help, she discerns that escaping from her own will, rather than Maleldil's, is the best option. In times of temptation, our judgment and understanding can be clouded by a lack of information or by our own desires. With our choices so uninformed, we, too, might easily be led astray. Then, what we choose seems right only because we are unfamiliar with a better option.

What is the better option? How can we "walk out of our will" when temptations come, the Weston-like temptations that beckon slyly or appeal to the intellect? Often we try to have a game plan for forestalling temptation: "This spring I will stop overeating to be in shape for summer!" or "This year I will quit smoking!" But even the strongest willpower has a tendency to flag as the months roll by.

We may feel anything but triumphant as the Ghosts of Failures Past mock our determination to win past the current temptation. But we must take heart. The apostle Paul had a viable plan for battling temptation. As he explained to the Corinthian believers, God is there to provide a way out—"a way to walk out of our will." This means choosing to obey God, following his light in the darkness of temptation, and making our choices according to his will.

Tempted? Rather than depending on your determination, recall the God who endured temptation and overcame it. God's strength and ability to get us past the temptation never fail. Don't believe it? Check out Matthew 4:1-11. Now, lean into his strength.

The temptations in your life are no different from what others experience. And God is faithful. He will not allow the temptation to be more than you can stand. When you are tempted, he will show you a way out so that you can endure.

I CORINTHIANS 10:13

7

[W]ith that "Now or never" he began to play on a fear which the Lady apparently shared with the women of earth—the fear that life might be wasted, some great opportunity let slip. CHAP. 10, P. 112

An old advertising campaign for the army, which challenged recruits to "be all that you can be," can provide insight for understanding the Green Lady's struggle—one to which women throughout time can relate. The temptation by the Un-man has led her to contemplate the great work that she might be missing out on. Suddenly her lot in life doesn't quite measure up to what it could be.

The mundane aspects of our lives can lead us to believe this as well. When we've carried out our least favorite task at work or cleaned up the sixteenth spill of the day, we might wonder, *Is this all there is? Am I really being all I can be?* We start to second-guess the decisions that led us to where we are—even if we know that our decisions had God's approval. And seeing others who seem more "successful" adds to our discontent.

Being "all that you can be" means doing whatever you're given to do "as though you were working for the Lord," as Paul admonished the believers of Colossae. It means joyfully going to the office or cleaning up the spill, if that is the work God has for you. It means praying for God to point out the opportunities he has for you. It also means taking your eyes off those who seem to "have it all" or those who express doubts concerning the quality of your life according to their standards. Above all, it means being content with where God has placed you right now.

Contentment comes by being satisfied with what we have been given. Often the things we long for cannot fulfill us for very long; they are the things that moths and rust destroy or thieves steal (see Matthew 6:19-20). God alone is the good that cannot be taken from us. If you are content with him, becoming content where you are is a real possibility. Be all that you can be right where you are.

Work willingly at whatever you do, as though you were working for the Lord rather than for people. COLOSSIANS 3:23

8   *He could not understand why Maleldil should remain absent when the Enemy was there in person.*   CHAP. 11, P. 119

When was the last time you found yourself on the ragged edge of exhaustion? In his constant vigilance over the Green Lady, Ransom finally reaches a state of utter weariness. The relentless arguments of the Un-man and his petty, compulsive use of Ransom's name have caused Ransom to feel forsaken by Maleldil.

As Lewis revealed in *Perelandra*, the plans of the enemy aren't always grandiose—the threat of the utter annihilation of a civilization via a nuclear bomb, for example. Instead, his plans often involved petty details that resulted in confusion, discouragement, and fatigue.

In our world, the presence of Satan—the enemy of believers in Christ—is keenly felt. There are increases in school shootings and other crimes involving innocent victims, media content that pushes the envelope far beyond the boundaries of good taste, and other strong reminders. Perhaps you, like Ransom, wonder where God is when the presence of evil seems so pervasive. Like David—and Jesus, who echoed his cry while on the cross—perhaps you're ready to say, "My God, my God, why have you abandoned me? Why are you so far away when I groan for help?" (Psalm 22:1).

Exhaustion can cause havoc with our faith and color everything a dismal gray. We feel Job-like in our suffering. But those times of exhaustion are when the enemy chooses to strike. "Like a roaring lion" (1 Peter 5:8), he seeks us when we're at our weakest and more apt to fall victim to his relentless attacks. But we can remember what David and Jesus knew—that God is still present. At the ragged edge of our exhaustion, he's waiting to catch us before we fall. The writer of Hebrews reminds us that God would never abandon his people. Sometimes he seems distant in order for us to rise up and walk toward him.

I will never fail you. I will never abandon you.   HEBREWS 13:5

9

The eldila of all worlds, the sinless organisms of everlasting light, were silent in Deep Heaven to see what Elwin Ransom of Cambridge would do. CHAP. II, P. 121

You would probably be stunned if a virtuoso pianist stood back and allowed an eleven-year-old to play the piano instead of him or her. But if playing the piano just then was an important step in the child's progress, perhaps you wouldn't be as shocked.

Ransom realizes that all heaven waits for him to do something to rid Perelandra of the evil that threatens to destroy it. Just imagine a colony of virtuoso performers, waiting for a novice like Ransom to perform. Though he doesn't know exactly what to do, he knows that at some point he will have to act. Key moments of decision—the Roman emperor Constantine as he contemplated Christianity, the legendary Roman soldier Horatius as he defended a bridge against the invading Etruscans, and Eve as she contemplated the forbidden fruit—run through his mind. At each of these moments, Ransom imagines, all heaven quietly waited for the decision to be made.

At times we all feel like novices. We're afraid to make a move, fearing that we'll fail. Little do we know that our stumbling, halting steps—like those of a baby taking his or her first steps—are infinitely precious to the Father. He cheers us on as we take those first necessary steps of faith and supplies what we need, as the apostle Paul reminded the Philippian believers. It's all part of the faith journey—we have to take steps.

When you know that you can perform a task well, you don't hesitate to do it, do you? Paul's words remind us that we're capable of anything God calls us to do, thanks to the ultimate virtuoso living within us—the Holy Spirit.

How will you act this week to the glory of God? Perhaps you might be led to step out of your comfort zone and speak about Christ to a coworker or help someone you wouldn't normally notice. Remember: you can do it—*through Christ.*

I can do everything through Christ, who gives me strength. PHILIPPIANS 4:13

10 *When Eve fell, God was not Man. He had not yet made men members of His body: since then He had, and through them henceforward He would save and suffer.* CHAP. II, P. 123

"We are his hands"—or so the song goes. Through us—the body of Christ—God effects change in the world. This is the lesson Ransom discovers as he contemplates what to do about Weston, the Un-man. Ransom is, in a sense, Maleldil's "hands." This is why Ransom cannot fully rest until he acts to fight the influence of Weston and help the Green Lady.

In a human body, all parts work together to perform individual functions. The heart pumps blood; electrical impulses sizzle across the synapses. The body is in motion because different parts work together. And when one part misfires or breaks down, other parts fail to work as well too.

In the same way, the body of Christ is designed to work together. Each Christian is a vital part of the body. The gifts and abilities we have (preaching, teaching, administration, healing, and so on) help the body to operate. And as the apostle Paul observed, we suffer when other members of the body suffer, though sometimes we think we can function even when others falter. We were made to be in community—to be involved in one another's lives. Yet we fear getting involved, getting our hands dirty, being inconvenienced, or inconveniencing others. Or we sit back and wait for someone else to take up the cause. But the amazing thing is that the all-powerful God willingly acts through his flawed people. We miss out if we choose to ignore that truth and fail to do our part to help the body. We are truly in this together.

God has put the body together such that extra honor and care are given to those parts that have less dignity. This makes for harmony among the members, so that all the members care for each other. If one part suffers, all the parts suffer with it, and if one part is honored, all the parts are glad. I CORINTHIANS 12:24-26

CHAPTER 8

A Preface to Paradise Lost

LEWIS WROTE *A PREFACE TO PARADISE LOST* as an introduction to John Milton's great poem. As is evident in a debate he had with fellow scholar E. M. W. Tillyard (recently republished as *The Personal Heresy*), Lewis was concerned that some critics of Milton never analyze the text, choosing instead to engage in a discussion of Milton's personality at the time he wrote the book. Lewis was clear in his condemnation of this kind of literary critical approach because, he said, the critic never gets to the text; therefore, the so-called analysis of the author's personality is little more than a projection made by the critic. Lewis thought it necessary to write about the text of Milton's *Paradise Lost* for those interested in the actual content of the poem. His goal was to counter poor critiques of Milton.

It was Lewis's attention to Milton's content, as well as to the background and analysis he supplied, that made *A Preface to Paradise Lost* relevant to these reflections dealing with temptation and triumph. Lewis began his work with a discussion about types of epic poetry, recognizing that Milton, like Virgil before him, chose a form of poetry that best fit the kind of story he was seeking to tell. To understand epic poetry, as well as Milton's use of this literary form, it was necessary to interpret the story itself. Milton's epic is about Creation and the Fall; it is the story of Adam and Eve, their choice to disobey in the Garden of Eden, and the unfortunate consequences that followed. Lewis explained that the style in which Milton wrote allows the reader to enter into the experience of the story of the Fall—in a way, to feel the weight and gravity of it. The style, not unlike a ritual, focuses or concentrates the reader's attention on that which is described. Milton's account of the Fall revealed what was at stake in Eden and recaptured the devastation that took place there. Perhaps Lewis's faithful assessment of Milton and his willingness to take the themes of *Paradise Lost* seriously allow his readers to see why the pursuit of triumph in the teeth of temptation is so important in the first place.

1   *Our life has bends as well as extension: moments at which we realize*
that we have just turned some great corner, and that everything,
for better or worse, will always henceforth be different.   CHAP. VI, P. 34

Ever feel nostalgic for the way things used to be? In the summer some of us long for the lazy days of vacation we had as students. Others think about how "carefree" life seemed to be before marriage and kids. The fact is that life sometimes involves transformation—a bend in the river. The Greek poet Virgil dealt with such world-order transformations in his epic *The Aeneid*. And Lewis reminded us that Milton's epic *Paradise Lost* describes just such a transition, from which there was no turning back. Consider the fall of Pompeii or the example Lewis gave in this context: Virgil's description of the arrival of the Trojans at Actium.

Other bends in the river could be sudden chronic illness, the loss of a family member, or other crises or permanent changes to our lives. In such cases we may feel as if we're struggling against rapids rather than being smoothly swept along a current. It's then that we long for the way life used to be. That's why the apostle Paul advised the Roman believers and others to avoid mirroring the reactions of the world. The world's reactions include bitterness, resentment, desires for revenge, and so on. None of these reflect a life transformed by God. Instead, they reflect a desire to resist or cling to the status quo.

We must choose to be transformed—to be carried along the river. If not, we might find ourselves dashed against the rocks of bitterness, fear, or resentment. Choosing to be transformed starts with our mind-set—our willingness to be led by God and accept whatever change he brings. Are you willing?

Don't copy the behavior and customs of this world, but let God transform you into a new person by changing the way you think. Then you will learn to know God's will for you, which is good and pleasing and perfect. ROMANS 12:2

2 *This is the very portrait of a vocation: a thing that calls or beckons, that calls inexorably, yet you must strain your ears to catch the voice, that insists on being sought, yet refuses to be found.* CHAP. VI, P. 37

As Lewis reminded his readers, some characters in epic poetry sense a call to action or a call to journey to a specified place that may or may not exist or that existed in the past. Throughout the epic there are glimpses of this land that tickle the sensibilities of the hero or heroine. There is also a sense of nostalgia for the way things were (for example, the innocence of the Garden of Eden).

If you are a believer, you can't help thinking of heaven—the place for which we're bound, which does exist but exists outside our reach on this side of life. It is the Celestial City in Bunyan's *The Pilgrim's Progress* and the pre-sin Garden of Eden in Milton's *Paradise Lost*. You feel the call or pull to this place, which is now your rightful home. It beckons to you as you go about your daily tasks. This destiny even informs some of your decisions. While the pull might seem faint sometimes, especially in times of doubt, it is always there. It outlines in gold even the tasks we think are mundane, especially if they're done in the name of Jesus.

As Paul explained, his pressing on had a purpose: to fulfill his call to journey toward heaven. It kept him steady through many hard times as a missionary and his eventual martyrdom. He knew that someday he would reach that "perfection" of which he caught a glimpse on the road to Damascus.

We no longer have to mourn the loss of "paradise." We're heading toward it right now. Like Paul, we just have to press on.

I don't mean to say that I have already achieved these things or that I have already reached perfection. But I press on to possess that perfection for which Christ Jesus first possessed me. . . . I press on to reach the end of the race and receive the heavenly prize for which God, through Christ Jesus, is calling us.

PHILIPPIANS 3:12, 14

3 *These references to the obvious and the immemorial are there not to give us new ideas about the lost garden but to make us know that the garden is found.* CHAP. VII, P. 49

If you've ever found yourself stirred by a piece of music and were not really sure why, the quote from *A Preface to Paradise Lost* above hints at timeless truths behind the stirring. The music might be a reference to the "obvious and the immemorial"—something that points to an archetype, such as heroism or paradise. We recognize the brassy strains as the hero's call to action or the soft violin pieces that signal love, because these sounds are generally used as cues for these virtues. But if the sounds were reversed—the brass for love and the soft violin for a hero stirred to action—we would be badly jarred.

As Lewis described in *A Preface to Paradise Lost*, the familiar images of the Garden of Eden in *Paradise Lost* help us know not only what we're looking at and what was lost but also what we can hope for. We know from the Creation account in Genesis 2 that the lost garden was paradise before the corruptive influence of Lucifer. We expect we would have been dazzled by the grandeur of nature—something beyond even the most beautiful garden on earth. We can't help mourning the loss of such an idyllic place through sin.

Many times, we try to recapture what we lost in the hopes of hanging on to it. With Eden, there's no going back. But we can look forward to heaven. There we'll have a fully realized and unending paradise.

That's why we can't help thrilling to the apostle John's description of heaven and the new city of Jerusalem. The pure, natural, and noncursed elements described in the passage below accord with our view of the paradise we have lost. We recognize the place, even though we've never seen it. Yet this "paradise" will be found by all who trust in Jesus. Do you trust in him? If so, someday he'll welcome you home to such a setting. It will no longer be an ideal only longed for, but a reality.

The angel showed me a river with the water of life, clear as crystal, flowing from the throne of God and of the Lamb. It flowed down the center of the main street. . . . No longer will there be a curse upon anything. For the throne of God and of the Lamb will be there, and his servants will worship him.

REVELATION 22:1-3

4 *Those who will not be God's sons become His tools.*

"Why does God allow so much evil in the world?"

Perhaps you've heard someone voice this question lately while contemplating the latest atrocity in the news; maybe you voiced it yourself after experiencing the pain of someone's wrongdoing. As you read Lewis's analysis in *A Preface to Paradise Lost* of Satan's plans for evil and the good that God brought out of those plans, the question of God's sovereignty comes to mind.

Here Lewis recalls a mixture of doctrine from Milton as well as Augustine, the great bishop of Hippo. Even the greatest evil can become a tool for good in the hands of the God who has ultimate control over everything. This idea that God retains control over everything is impossible for the human mind to fully comprehend. We might struggle to believe that God was still in control during the Holocaust or today when children are murdered. Yet under God's sovereignty, even the most evil actions can be turned around for good.

Many people in the Bible understood this issue. As Joseph contemplated his position in Egypt—a position brought about through the actions of his jealous brothers—he confronted them with truth. They had been the very tools God used to bring Joseph to Egypt and thus save the family during a time of great famine. Job understood this issue all too well, when God allowed Satan to have his way with him; Satan was the unwitting tool that God used to further plane his instrument Job. And Old Testament prophets such as Jeremiah and Ezekiel knew firsthand that God allowed enemy nations to conquer Israel in order to teach his wayward people a lesson.

As we contemplate the wrongs others have done to us or the stumbling blocks in our lives, God offers another perspective: they could be tools God uses to shape us.

You intended to harm me, but God intended it all for good. He brought me to this position so I could save the lives of many people. GENESIS 50:20

5 *The Fall is simply and solely Disobedience—doing what you have been told not to do: and it results from Pride—from being too big for your boots, forgetting your place, thinking that you are God.* CHAP. X, P. 69

"Majoring in the minors" is a charge we might lay before someone who is focusing on the unimportant details of a situation. In a sense, this was Lewis's argument as he discussed the exact nature of the fruit eaten by Adam and Eve in Book IX of *Paradise Lost.* The fruit itself doesn't matter, Lewis averred. What matters is that Adam and Eve disobeyed God—plain and simple.

We're sometimes tempted to major in the minors in another sense. Attempting to minimize the magnitude of our sins, we might claim that we couldn't help ourselves or are not as bad as other people nowadays. We would rather not talk about pride—or, as Lewis put it, "forgetting [our] place"—even if that's our hidden agenda. If we focus on these other details, we might feel helpless to change. And if *we* can't change ourselves, can anyone?

What we forget is that pride is a poison, and the antidote it requires is grace and humility. God's grace allows us to forsake any pretense of wholeness and make an admission of sin—and that humility always takes pride down a notch. The fragrance of humility is sweet to God. In Jesus' parable of the Pharisee and the tax collector, the humble prayer of the tax collector "justified" him before God, whereas the prayer of the Pharisee simply reinforced his own pride.

If we really want to be justified, we can admit when we've done wrong and seek God's mercy. This strategy worked for the tax collector and will help us keep our focus off minor details.

The tax collector stood at a distance and dared not even lift his eyes to heaven as he prayed. Instead, he beat his chest in sorrow, saying, "O God, be merciful to me, for I am a sinner." I tell you, this sinner, not the Pharisee, returned home justified before God. LUKE 18:13-14

6

It is like the scent of a flower trying to destroy the flower. As a consequence the same rebellion which means misery for the feelings and corruption for the will, means Nonsense for the intellect.

CHAP. XIII, P. 94

The plot to overthrow the hierarchy of heaven (Book V of *Paradise Lost*) seems as ludicrous, as Lewis describes it, as one of those "world's worst criminals" shows. These delight in detailing the ludicrous mistakes of criminals—mistakes that led to their capture, such as the bank robber who wore a work shirt with his name scrawled across it during a robbery or the thieves who posted pictures of their exploits on the Internet. The phrase "shooting oneself in the foot" comes to mind when we hear of such cases, as when we read Milton's descriptions of angels created by God and now seeking to overthrow his rule.

This sort of blindness fits the prophet Isaiah's description of Judah's blind disobedience. The leaders of Judah sought alliances with nations such as Egypt, believing they could get by without God. The same is true today. You've undoubtedly heard someone proclaim doubt about God's existence, expecting God to prove himself or else the doubter will have nothing to do with the idea of him. Or, you've heard others delight in the wrongs they've done, believing that God—if he exists—was powerless to stop them. But as with the rebellion in heaven and with Judah, God allows rebellion only for a time. He merely awaits an opportune moment before he judges. And that's mercy.

One of the Holy Spirit's tasks is to convict us of wrong. However, as the writer of Hebrews warns, "Today when you hear his voice, don't harden your hearts as Israel did when they rebelled, when they tested me in the wilderness" (Hebrews 3:7-8). Do you hear his voice? Don't harden your heart.

Surely you have things turned around!
Shall the potter be esteemed as the clay;
For shall the thing made say of him who made it,
"He did not make me"?
Or shall the thing formed say of him who formed it,
"He has no understanding"?

ISAIAH 29:16, NKJV

7

Heaven understands Hell and Hell does not understand Heaven.

CHAP. XIII, P. 98

In the last movie or television show you saw, who was the more memorable: the hero or the villain? Many actors express their preference for playing the villains in movies; for them, playing Macbeth would be preferable to playing Macduff. Such parts are often more colorful and much more memorable for viewers.

Is it any wonder that Satan seems the most complex character in *Paradise Lost*? He's more vivid and therefore easier to understand. As Lewis explained, villains seem easier for an author to describe than the heroic ones. This is all due to our sin nature. On this side of the Fall, we can relate to the motivations of some story villains, who often don't think of themselves as villains at all.

Because of this tendency of ours, we can see why God declares through the prophet Isaiah that his thoughts are not like ours. Being born with a sin nature, we can't comprehend what it's like never to sin, never even to make a mistake. Sadly, this very nature leads us to underestimate God. If we can't imagine infinite love or compassion, we doubt that we could ever experience it—and we don't quite recognize it when we do.

This description of God's thoughts was not meant to cause embarrassment or slight but to encourage us. In just the previous verse, Isaiah described God's mercy. Although we don't understand his higher ways, our all-knowing, all-seeing God understands our weaknesses and doubt. Acknowledging his omniscience, we can trustfully rest.

Trying to wrap our minds fully around the infinite leads only to a headache. Sometimes instead of trying to "get it" in our minds, we need simply to accept the truth in our hearts.

"My thoughts are nothing like your thoughts," says the LORD. *"And my ways are far beyond anything you could imagine. For just as the heavens are higher than the earth, so my ways are higher than your ways and my thoughts higher than your thoughts."* ISAIAH 55:8-9

8 *They know they will not repent. That door out of Hell is firmly locked, by the devils themselves, on the inside; whether it is also locked on the outside need not, therefore, be considered.* CHAP. XIV, P. 102

We have all seen people dig in their heels on a particular issue. Whether it's a position, a political ideal, or some other uncrossable line that brings out stubbornness, their faces are like a locked door to which the key has been thrown away.

In *Paradise Lost*, Satan and his minions have locked the door to repentance and thrown away the key. Lewis wrote of the way of humiliation and repentance as the way out of hell for humans; Satan's devils will never take that route. They will never yield, never return to a life of service to the Almighty. Their willfulness is a powerful reminder of the pharaoh of Egypt during Moses' time. Throughout Exodus 7 to 10 is a constant refrain: "Even so, Pharaoh's heart remained stubborn, and he still refused to let the people go" (Exodus 9:7). In chapter 11 the refrain changes: "The LORD hardened Pharaoh's heart, and he wouldn't let the Israelites leave the country" (Exodus 11:10). The door has now finally been locked.

We all have moments of stubbornness—our "locked-door" moments. But David, the psalmist-king, offered a remedy: good, old-fashioned repentance. This is a voluntary releasing of pride and a willingness to change. No stranger to stubborn stances (see 2 Samuel 11), David at least knew when to own up to his wrongdoing. His psalm of contrition is a textbook lesson on repentance. Instead of continually cramming things in his spiritual closet and trying to force the door shut, he invited God to clean everything out.

What's in your closet? Need God to clean it out? You have to unlock and open the door first.

Create in me a clean heart, O God. Renew a loyal spirit within me.
PSALM 51:10

9 *For everything that has been lost, you can find something else that will do quite as well.* CHAP. XIV, P. 103

What would give a crack house that "homey" touch? New curtains? Knickknacks and nicer furnishings? Perhaps a doorbell with a lovely chime? The idea is ludicrous, is it not? You could decorate it and give it a new paint job, but it would still be a crack house—a place of addiction and death.

In Book II of Milton's *Paradise Lost*, Satan is discussing with his minions the possibility of another war with the army of heaven when Mammon, one of the fallen angels, brings up the idea that their place of residence could be just as good as the heavenly home now lost forever. He reasons that they could find a substitute for the light of heaven that would be just as good as the real thing.

Not likely! Yet how many times have we had similar thoughts? In *A Preface to Paradise Lost*, Lewis wrote of similar substitutes made in the hopes of regaining what was lost—love or honor or some other good. We think, *I can sleep with him and gain a semblance of love, even though we're not married.* Or, *I can make amends for the money I stole by giving some of it to charity.*

The apostle Paul pointed out this penchant for substitutes in his letter to the Roman believers. God's wrath was kindled against those who would prefer to worship people or sinful desires instead of worshiping God. Unwilling to attain heaven by repenting and obeying God, they preferred a "decorated crack house" existence. Their mantra: "I'd rather rule in hell than serve in heaven," or "Sin boldly." The heart of the matter is control— preferring one's own instead of God's. But control is merely an illusion— like the high of a drug, which always ends in a crash.

We fool ourselves when we believe that any way other than God's is a path to lasting satisfaction. We might have a form of satisfaction temporarily. But "trad[ing] the truth about God for a lie" ultimately leads to heartache.

They traded the truth about God for a lie. So they worshiped and served the things God created instead of the Creator himself, who is worthy of eternal praise! Amen.
ROMANS 1:25

10 *No man, perhaps, ever at first described to himself the act he was about to do as Murder, or Adultery, or Fraud, or Treachery, or Perversion.*

CHAP. XVIII, P. 122

Even after being caught with a hand in the proverbial cookie jar, many people will come up with a euphemism or some other rationalization. So we might hear of an "affair" or an "aggressive business dealing" instead of adultery or extortion. Like former president Nixon during the Watergate scandal of 1973, the defendant declares, "I'm not a crook."[1]

After being tricked by Satan, who was in the guise of the serpent specially chosen for this mission, Eve plucked and ate the fruit of the tree of knowledge (Book IX of *Paradise Lost*). And, rather than see Adam wedded to another if God elected to punish her for disobedience, she decided to persuade Adam to eat the fruit. Lewis described the motivations of both. Eve didn't think of herself as attempting to murder Adam. Yet her persuasion contributes to his spiritual and, later, physical death. And Adam, out of fear of losing Eve, agreed to eat the fruit. At that moment he preferred the created, rather than the Creator.

Instead of rationalizing like Adam and Eve did, Paul the apostle boldly declared himself in the wrong and incapable of doing the right thing in his own strength. Speaking of his sins, he didn't say he "made a mistake" or some other euphemism. Instead he took pride out of the equation and owned up to the wrong.

Who among us can't relate to Paul's frustration at his failure to do what was right? Consider the last time you tried to avoid a temptation but fell headlong into it instead. Paul's own transparency encourages us to be transparent before the God who sees all anyway—even when we try to cover up. Only God can help us triumph over our wrongful desires.

I don't really understand myself, for I want to do what is right, but I don't do it. Instead, I do what I hate. ROMANS 7:15

CHAPTER 9

The Screwtape Letters

THE SCREWTAPE LETTERS is one of C. S. Lewis's most popular and creative books. The fictional Screwtape is a senior devil writing instructional letters to his nephew, Wormwood, on how to tempt an unsuspecting human "patient." The letters were first published in installments, one per week, in the London newspaper *The Guardian*. When completed, they were bundled together and released in book form in 1942, running through multiple printings that very year.

Everything in the book is written in an upside-down manner. Screwtape fashions himself in the right: he refers to Satan as "Our Father Below" and God as "the Enemy." All his advice is nefarious. Lewis's cleverness is readily on display, and a reader cannot help but wonder how it was possible for him to know the twists and turns of such devilish thought. Lewis conceded that any and all of us are, in fact, much closer to the diabolical than the angelic. Lewis simply wrote honestly about the human condition, glossing over none of the wiles of human depravity. Consequently, the book is not merely one of great spiritual insight but of deep psychological insight as well.

The great sins are not necessarily those of the flesh. In fact, the greatest sinner of all time, the devil himself, is an unembodied being: he has no flesh. His sins—such as envy, jealousy, pride, anger, resentment—are all sins of the spirit. But this is no encouragement for those engaged in the sins of the flesh; on the contrary, fleshly sins can be rationalized and justified, and they, too, can morph into the sins of the spirit. Whatever the category, all sins involve the will; all are harmful; all are contrary to God's design and character. Lewis let no one off the hook: the churchgoer as well as the secularist can find hints of his or her own struggles dissected and repudiated in these letters. The letters serve as a mirror of the soul. They are not written for the fainthearted. But, if anyone dares to look, it is possible to gain an honest evaluation of oneself and to repent.

Lewis claimed that he got the idea for these letters while attending a Sunday morning service at his parish church, Holy Trinity in Headington Quarry, just outside Oxford. One cannot help but wonder what Lewis must have thought of the sermon that morning! Whatever his inspiration, this one thing is sure: those who read *The Screwtape Letters* will be constantly reminded of the wiles of the devil and of how desperate is the need for God and his grace.

1 *The simplest is to turn their gaze away from Him towards themselves.*
CHAP. 4, P. 16

In this line of Screwtape's, Lewis alluded to a fundamental truth of human existence: we all start out self-absorbed. Each of us is born folded inward, like a rose in bud. As fallen creatures, we are born self-focused. But gradually, if we are growing properly, we begin to unfold, petal by petal, becoming more and more aware of others. We also begin to recognize the divine presence of the ultimate other: God. Learning that the universe is not centered on ourselves is the first step toward learning that it centers on God. Screwtape advises Wormwood to reverse this foundational truth: to deflect a focus on God and others by directing it to the self.

Both psychological growth and spiritual growth are outward and upward, toward God and others. If we stop unfolding and turn inward again, we isolate ourselves and stunt our growth. And as Screwtape observes, this is the simplest way to severely hinder spiritual growth. God is self-existent, the Creator, Sustainer, and Center of all reality. He is as sun, rain, and soil are to a plant. To refuse him is to refuse life. But if we continue to unfold, we will find ourselves growing into the image of Christ, becoming more loving, more accepting, more understanding of others, and more in tune with the will of God. This principle is illustrated in those whom we most admire—people such as Mother Teresa and Henri Nouwen, who, for the love of God and in gratitude to Jesus, gave their lives for others.

Consider the past few years of your life. What pattern do you see? Are you drawing closer to God and others, or are you withdrawing into yourself? Are you turning inward, or unfolding more and more into the image of Christ?

If we love our Christian brothers and sisters, it proves that we have passed from death to life. . . . We know what real love is because Jesus gave up his life for us. So we also ought to give up our lives for our brothers and sisters. 1 JOHN 3:14, 16

2

Do not let him suspect the law of undulation.

CHAP. 9, P. 45

Since Screwtape and Wormwood are spirits (fallen, to be sure), the inexperienced Wormwood must be reminded that the emotional, mental, and physical lows of his human "patient" are not necessarily the result of his own diabolical work as a tempter. Rather, they are part of being human and very much in God's design: so much so that this may be called a "law."

We live in time and in process; we constantly change as bodies age, emotions waffle, intellects cloud. Life has its seasons, bodies have their cycles, hours and days have their moods. No, Screwtape cautions, such undulations are no advantage to hell unless they become the occasion for bad choices. Ups and downs are not intrinsically sinful. Even our spirituality is something like the phases of the moon or the seasons. Our fervor may wax and wane; we may go through a time of winter, when all seems bare and dead, to one day seeing the barren place give way to the delicate new budding of spring. This "undulation" is right and natural and good; God uses the different phases and seasons for his purposes. What he does in a summer season of our spirituality may be vastly different from what he does in winter.

The danger comes, as Screwtape knows, in our failing to see and embrace the seasons, in believing that all times of our lives must be the same. We cannot claw and scramble our way back to summer or quickly leave a harsh winter season. And, as with the phases of the moon and the seasons, we must embrace the place where God has brought us, find the meaning and lessons to be learned in that place, and then be willing to move on when that season is past.

We can enjoy the summer and remember that winter will one day give way to spring. If we remember the law of undulation, we will find grace and peace in the journey.

For everything there is a season, a time for every activity under heaven.

ECCLESIASTES 3:1

3   *It is during such trough periods, much more than during the peak periods, that it is growing into the sort of creature He wants it to be.*

CHAP. 8, P. 40

Emotional ups and downs—peaks and troughs—come to all. As the demon Screwtape knows, troughs are times of vulnerability to temptations ranging from sensuality to self-pity. But troughs are also where godly character is usually formed, by choosing God and obeying him when times are tough.

Godliness is a matter of the will: doing what is good when everything seems to be going wrong. Screwtape knows that we often evaluate our spiritual lives based on how good we feel. If we feel close to God, happy, contented, and generally cheerful, we believe this must mean we are in the best spiritual state. When we are depressed, in need, in turmoil, or lonely, we believe we have somehow fallen off the "God-wagon" and have gone astray.

Although the emotional peaks are bright and lovely and certainly more enjoyable, that doesn't mean the trough is the wrong place for us. The truth is that God is often most at work in the troughs—the hard places where we feel most desolate and alone. Sometimes when we're trying to clamber back up to the peak, God may be calling us to stay awhile in the trough.

At these times we often feel full of confusion, fear, and sadness because we cannot see God's hand at work, molding us by the very things we wish to escape. It is often only afterward, when he has moved us to a different place, that we can look back and see how he was working in the midst of the difficult spots. If you are in a trough, seek God there. Ask him what he is trying to do. Don't automatically assume that it's wrong for you to be there, but listen for his voice in the darkness. He may be doing something good in you.

Our present troubles are small and won't last very long. Yet they produce for us a glory that vastly outweighs them and will last forever!   2 CORINTHIANS 4:17

4 *An ever increasing craving for an ever diminishing pleasure is the formula.* CHAP. 9, P. 44

Lewis gives an excellent description here of addiction as a vicious cycle of craving more and more of things that satisfy less and less. We think immediately of "big" behavioral sins—such as pornography, drug abuse, and alcoholism—which certainly fit this pattern. But we don't often think of addiction in relation to the more invisible sins such as the lust for power in relationships or for recognition, things that on the surface can seem like mere motivation, even healthy ambition.

Often addiction comes cloaked as a coping mechanism. Cravings for food that are not based on hunger, a constant need for entertainment and diversion, a preoccupation with physical appearance and maintenance of youth and beauty, an overwhelming desire for romance—these are all indicators of addiction, an increasing craving for something that satisfies less and less.

The reason for these cycles? Some deep need in us is not being met. Somehow we are not fulfilled, and we try to fill this need ourselves—but with things that do not satisfy us. It may be connected to pain from the past or from disappointment in the present, from deep loneliness or insecurity. Whatever the root cause, trying to fill these needs by our own "lust cycle" is like trying to bail out a sinking boat by drilling more holes in the bottom: we're just sinking faster.

Pause for a moment and ask God to reveal any such cycles in your life. Is there something that needs to be surrendered to him? Only God can uncover, heal, and fill the places we try to fill ourselves. We cannot do that on our own.

Since you have heard about Jesus and have learned the truth that comes from him, throw off your old sinful nature and your former way of life, which is corrupted by lust and deception. Instead, let the Spirit renew your thoughts and attitudes.

EPHESIANS 4:21-23

5   *It does not matter how small the sins are, provided that their cumulative effect is to edge the man away from the Light and out into the Nothing.*

CHAP. 12, P. 60

As Lewis explained through Screwtape, small sins can add up to a load of guilt increasingly difficult for the patient to bear. This is the "cumulative effect" of sin. It is the lever that pries a Christian away from God.

God has given each of us a conscience—a quiet little nudge or voice in our hearts that indicates when we are going astray. It is certainly not the only way God shows us right from wrong, but it can be an excellent guide in keeping our hearts right toward him.

We can choose to obey our conscience or to ignore it; we can simply drown out the quiet voice and ignore the uneasiness in our hearts. Yet ignoring our conscience on even the smallest matter is sin and edges us, as Lewis put it, "away from the Light and out into the Nothing." The conscience is a guide for keeping our hearts and actions right toward God. Every time we ignore it, we harden our hearts just a little more against God and turn to self. Without repentance, we will keep ourselves from a close relationship with God and go further and further astray.

Take a moment and consider: is there anything stopping you from standing with a clear conscience before God? Set that thing right, or you will continue edging further "from the Light and out into the Nothing."

Cling to your faith in Christ, and keep your conscience clear. For some people have deliberately violated their consciences; as a result, their faith has been shipwrecked.

I TIMOTHY 1:19

6   *Indeed the safest road to Hell is the gradual one—the gentle slope, soft underfoot, without sudden turnings, without milestones, without signposts.* CHAP. 12, P. 61

Too often we hear of a scandal involving a Christian leader caught in serious sin, and we wonder how it could have happened. Generally, people who end in spiritual ruin do not just go running off the edge of a moral cliff knowing they are heading for disaster. Only a fool would do such a thing. No, the ruin comes in much more insidious ways, ways Lewis described as soft and gentle and so slight that they look almost perfectly safe. And this can happen to any of us.

We can be lulled by complacency or enticed by what seems like the tiniest indulgence. We justify it by thinking, *Okay, it isn't good for us, but what will it really hurt?* This is the beginning of a slippery spiritual slope that leads us away from God. We don't want to look back one day and wonder how we have wandered so far from God or find, like so many fallen Christian leaders, that our series of choices has led to our downfall. So how can we recognize the signposts leading to this path?

One helpful practice is to do regular spiritual checkups. Just as we have regular physicals, we should also have times when we review our spiritual progress, assessing whether we are growing closer to God or moving away from him.

You might keep a journal to record thoughts, feelings, and actions. Looking back through it can be greatly encouraging, as well as offer a good overview of ways you might be slipping. Having a good friend who can offer an outside opinion can also be helpful. Ask him or her how you have grown in the past year. Ask yourself questions such as, "Am I closer to God than I was last year?" "Have I gone backward in any area?" "Are there areas of my life I am not giving to God?"

Regular spiritual checkups will help guard us from looking up one day and realizing that we are far down the slope and far from God.

Keep watch and pray, so that you will not give in to temptation. For the spirit is willing, but the body is weak! MATTHEW 26:41

7

We want a whole race perpetually in pursuit of the rainbow's end, never honest, nor kind, nor happy now. CHAP. 15, P. 78

Generally, people are about as happy as they make up their minds to be. Circumstances certainly can play a part. Wouldn't they be happier being healthy than being sick? Wouldn't they generally feel a lift in their spirits if their relationships were going well, their homes were peaceful, and they excelled at their jobs? But we make a mistake when we allow circumstances to determine our level of happiness.

Lewis reminded us that one of the biggest traps of the devil is to make us discontent with our present circumstances and long for circumstances that might be more conducive to happiness. We think, *If . . .; if . . .; if . . . If only this or that would happen, then I would be happy.* But as Lewis pointed out, while we pursue the rainbow's end, we rob ourselves of happiness and contentment now.

Even in less than ideal situations, we can choose to be happy. The beautiful truth about being a Christian is that, even more than happiness, we can choose joy. Some of the most joyful Christians are also in some of the most trying circumstances. Through diseases that cripple their bodies, through financial hardship, loss, and sorrow, they have learned that happiness is found not in their circumstances but in their attitudes and the joy found in the presence of the Lord.

Are you waiting for the "ifs" to become realities before you let yourself be happy? Have you found the joy that comes through the presence of the Holy Spirit even in the midst of trials? If not, how long will you wait for the rainbow's end?

We are ignored, even though we are well known. We live close to death, but we are still alive. We have been beaten, but we have not been killed. Our hearts ache, but we always have joy. We are poor, but we give spiritual riches to others. We own nothing, and yet we have everything. 2 CORINTHIANS 6:9-10

8   *[N]othing throws him into a passion so easily as to find a tract of time which he reckoned on having at his own disposal unexpectedly taken from him.*   CHAP. 21, P. 111

Screwtape's next suggestion for the corruption of Wormwood's patient is through unexpected interruptions in the patient's day. We've all experienced those. Having made plans for a specific period of time, we're thrown for a loop when our time is infringed upon by chattering co-workers or fighting children demanding a referee.

As Wormwood knew, many of us are quick to claim ownership of time. A recent seminar on time management gave tips on how to manage people so they do not infringe upon "your" time. The tips included standing at the door of your office so they could not enter your space and also scheduling your day in fifteen-minute increments so as to never let someone overstay his or her allotment. While these are no doubt efficient techniques, if we were to live by them, we would be crippling ourselves as effective disciples of Christ. All that happens in our spiritual lives happens in relationship, whether with God or with other people. If we so closely guard and manage our time, we are in danger of leaving little room for the Holy Spirit to use us in ways not scheduled in our planners.

David, the writer of Psalm 31, saw time in a different way: everything is under God's control. Having spent many years wondering when his time would come to be king of Israel, David had confidence that time is truly God's province.

In today's world, many people have been left wounded and bruised by pain and suffering. They are searching for answers and for hope. How tragic it would be if someone approached us genuinely seeking Christ and we did not take the time to help. Are we leaving room to do the work if God should bring us someone in need? Or are we guarding our time so carefully that we will miss the opportunities God may bring today?

My times are in Your hand.   PSALM 31:15, NKJV

9

And all the time the joke is that the word "mine" in its fully possessive sense cannot be uttered by a human being about anything.

CHAP. 21, P. 114

One of the earliest words we learn as children is *mine*. In kindergarten we gradually learn to share, but the "mine" remains. We need only have someone infringe upon our personal space or possessions to see how deeply imbedded this concept is in us. Missionaries speak of going to certain other cultures in which tribes share belongings and their difficulty in getting used to people walking into their homes and borrowing things without asking. Almost from the cradle, a sense of personal possession is very strong in Western culture.

This applies not just to belongings, however, but also to ourselves. Our language is full of examples: "a self-made man," being "self-possessed," having a strong "sense of self." These all imply that fundamentally we own our selves, that the basic unit of personal possession is self. As Lewis pointed out in this letter of Screwtape's, such thinking is fundamentally absurd because God is the author and creator of all things. Everything we have, even our very selves, comes from his hand. It is true that we can choose to turn our backs on God because, in his goodness, he has given us free will—the ability to choose our own course; we can make decisions for ourselves. But even free will is a gift from him.

As Christians, we have chosen to freely give ourselves back to God. Unfortunately, we don't always live that way. Like a child who tries to take back a present once given, we want to take back our lives after we surrender them to God. But they are no longer ours to take back. They belong to Christ.

Are we putting stipulations on our gifts? Are we trying to sneak back control, not sure we're quite ready to really give ourselves? Only God can truly utter the word *mine*.

Are you letting him say that about your soul?

I made a covenant with you, says the Sovereign LORD, and you became mine.
EZEKIEL 16:8

10

Substitute for the faith itself some Fashion with a Christian colouring. Work on their horror of the Same Old Thing. CHAP. 25, P. 135

In Christianity there is no end to the good works and causes we can embrace. We can focus on social justice or political activism regarding issues such as abortion and homosexuality, resettling refugees, caring for the environment, and so forth. We can read the latest Christian blockbuster, join the choir, or make Bundt cakes for the youth group bake sale. We can find any number of things to do for God. Some are things our parents and grandparents have done before us; others are merely an escape from what we see as the "old" way of thinking, having a "horror of the Same Old Thing." There are so many options that we could spend every waking moment involved in Christian activity for God if we so chose. And all these activities have merit. They build Christian community, raise awareness of injustice in the world, help the poor. They are good works.

But in the midst of this whirl of activity, we need to check ourselves. Are the things we are doing, as Lewis's quote alludes to, just substitutes for faith? Faith is not measured by how busy we are for God or by how many good works are penciled into our calendars. Faith is the heart-to-heart intimacy between God and us. Good works will naturally spring from faith, but they are not faith in and of themselves.

Are our good works springing from our faith, or are they substituting for it? Works can put muscle to our faith, but faith must be the heart. If our works spring from faith, they will be God-honoring and right. If they are a substitute for it, they serve only to distract us from the state of our souls.

Take a moment to reflect on your activities. From what source do they spring?

We keep on praying for you, asking our God to enable you to live a life worthy of his call. May he give you the power to accomplish all the good things your faith prompts you to do. 2 THESSALONIANS 1:11

CHAPTER 10

Letters to Malcolm: Chiefly on Prayer

AFTER WRITING *THE SCREWTAPE LETTERS*, C. S. Lewis thought of writing a sequel. The first book contained letters of a senior devil writing to a junior devil, advising him as to how he should go about his tempting business. The plan for the second book was to feature correspondence from a senior angel advising a junior angel on how to go about nurturing a mortal toward sainthood. The second book was never written (though a separate essay called "Screwtape Proposes a Toast" was), for Lewis realized he did not have the capacity to write it. Who does? Each of us is far closer to the diabolical than we are to the angelic; it is but a pretense or deception to suggest that there is a natural inclination toward a consistent expression of divine good.

At the very end of his life, however, Lewis did write a very modest and utterly unpretentious sequel to *The Screwtape Letters*. This book is called *Letters to Malcolm: Chiefly on Prayer*, which mirrors *The Screwtape Letters*. In it Lewis wrote to Malcolm, a fictitious character. Only Lewis's side of the correspondence is found in the book; issues relative to the other side of the correspondence are inferred. Still, *Malcolm* is a book about two men seeking to dialogue and encourage each other to follow Christ more closely. Though it touches on many themes, prayer is a dominant one throughout. This is a book that raises questions and expresses doubts—they are not discussed with rancor or cynicism, but rather as the kind of question that opens the door to curiosity, wonder, awe, and eventually worship.

After *A Grief Observed*, in which Lewis chronicled his own winding pilgrimage through the regions of grief and great sorrow, some thought he never recovered but lived his last days with mere vestiges of faith, limping his way toward eternity. No one who reads *Malcolm* could ever think that for long. Some of the questions in *A Grief Observed* that arose from heartache and struggle are revisited in *Malcolm* as promptings toward adoration. The best way to triumph over temptation is to cultivate an honest trust in God that transcends any kind of pull away from him. *Malcolm* is a valuable resource for anyone longing for triumph, for it is a book full of humility, hope, and deep love for God.

1   *We must lay before Him what is in us, not what ought to be in us.*

CHAP. IV, P. 22

Each of us has a vision of what we have not yet become, what we could be, what we were created to be. The only glitch is that we are nowhere near attaining that vision. We still have many rough patches that need to be sanded smooth. We're internally conflicted because we know that we were meant to be better than what we are now. If we could just not get impatient in traffic or contribute to family arguments, if we were more generous, or if we could get a little golden halo to hover brightly above our heads, then, we think, we might be closer to the vision.

Sometimes we try to strong-arm the vision into reality before God. We put on our Sunday-best attitude to pray, willing ourselves to be pious and compassionate, to sit still and stop fidgeting. God sees through the pretense to just who we are, smudges and knobby knees and all. And he loves us completely for who we are right now.

But in order for us to grow in his embracing love, we must do what C. S. Lewis observed: we must bring to God who we *are*, not who we think we should be. If we hide what is in us, we lay a false thing before God, hindering our ability to draw close to him. If we have the courage to come to God in our anger and despair and in our pettiness and neediness, being honest about what is actually in our hearts, God can work in us. We do not have to arm wrestle our natures into a pretend holiness, trying to cover the stains and tears and act as though we are okay. Instead, if we honestly and openly lay before him the things in our hearts, he will continue the miraculous work of transforming us into the people we were created to be.

Search me, O God, and know my heart; test me and know my anxious thoughts. Point out anything in me that offends you, and lead me along the path of everlasting life. PSALM 139:23-24

2 *It seems to me that we often, almost sulkily, reject the good that God
offers us because, at that moment, we expected some other good.*
CHAP. V, P. 26

Children often determine the worth of a wrapped present based on size:
the bigger the package, the better the gift. Adults are swayed more by
overall appearance: Does the gift have a tag from an expensive store? gold
wrapping paper and a beautifully tied bow? Then it must contain something special. But white-elephant gift exchanges turn these criteria on end.
That large package might be nothing more than economy-size paper tow-
els. The expensive-looking Godiva chocolate box might contain denture
cleaner. And the oddly shaped, poorly wrapped package could conceal a
treasure.

The goodness of God often comes wrapped in strange packages. We
have our eyes on the Godiva chocolate box, sure it's going to be something
wonderful, and God hands us a little packet wrapped in last week's comics
and tied with yarn. "Here," he says, "I chose this just for you." And we look
longingly at the chocolate box, wishing for it instead.

As Lewis observed, often the blessings of God come in ways we would
not have chosen but are handed to us anyway. Sometimes they even come
wrapped in hardship and sorrow—caring for an elderly relative, moving
to a less-than-exciting location, experiencing an unexpected change in life
circumstances. It may take us years to see the good in these things. It may
seem that there is no good in it at all, so our hearts yearn for the Godiva
chocolate box, sure that it would have been better than this. The truth is
that we cannot see inside the packages of many life circumstances. But
God sees, and he chooses to give us the things that are best for us. What
we want is not always what we need.

All he does is just and good, and all his commandments are trustworthy.
PSALM 111:7

3   *If God had granted all the silly prayers I've made in my life, where should I be now?*   CHAP. V, P. 28

Let's consider Lewis's question: "If God had granted all the prayers I've ever prayed, where would I be?" For most of us, the answer would probably be, "Not where I am now!" We have lodged thousands of ungranted requests in our lives. As children, perhaps we prayed for curly or straight hair, or maybe for a horse. In high school we might have prayed each night to marry our first love, a petition that for most of us was not granted. As adults we ask for jobs and education and finances, for things that would enhance our careers or family life.

When we pray these prayers, we desperately want them to be granted, but in later years we can often look back with relief upon those ungranted prayers. "Thank God I didn't marry my high school boyfriend" or "Thank God I didn't move to France for that job" or "Thank God I didn't get that scholarship to the university." In the clarity of hindsight, we can see that, if granted, those requests would have taken us on rabbit trails, blocking the wonderful things that came after.

This process occurs throughout life. We are constantly petitioning God in prayer—as we should be. Some requests are granted. Many are not. It may be years before we understand how getting what we wanted would have negatively affected our lives. With some especially difficult or confusing situations, we may have to wait for that understanding until we stand face-to-face with Jesus.

Of course, we cannot know ahead of time which petitions would thwart God's best for us. With this in mind, as we continue walking with God let us try to hold our prayers loosely, remembering that we ask with limited understanding and that, in his wisdom and mercy, God can see what we cannot.

True wisdom and power are found in God; counsel and understanding are his.
JOB 12:13

4

We have no non-religious activities; only religious and irreligious.

CHAP. VI, P. 30

We generally don't think of all of life as being religious. The tendency to separate what goes on in our devotional lives and in church from the rest of our days is, as Lewis points out, a false dichotomy. We have no activity that is not religious in nature. That is, every activity is either glorifying to God or not glorifying to God.

But what about pumping gas, weeding the garden, or buying a pair of shoes? Surely some things are neutral! Though they may seem so, in reality they are not. We are so accustomed to the false dichotomy that we do not see that everything we do means putting our energies toward either building or not building the Kingdom of God.

Brother Lawrence, a lay brother in a Carmelite monastery during the 1600s, understood this principle very well. He spent many years of his life in the monastery kitchens. There he developed a remarkable life of prayer and intimacy with God. He chose to wash dishes to the glory of God, and in the midst of those mundane tasks day after day, he sought to draw closer to God. Lawrence's intimacy with God was the result of joyfully serving others as an act of worship and talking to God in the quiet and undistracted moments afforded by routine.

One of Brother Lawrence's secrets was in realizing what Lewis would one day also discover: that every activity can be either religious or irreligious. The difference is in our minds and hearts. What attitude do we have when we pump gas or shop for shoes? Those simple acts can have vastly different meanings if we are doing them with thanksgiving and praise as opposed to frustration and greed.

It is difficult to adjust to the idea that each of our actions has spiritual consequences, that the way we choose to think about and approach the activities of daily life bears fruit in our spiritual lives. Are we, like Brother Lawrence, taking every opportunity to draw near to God, whether elbow deep in soapsuds or singing hymns on Sunday morning? Let our attitudes about the actions of our daily lives lead us closer to our Lord.

As we pray to our God and Father about you, we think of your faithful work, your loving deeds, and the enduring hope you have because of our Lord Jesus Christ.

I THESSALONIANS 1:3

5 *The unfinished picture would so like to jump off the easel and have a look at itself!* CHAP. VI, P. 34

Like a fine painting, our lives and characters are formed stroke by stroke by the Master Artist, with a wide palette of colors. There are dark and somber shades and shafts of sunlit tints, all illuminating and adding depth to who we are becoming.

But we can be very impatient, wanting to see exactly how the picture is taking shape. As Lewis quipped here, we want to get down from the easel where God is at work and survey the progress. And in accord with human nature, we are not satisfied with that. We also want to see the end result.

It is natural that we should desire to see how we will end up. We want some reassurance that we're going to take shape the way we think is best. We also want to make suggestions, offer a little criticism, perhaps take the paintbrush and tweak the spots we don't particularly care for. "Don't use that color. Don't make that spot so dark and difficult. Why can't we put sunlight all over—make life easy?"

As we are reminded in Philippians 1:6, God is doing a good work in us and will complete it. In the painting of our lives, he is adding strokes we might not like. We may not understand what good that dark splash, that spot of somber green is really doing. But he is the only one who can see the whole painting and who is working little by little to bring it forth. We cannot see how our painting will turn out, no matter how hard we scrutinize the unfinished canvas. We must trust the Master Artist's hand and in obedience allow God to continue his work in us, believing that stroke by stroke he will complete us the perfect way.

I am certain that God, who began the good work within you, will continue his work until it is finally finished on the day when Christ Jesus returns.

PHILIPPIANS 1:6

6   *I am often, I believe, praying for others when I should be doing things for them.* CHAP. XII, P. 66

Do our prayers have hands? Lewis's observation above cuts to the core of a problem that has plagued Christians since the earliest days of Christianity: the dichotomy between word and action. How often do we pray for others with concern and compassion, but then stop short of doing anything else for them, using only our mouths and not taking any steps to physically help them? James 2:14-19 makes it very clear that faith must be accompanied by deed; deed must spring from true faith. The same holds true for prayer. It is a good thing to lift others up in prayer, but if we do nothing else, we may be stopping short. In prayer, we should ask God if he would like to use us in the situation brought to our attention. Often he may want us to be part of the solution. Prayer should be our first step; action, our second.

Is someone sick? Perhaps we could make a pot of soup or call to see if the person needs any errands run. Is someone in financial or emotional distress? A note, a visit, or an anonymous monetary gift could help alleviate his or her condition. Think for a moment. How long has it been since you gave your prayers hands and feet?

Too often prayer is removed from the actions of our daily lives. We tuck our prayers into a corner of our day and then live the rest of life with it tidily put away. But when we act in this way, we create that false dichotomy. Instead we should seek to be walking prayers, living out what we have been directed by God to do that day. Are we listening for instructions or just tossing concerned prayers to God and leaving all the results up to him? As we pray for others, let us take a moment and ask God if there is any way we can help them. In this way, we will pray as a whole—with mouths and hands, words and actions.

What good is it, dear brothers and sisters, if you say you have faith but don't show it by your actions? JAMES 2:14

7

Therefore of each creature we can say, "This also is Thou: neither is this Thou." CHAP. XIV, P. 74

All Creation reflects its Creator. Though marred by the effects of the Fall, nature can speak volumes about the character of God. The mountains attest to his strength and power, the oceans to the richness and complexity of his creativity. Even a little wildflower, with its delicate stem and translucent petals, reveals his meticulous attention to detail. Every creature reflects aspects of the person of God.

This is most true of people, for we were made in the image of God. Our interpersonal relationships, depth of emotion, capacity to think rationally, and individuality all wonderfully illuminate the nature of our Creator. This is true for all the marvelous people we come in contact with every day—our spouse, family, friends, co-workers. Though they certainly are not God, for no human could possibly contain all that God is, we can recognize God's fingerprints on them, the reflection of him in their lives. As Lewis observes, of each we can say, "This also is Thou: neither is this Thou."

However, the tricky bit is that this applies to people we do not like as well as to those we do. It's easy to acknowledge that the people we like are reflections of God, but we wonder why there can't be a special category for people who are just generally annoying, rude, or mean. Surely we do not have to look at them and echo Lewis's sentiment! But indeed we do. Their behavior—like ours—may not reflect God all the time, but they as humans intrinsically reflect their Creator.

The next time you interact with the one who most sets your nerves on edge, pause and consider that that person, like you, is a reflection of God. Are you treating him or her with due honor? It may be difficult, but a creature made in the image of God deserves no less.

God created human beings in his own image. In the image of God he created them; male and female he created them. GENESIS 1:27

8 *The prayer preceding all prayers is "May it be the real I who speaks. May it be the real Thou that I speak to."* CHAP. XV, P. 82

In some ways the world is like a carnival house of mirrors, reflecting back to us distorted versions of reality. When we look into the mirrors at a carnival, the person looking out has a tiny head and a huge body, or else is only five feet tall and almost as wide. It is a reflection of us, but not a true reflection. We are not seeing ourselves as we really are.

How true of our spiritual selves this is. Our past hurts, our recurring struggles with sin, our broken relationships all distort our true selves. We "look in the mirror" and see only ugliness, only brokenness: a twisted image of what was meant to be beautiful.

We do the same with God's image. The things that distort our image in our own eyes distort the image of who God is, too. A painful church experience, family discord, shame over past sin, a sense of failure—all these contribute to a skewed perception of God. Just as the distortion we saw in the fun-house mirror, we see a God of cold, sterile judgment, a God who loves impersonally and only a little, a God who is keeping score. But we cannot trust our eyes. They have been deceived by a million little distortions in our lives. Lewis's quote cuts through the distortions, acknowledging them as false and asking God what is true.

It is only through God that the images become true again. As we draw closer to him, we open our hearts for realignment. We begin to see glimpses of the real us and the real God. Our hearts begin to be aligned with the truth. Let us begin each prayer echoing Lewis's prayer, acknowledging that we live in a house of mirrors and asking God to daily bring us closer to the truth of who he is and who we are.

You will know the truth, and the truth will set you free. JOHN 8:32

9   *These pure and spontaneous pleasures are "patches of Godlight"*
in the woods of our experience.   CHAP. XVII, P. 91

When was the last time you remember finding a moment to gaze out a window and take a deep breath, purposefully breaking out of the routine of life to just be still? We do not stop to breathe and look around very often. Always pressed for time, we live gazing straight in front of us, looking to the next task. We live by lists, checking off item after item, always in a hurry. With so narrow a view, what do we miss? If we do not look up, we cannot admire the blossoming cherry and magnolia trees around us. If we do not look down, we miss a chipmunk in the yard and that tiny row of ants crossing the sidewalk in single file.

Occasionally something breaks our routine. It could be a shaft of sunlight, the first fireflies of the year, the smell of cut grass in summer. These, as Lewis noted, are "patches of Godlight"—moments when the transcendent touches us and we simply behold with awe and wonder a pure and simple thing. They remind us that our lives are touched by the divine. Beckoning us to turn our eyes from minutes and seconds and tasks, they invite us to stop and simply be, to fully inhabit a time and place and enjoy it.

These moments also give us a foretaste of what is to come after this life. We will behold something more clear and lovely and brighter than anything on earth. Heaven will be radiant and filled with the beauty we glimpse in these transcendent moments, but spotless and without end.

Earth is a pale and worn shadow compared to heaven. The world, with its cares, can entrap us into unhealthy cycles and myopic vision. But if we are looking for the patches of Godlight, we will find a foretaste of heaven amid the toil and care of earth. Today, keep an eye out for those moments when you can glimpse heaven.

I saw the holy city, the new Jerusalem, coming down from God out of heaven like a bride beautifully dressed for her husband.   REVELATION 21:2

10 *Joy is the serious business of Heaven.*
CHAP. XVII, P. 93

Do we take joy seriously? How many of us stood in vacation Bible school in younger years, clapping and singing, "The joy of the Lord is my strength," feeling anything but joyful and just wanting to get to the good part—the snack? Many of us were not taught to take joy seriously as children, and we take it no more seriously as adults.

One problem is that we don't have a good idea what joy really means. We think joy is something we're supposed to have when we aren't happy but are expected to have a good attitude anyhow. For most of us, joy seems more like a martyr complex than like the wild celebrations described in the Bible. People danced uncontrollably with joy, wept with joy, made music, and had feasts. Joy is not meant to be a grin-and-bear-it situation. It is exuberant and free and more than happy—not less than. And joy, says Lewis, is the serious business of heaven.

What a crazy thought! Isn't the serious business of heaven . . . serious? Like chanting in Latin or serenely playing a harp—everyone calm, no one really *happy*. If that's what we think, how much we have missed! We often imagine heaven to be like an exercise in spiritual discipline, but we forget that one of the most neglected spiritual disciplines is celebration, which is directly linked to joy. If the serious business of heaven is joy, then imagine the levity and the laughter we have to look forward to: heads thrown back and dancing with an exhilarating kind of joy. Perhaps we can take a cue from David (and others in the Bible), as well as from Lewis, to begin practicing now for this most serious business of heaven. Why not be daring and begin today? With laughter, celebration, thanksgiving, and praise, we can join the host of heaven in the delightful practice of joy.

Let all who take refuge in you rejoice; let them sing joyful praises forever. Spread your protection over them, that all who love your name may be filled with joy.
PSALM 5:11

CHAPTER 11

The Abolition of Man

LEWIS BELIEVED HIS THREE BEST BOOKS were *Perelandra*, *Till We Have Faces*, and *The Abolition of Man*. Philosopher Mortimer Adler also thought highly of *The Abolition of Man*, including it in his Great Books of the Western World in 1968. Even the behaviorist B. F. Skinner invested a significant portion of his *Beyond Freedom and Dignity* reacting to this particular Lewis book. What made this book interesting to such thinkers?

In it Lewis argued that there is such a thing as objective value; that we live in a universe in which there are knowers as well as things to be known; that it is *thinking* objects in addition to mere material ones that make up reality; that truth does not equal reality—truth is what a person thinks *about* reality only when he or she thinks accurately about it.

Lewis was saying that what we think can in fact be measured against some objective reality. This means that thoughts failing to conform to the objective world are false; they have no support in the real world. Furthermore, Lewis believed that our emotions, too, should also conform to reality—here he refers to proper emotions as "*just* sentiments"—as should choices of the will. Thus the mind, the emotions, and the will can also be evaluated according to their conformity to an objective standard, and this standard is one that transcends rulers and the ruled alike. And for brevity, he referred to the whole of this doctrine of objective value as the *Tao*, after the Chinese concept of "the greatest thing."

Certainly no one will ever get to the bottom of all truth. But it is foolish to think, by contrast, that truth cannot be known at all. In *The Abolition of Man*, Lewis proclaimed the idea that to abandon objective reality is actually to devalue all things that objective value dignifies. Maturity comes when one is responsive to the real world in ways congruous with it—emotionally, rationally, and volitionally. And failure on this point actually diminishes a person and a culture. It leads to the "abolition of man," the loss of human dignity. Right response to reality, however, allows for the proper development of character in a way congruous to honesty and humility.

Lewis's reason for writing *The Abolition of Man* was to counter the tendency toward subjectivism that isolates individuals not only from objective reality but also from one another. He had observed the loss of human dignity when this occurs. Triumph over temptation requires an accurate assessment of oneself as well as a proper grasp of the real world.

1 *The task of the modern educator is not to cut down jungles but to irrigate deserts. The right defence against false sentiments is to inculcate just sentiments.* CHAP. I, P. 24

Is it wrong to experience and express our emotions? Some people believe that all ordinary human emotions are against reason and thus should be held in contempt. Since emotions are subjective, they are deemed trivial and should be eradicated. Young people, especially, are encouraged to reject the lure of such sentiments. In a technological world swallowed by emotional propaganda, should not our Western, sentimental youth have their minds strengthened to resist such manipulative emotion?

A response to such a claim may be found in *The Abolition of Man*. In it Lewis drew from his experience as a teacher to argue that though some might need to be shielded from such excesses of sentimentality, what the majority of students need is to wake up from their sleep of chilly crudeness. Educators need to water the arid wastelands of youthful minds starved of certain experiences that develop generous and fruitful human beings. Lewis saw the debunking of this traditional value system, with the possibility of starting all over again with a new set, as an attempt to cut out the very soul of humanity.

To devalue feelings is to suggest an insidious assumption to people that immunizes them against the pleasures of life with its tenderness, love, and affection. As Lewis proposed, the result of such neglect is a pragmatic person with an inflated opinion of his or her own knowledge and a hardened heart toward humanity and God. And such withdrawal of values, emotions, and experiences makes people easier targets of propaganda.

Jesus was not reluctant to show "just sentiments." On one occasion, as he overlooked the city of Jerusalem, Jesus began to feel sorrowful, and he expressed his feelings about a people who had hardened their affections toward a loving God and his servants. Like Jesus, we, too, need to express our feelings and emotions concerning experiences that touch our lives, and in so doing, keep our souls soft and tender toward God and humanity.

O Jerusalem, Jerusalem, the city that kills the prophets and stones God's messengers! How often I have wanted to gather your children together as a hen protects her chicks beneath her wings, but you wouldn't let me. LUKE 13:34

2   *It is the doctrine of objective value, the belief that certain attitudes are really true, and others really false, to the kind of thing the universe is and the kind of things we are.*   CHAP. I, P. 29

Certain aspects of nature should merit emotional reactions of either approval or disapproval, reverence or contempt. That is, specific human responses to nature are more appropriate than others. Beautiful objects of our world should foster expressions of ecstatic thanksgiving as we appreciate the grandeur before us, our souls nourished by the experience, while ugly objects should give rise to distaste, blame, or even hate. The same should apply to those works of humanity that are ill-made or perverse.

In *The Abolition of Man*, C. S. Lewis considered that this idea—which is present in all its variations in the writings of Plato, Aristotle, and Augustine; in Chinese and Indian philosophies; and in the Hebrew and Christian religions—should be called "the *Tao*." It is the way in which the universe is meant to function and the pattern to which all human activities should conform. This is the doctrine of objective value. In practice, this means that certain views are true while others are false—that particular knowledge is objectively true. Certain things are knowable to us as human beings, and through engagement with them we understand what it is to be human.

Furthermore, human sensibility has a range of emotional sensitivity and should be used accordingly to render what is worthy of esteem and value, since every object has an appropriate degree of value associated with it. Lewis suggests that educators should train students in making right decisions about what is valuable or not, what is to be liked or disliked in the world. There needs to be training in how to feel pleasure, dislike, or disgust at those things that are pleasant, dislikable, or disgusting.

The author of Hebrews had a similar concept in mind when he encouraged his readers to train themselves to distinguish good and evil. Living a godly life, they were to keep moving forward in mature understanding of the faith and not to merely dwell on the very basics of Christianity. God desires that we, too, might walk daily in his wisdom to know what is of the Lord, of humanity, or of Satan so that we can embrace godly beliefs about God's universe.

Solid food is for those who are mature, who through training have the skill to recognize the difference between right and wrong.   HEBREWS 5:14

3   *[E]motional states can be in harmony with reason (when we feel liking for what ought to be approved) or out of harmony with reason (when we perceive that liking is due but cannot feel it).*   CHAP. I, P. 29

The doctrine of objective value is the conviction that certain attitudes are true while others are untrue. For instance, as Lewis argued, the notion that children are delightful is not merely a momentary psychological recognition of parental emotions; it is an objective value that is beyond ourselves whether we know it or not. Since each individual appreciation is a response to objective value, it is possible to have right emotional feelings that align with reason, as well as misaligned emotions. Conversely, emotions might be disharmonious if they fail to conform to logic. In *The Abolition of Man*, Lewis claimed that the possibility of a reasonable emotion exists—but that reasonable emotion is dependent on that emotion's conformity to something else beyond the sensation itself.

Lewis suggested that emotional states are *alogical*, beyond the scope of logic—that is, one can't prove anything by them—although some emotions may be in harmony with reason and others are without such harmony. Emotions may be considered in harmony with reason when objective reality supports the emotional state: tears at a funeral, laughter at a party. In this way it can be truly said that there are both right and wrong emotional states; the supporting context validates the proper emotion. Emotions may be valuable indexes to reality. Lewis appreciated the emotions, and in *The Abolition of Man* he took to task an educational theory that sought to eliminate the sentiments rather than understand their true value. Emotional states can be in harmony with reason, and life is richer when they are. Lewis believed in just sentiments; that is, emotions that render to circumstances their due.

Jesus stood at the grave of his friend Lazarus and wept. In his humanity, the Lord expressed emotion, even while knowing that he would bring Lazarus out of the tomb. Those who saw his tears commented on how much Jesus loved his friend. Then Jesus spoke words beyond the veil and caused his friend's soul to be reunited with his decayed body—resurrection words that brought the brother of Mary and Martha back to his grieving family. In sorrow and in celebration, Jesus demonstrated right emotion in harmony with reason.

Jesus wept.   JOHN 11:35

4 *We laugh at honour and are shocked to find traitors in our midst.*
We castrate and bid the geldings be fruitful. CHAP. I, P. 35

Modern education was the target of Lewis's criticism delivered in three lectures at the University of Durham and later published under the title *The Abolition of Man*. Parallel to this condemnation was his fictional work *That Hideous Strength*—a satire on the results of modern education. In Lewis's opinion, the scientism being practiced in state schools, in which the Western world placed so much hope, was antihuman and would eventually lead to the eradication of human beings. Lewis strenuously objected to teaching that encouraged students to be afraid of emotions or feelings.

In fact, Lewis claimed that people need to have their emotions trained, since the intellect is helpless against the physical nature of humanity. To shape our emotions into stable sentiments, we must submit them to reason, which is led by the Spirit and nourished by God's Word. Communication between a person's intellect and instincts is then achieved through feelings. In other words, the mind governs the natural instincts through the emotions.

Meanwhile, society is constantly demanding qualities of character that it believes is nonexistent: goodness, righteousness, integrity, and honesty. Yet a sort of operation has taken place on the souls of humans whereby the means of achieving these virtues was removed. We make people passionless, yet expect them to be of the highest character and endeavor to be good.

Jesus spoke to this issue when answering a Pharisee's trick question about the greatest commandment. Quoting from Deuteronomy 6:5, Jesus insisted that we love God with our whole being: our *hearts*, which is another expression for our emotions; our *souls*, which includes volition, intuition, and conscience; and, as he put it in Matthew 22, our *minds*, or reason.

In this life, we are to obey God in love with the totality of who we are as human beings, not allowing ourselves to be conditioned by the thought police, who reject God-ordained standards. We need God's wisdom and strength to walk the narrow path between inflexible reason, which veers toward cold legalism, and impulsive sensuality. As we love God with all the fullness of our humanity, we will subsequently love our neighbors as ourselves (see Matthew 22:39) and display the virtues that society so desperately needs.

Jesus replied, "'You must love the LORD your God with all your heart, all your soul, and all your mind.' This is the first and greatest commandment."

MATTHEW 22:37-38

5   *Their scepticism about values is on the surface: it is for use on other people's values; about the values current in their own set they are not nearly sceptical enough.*   CHAP. 2, P. 41

Lewis's context was the whole system of values that many educated and professional people accepted uncritically during the period between World Wars I and II; conditions of comfort, democracy, security, tolerance, and peace were more highly prized than honor, bravery, and loyalty. People were more concerned with their material welfare than with virtues that contributed to the common good of humanity—peace at any price, including contempt for authority and belief in all that the mass media presented. Any spiritualizing of sentiments was mocked.

It was within this milieu that C. S. Lewis confronted the gullible dogmatism of his time, exposing a double standard of skepticism in the prevailing society: a cynicism toward traditional values without reciprocal doubts about their own. Many of those who attacked conventional principles held standards that they supposed were beyond criticism. As they stripped away patriotic and aesthetic sentiment, religious authority, and cultural taboo—supposedly to allow the real or basic values to emerge—they assumed the critical immunity of their own principles.

In Lewis's *That Hideous Strength*, Jane Studdock is such a person. To distance herself from women in fashionable clothes whose concern is physical attractiveness, Jane prides herself in dressing like an intellectual—ironically, just another mode of conformity. Blinded by her prejudice, Jane does not realize that she enjoys shopping for clothes (just a different kind) as much as the women she holds in contempt.

Jesus spoke to the Jane Studdock in all of us when he declared that, before we judge others, we should be careful to check whether we have a similar problem in a different guise. In psychology, it's called "projection": we quickly criticize those who remind us of faults we would rather deny in ourselves. To avoid condemning ourselves, we condemn others, finding reasons in superficial differences or our own adherence to culturally acceptable norms. God wants us to first get rid of the dust lodged in our own eyes that blinds us to our own faults—individually and collectively.

Why worry about a speck in your friend's eye when you have a log in your own? . . . First get rid of the log in your own eye; then you will see well enough to deal with the speck in your friend's eye.   MATTHEW 7:3, 5

6   *Telling us to obey Instinct is like telling us to obey "people." People say different things: so do instincts. Our instincts are at war.*

CHAP. 2, P. 48

What happens to a society that strips away all emotions, values, and traditional beliefs from its system to try to obtain a set of core rational values? Appeals to love, honor, and shame would now be excluded from the process. We cannot return to sentiment, because it is cut away and only reason remains. Yet the concept of pure reason lets us down when attempting to explain such values as the preservation of society. The choice to sacrifice oneself for the good of the community is neither rational nor irrational: it is only through desire or duty that such a choice is made.

Many would argue that instinct (spontaneous, superficial human impulse) supersedes reason and that humans have no choice but to obey instinct. We have an instinctive drive to preserve our own species, so we strive to protect society. But we also have an instinct for self-preservation. Why should we obey one instinct above another? In fact, our instincts are telling us all sorts of things, and each one speaks as if it is the most important of all and should be obeyed. There is no rationale for preferring one instinct above another; with our instincts at war, our choice ends up as a value judgment.

As a formerly zealous member of the Pharisees, who demanded the strictest obedience to the Jewish law, the apostle Paul knew about this war within. In Romans 7, he wrote that our very nature is at war against itself and God. How can we overcome the internal stresses that wrestle within us and make us slaves to sin? The answer to the dilemma is that God created us in his image and wrote his law in our hearts (see Romans 2:15). We know which impulses to obey because we have God's Word. From the indwelling Spirit, we have the desire and power to obey. By these God-ordained means, the conscience he put within us may be trained and strengthened, and the internal and social conflicts resolved.

I have discovered this principle of life—that when I want to do what is right, I inevitably do what is wrong. I love God's law with all my heart. But there is another power within me that is at war with my mind. ROMANS 7:21-23

7

All value will be sentimental; and you must confess (on pain of abandoning every value) that all sentiment is not "merely" subjective.

CHAP. 2, P. 53

Very few people think about society's future well-being, let alone have inclinations toward safeguarding the species. If this is so, then how could we attribute to instinct such a negligent attitude? In *The Abolition of Man*, Lewis alleged that most people have a stronger drive to preserve their immediate family. If instinct is the source of value, then preserving the future is less urgent and compulsory than, say, a parent's concern for a child. Lewis argued the impossibility of justifying the care for posterity as a superior instinct; thus, the foundations of society can never be established upon instinct alone.

But preservation of society is, in fact, among the viable beliefs that make up the *Tao*, the doctrine of objective values. They are premises (givens)—not conclusions—for the human race, and we must embrace them for what they are. Like the existence of God, reason, and morality, the preservation of society is so foundational that it is beyond the possibility or necessity of proof.

In his preface to the novelistic *That Hideous Strength*, Lewis said that he had the same solemn purpose as previously asserted in *The Abolition of Man*. In his fictional work, Jane and Mark Studdock are typical products of modern education: they have a subjectivist and relativistic approach to values. Yet the development of values is inescapable—so the new basis for morals becomes the instinct to preserve the species. But in truth, this type of education prepared people to accept the conditioning and control of the majority by the powerful few: humans taking charge of humans. *That Hideous Strength* shows the dehumanizing and socially disastrous results.

By contrast, the Lord Jesus Christ invaded our world and demonstrated the supreme value of love by serving the powerless in first-century Palestine: children, the poor, Samaritans, shepherds, and widows—all the socially disenfranchised. Instead of dominating people—the goal of the "conditioners" in both *The Abolition of Man* and *That Hideous Strength*—the Messiah showed concern by surrendering his divine right and accepting the posture of a humble servant.

Rather than unjustly manipulating others to selfish advantage and "playing God"—which is anything but—we can follow Christ as our example and dispense God's grace and mercy to the marginalized in society, and so preserve society for future generations.

You must have the same attitude that Christ Jesus had. PHILIPPIANS 2:5

8 *If nothing is self-evident, nothing can be proved. Similarly if nothing
is obligatory for its own sake, nothing is obligatory at all.*

CHAP. 2, P. 53

In many ways, the most valuable part of *The Abolition of Man* is its appendix. There Lewis illustrated the universality of the moral law (*Tao*), drawing on examples diverse in time, place, and culture—including Egyptian, Babylonian, Chinese, Jewish, Hindu, Christian, Indian, Norse, Greek, Roman, and other cultures. All have moral strictures on such things as killing, marriage, duty to parents, justice, and charity. As these examples demonstrate, morality is not an accident of biology, nor is it socially constructed. If they were not objectively true, then morality and ethics would be a matter of preference or biological determinism, and rationality itself, under such assumptions, would make no sense.

The place where all moral reasoning begins is the *Tao*—the reality of objective values—which is self-evident and obligatory; we must accept it as being essential to the world we know. These values govern moral education, marriage, relations between people, and the relationship between emotion and reason. To not accept these is to be without sensible morality. Lewis's point was not that all religions are the same nor all ethical codes equal—far from it; rather, that there is a natural law that makes demands on all people at all times. Human nature is constant, and though there have been many cultures, there has really been only one civilization. We are all created in the image of God and share foundational moral beliefs that flow from his character. There is nothing arbitrary about the moral law.

By contrast, teaching that is subjectivist and relativist about values empties humanity of any spiritual awareness of God. Lewis sought to reaffirm that awareness. Christ's purpose was to unveil the Father so that people would set their eyes on the living, personal God and come to know him. Often the first step toward God is the awareness that the moral law exists and that not one of us has kept it. The truth of this is attested by nothing less than the Holy Spirit of God.

His Spirit joins with our spirit to affirm that we are God's children.

ROMANS 8:16

9 *When all that says "it is good" has been debunked, what says "I want" remains. It cannot be exploded or "seen through" because it never had any pretensions.* CHAP. 3, PP. 77–78

The scientism of the Western educational system was built on the supposition that existence is its own justification and that developmental change—evolution—is defensible as a characteristic of the natural order of the world. Lewis argued that modern education, far from orienting the mind to the natural order, was reconditioning it in such a way as to be freed from all that was natural—procreation, birth, death, relationships with fellow humans—with the aim of taking control of humankind's destiny.

A wholly instinctive approach to values explains why people do such things as lie, rape, and murder: obeying their instincts alone, they have no innate motivation to tell the truth, to respect an individual's person, or to embrace the sacredness of life. If the preservation of the species is the ultimate end of humankind, then anything that conflicts with that can be swept aside. This further explains the contemporary sexual immorality of Western society, for example, which discards traditional values and promotes sexual appetites as natural and—here is the key—thus needing to be gratified as long as they do not interfere with the safeguarding of the species.

The church of the twenty-first century is incredulous toward the unpretentious appetites of power and greed of eighteenth-century Christian believers who condoned and practiced human slavery. Yet in one hundred years' time, how will the church view contemporary Western believers? Will they be astounded at our indifference, greed, and lack of compassion toward those in the majority world chained to poverty, starvation, and industrial exploitation? Operating on instincts alone does not lead to concern over such blights on the global landscape.

In a tangible example of servanthood, the Lord Jesus took off his outer garment and washed the feet of his followers. Even though the disciples knew the custom of washing feet before a meal, and even though the basin of water and towel sat in the room, no one else had volunteered to do the job. And as we sit in our comfortable, cushioned seats and wait for God to come around to our way of living, God still looks for a multitude of followers to give up their pampered lives and come around to his way of serving.

Since I, your Lord and Teacher, have washed your feet, you ought to wash each other's feet. I have given you an example to follow. Do as I have done to you.
JOHN 13:14-15

10 *A dogmatic belief in objective value is necessary to the very idea of a rule which is not tyranny or an obedience which is not slavery.*

CHAP. 3, PP. 84–85

In *The Abolition of Man*, Lewis declared that an educational system producing students with untrained emotions and thus no appreciation of values would lead to the downfall of the civilization that accepted it. When Lewis's novel *That Hideous Strength* was published in 1945, it was clear that he had written a novel to parallel the ideas of *The Abolition of Man*. He must have had in mind the kinds of tyrannies present in both fascist and socialist states as he developed his story of devilry.

One of the potential problems of Lewis's novel is its placement of science, sociology, and technology on the side of the demonic over against the enslaved spiritual and classical traditions—which opened it to the charge of taking a simplistic approach and suggesting that these social and cultural dimensions were more than usually susceptible to satanic conflict. Lewis sought to disclaim that very objection in the novel's preface, explaining that he wrote about the profession he knew best—his own. But he also believed that there was a dangerous infection plaguing society and that educational institutions were at the center of the battle for the lives of those inoculated by the sin of pride. So-called civilized and educated professionals were being manipulated by dehumanizing, even demonic, forces. The battle was for individual minds, but it was of national proportions.

Lewis proclaimed that society needed to wake up from the evil enchantment of worldliness—a strong spell that had been upon the Western world for a number of centuries. The whole of Western education was under this magic charm as it aimed to silence the still, small voice of God and convince people that humanity essentially was good.

One reason Jesus came from heaven to earth was to render powerless the works of Satan and rescue people from the bondage of spiritual and physical disease. Much of his ministry in first-century Palestine was comprised of encounters with demonic forces, which recognized his eternal calling long before his followers did. Christ's work on the cross has already given the church victory over Satan, although the full consummation is yet to come when Christ returns again. As followers of Jesus, we are to stand against the wiles of the enemy and declare Christ's lordship over the nations of this world, who belong to God through the Messiah's saving work.

We are not fighting against flesh-and-blood enemies, but against evil rulers and authorities of the unseen world, against mighty powers in this dark world, and against evil spirits in the heavenly places. EPHESIANS 6:12

CHAPTER 12

That Hideous Strength

IT WAS LEWIS HIMSELF who first connected *That Hideous Strength* and *The Abolition of Man*. He often set out to make similar points in both a work of fiction and a work of nonfiction. His interest in doing so was rhetorical; the more complex the point, the more necessary to come at it from a variety of literary angles. Thus, he made a claim in propositional language that he later depicted in figurative language. In *That Hideous Strength* (fiction) Lewis made a point he had set up in *The Abolition of Man* (prose): that those who step outside the dictates of reality will literally have hell to pay for their rebellion against the moral order.

In this book, Lewis contrasted two groups. One group is centered on Elwin Ransom, the primary character in Lewis's science fiction trilogy. Ransom's party is headquartered at a manor called St. Anne's. This group is inclusive of all types. There are men and women, wealthy and poor, educated and uneducated, upper and lower classes. There is room for a skeptic and even for animals: a bear named Mr. Bultitude and a common bird, a jackdaw. The people at the manor are life givers and draw energy from one another. By contrast, the second group is a nefarious one called the N.I.C.E. ("the National Institute of Co-ordinated Experiments"). It is a gathering of evil people who have developed an inner ring, a clique, that is exclusive and given to using others for their own interests. There is no willingness on the part of the N.I.C.E. to adjust their designs and plans to suit others. Furthermore, they have denied the demands of reality and have lost their own humanity in the transaction.

The two groups are further contrasted by a husband and wife who are drawn into them: Mark Studdock into the N.I.C.E. and his wife, Jane, into Ransom's group. Lewis presented the Studdocks' marriage as a product of modern education. They fear emotion, lack integrity, and are focused on their own personal needs. Mark's pride, shown in his craving to be an insider, and Jane's fear of being vulnerable and open constrict the possibility of a loving marital union. The Studdocks serve as Lewis's guides to the good and evil worlds of St. Anne's and Belbury (Jane and Mark, respectively). And the couple's eventual redemptive change to accept the good (or "the Normal") serves as an example of choices we can make.

What Lewis allows his readers to see in *That Hideous Strength* is the contrast between a group that gives life and a group that takes life. All of us are moving toward one of these two kinds of subcultures: givers or takers. Here, perhaps more than in any of Lewis's other novels, is this contrast displayed: the temptation to take what is not ours is destructive; the practice of giving leads to triumph and life.

1

The purchaser [of Bragdon Wood] was the N.I.C.E., the National Institute of Co-ordinated Experiments. CHAP. 1, SEC. 4, P. 21

The N.I.C.E. is a scientific institute at Belbury. Mark Studdock, a sociologist at Bracton College—a small British university in Edgestow—joins the staff and eventually writes newspaper propaganda. Studdock takes this position after wrestling with the uncertainty of his responsibilities and the questions he has concerning the people at Belbury and certain circumstances: the murder of a colleague and the confrontational strategy of the N.I.C.E. in taking over Edgestow. These circumstances serve as warnings, foreshadowing the devilish conspiracy of the N.I.C.E. against humankind. Eventually Studdock is told of its Head and his totalitarian goals and is asked to lure his wife, Jane, to Belbury in an attempt to control her gift of foreseeing the actions of the enemy.

One point to be taken from the book's beginning is that external appearance does not always accurately represent reality. Quite often we find that institutions and individuals pretend to be what they are not. Our own pretense might start slowly and innocently, but if we continue to water the falsehood, it grows quickly into justification and rationalization of our sinful struggles. Similar to the religious leaders of first-century Palestine, we may present a grandiose facade while harboring all kinds of impurities and the stench of sin.

Yet as followers of Jesus we do not have to succumb to pretense and hypocrisy. Our Savior promised that the Holy Spirit would come alongside and lead us to truth. In dynamic and functional union with him, believers can receive warnings (through the conscience) of drifting currents of thought that would lead us to run aground on sandbars of sin. If we continually listen to and obey the cautions of our Master Pilot, the Spirit of God will empower us to overcome temptation and guide us to secure harbors.

If we let God soften our hearts, we will be able to hear him prompting us away from a cul-de-sac of conscience or an endless cycle of hypocrisy. Today we need a fresh infilling of his Spirit, so that we might be his obedient children who walk a straight path in wholeness of heart and mind.

What sorrow awaits you teachers of religious law and you Pharisees. Hypocrites! For you are like whitewashed tombs—beautiful on the outside but filled on the inside with dead people's bones and all sorts of impurity. MATTHEW 23:27

2   *If he guessed very little of the mal-adjustment between them, this was partly due to our race's incurable habit of "projection."*

CHAP. 2, III, P. 52

In an early morning interaction between the newly married Studdocks, Jane is annoyed about her hair not doing as she wished, angry at her lack of emotional strength concerning her dreams, and on top of it all, disappointed in her husband's deficiency of compassionate support. But Mark is practically oblivious to any of these currents flowing through his wife because he is sexually aroused by her and falsely assumes that Jane's sensations are the same as his own. His imaginary projection masks the disharmony between the couple, preventing any resolution of it. Each one's problem with the other is essentially a failure of imagination.

Lewis understood the importance and power of the human imagination. For the readers of *That Hideous Strength,* he often used satirical fantasy to kindle in imaginations the possibility of a supernatural Christian world. He believed that myth could be divine truth touching the human imagination with what is real, evoking a longing of an actual otherworld of possibilities. He used various mythical images from the traditional Arthurian legends such as ancient Logres, Pendragon, and Merlinus Ambrosius, as well as an original myth regarding Elwin Ransom's travels in the heavens and his interaction with the Oyéresu—the ruling powers of heaven. Lewis's purpose was to direct the modern imagination toward the reality of the supernatural as a prelude to the gospel.

In the Gospels, human imagination often runs contrary to divine will. Instead of an imagination converted to God's desires, the traditional messianic myth anticipated a conquering king dictating militant action. But Jesus rejected this misplaced imagery, walking away from celebrity status and political power in order to be alone with God (see John 6). We need God to baptize our imaginations, as Lewis put it, so that we might see God as he is, in his glorious splendor but removed from human myths of manipulative self-centeredness.

And seeing God as he truly is, according to his account of himself in the Bible, becomes the first step toward seeing ourselves and our fellows as we truly are.

When Jesus saw that they were ready to force him to be their king, he slipped away into the hills by himself.   JOHN 6:15

3   *There are a dozen views about everything until you know the answer.*
Then there's never more than one.   CHAP. 3, IV, P. 84

As Mark Studdock tries to work through his doubts and understand what his role at the N.I.C.E. would be, he speaks to his colleague Bill Hingest at dinner. Bill, aka Bill the Blizzard, tells him that the organization's purpose is not science but political conspiracy. But through his sociological lens, Mark interprets the aim of the N.I.C.E. as social planning and assumes that Bill is merely prejudiced by his own academic discipline. Bill warns the young sociologist against becoming involved with the N.I.C.E., a warning Mark dismisses by saying there are two views about everything. Part of Bill's reply is quoted above.

Mark does not want to listen to the truth. He has misgivings concerning the people of the N.I.C.E. and its manipulative vision, but his self-centered pride in longing to belong to the inner circle muffles such cautions as Bill's, while justifying his own interpretation because of his educational experience. Lewis contended that Studdock's education—being neither scientific nor classical and lacking honor, nobility, and depth—allows him to be ensnared by the evil world of the N.I.C.E., with its intended reconditioning of humanity and destiny control.

It is true that there are always a dozen ways to view any reality; our opinions are frequently colored by the lenses of personal experiences, education, traditions, and situational contexts. Critical realists believe that they have some truth and seek to obtain more, naive realists think they know all things, and subjective realists propose that there is no truth except in themselves. Nonetheless, there is absolute truth. But Studdock is not prepared to receive information contrary to his prejudices or to plumb deeper into the truth about the N.I.C.E.

In our postmodern Western world, many people have the same attitude toward the truth about Christ. Ironically, they restrict their opinions in reaction to the narrowness of Christianity without any serious investigation of biblical truth. Even Jesus is seen as being bigoted when declaring that he is the only way to God the Father. Yet there is only one spiritual truth, and that way is narrow by the very nature of reality. We need to invite God's Spirit to come and guide us to this certainty and show us the truth in Christ.

I am the way, the truth, and the life. No one can come to the Father except
through me.   JOHN 14:6

4 *"And what are you going to do?" asked Jane.*
"Heaven knows!" said Mrs. Dimble. CHAP. 4, I, P. 88

Margaret Dimble's retort to Jane Studdock concerning her sudden house eviction by the N.I.C.E. at Belbury is followed by a description of legal inquiries by her husband, Cecil. The adage—"Heaven knows"—is often said in desperate situations without sufficient thought to its truth. Heaven is where God dwells, and God knows all truth. He *is* truth. He knows all because he is eternal—living in the past, present, and future.

As a novelist shapes a story, he or she simultaneously lives in each episode of the story. So God, the author of life, understands the full picture of our existence—the beginning, middle, and end. There is nothing that he does not know concerning the universe, our planet, the history and future of humanity, and the nations. All is revealed to him who knows and sees all.

This awareness of the omniscience (all-knowingness) of God should provide comfort and encouragement to all who love him. Whatever the situation we face, whether financial or relational or vocational—even being turned out of our homes like a sparrow falling from its nest—our heavenly Father knows what we are going through. His knowledge of our lives is so detailed that he even knows the number of hairs on our heads. Jesus taught that we should not be afraid in such circumstances but realize that our Father deeply loves and values us. He cares, no matter what we may feel about our circumstances.

The all-knowing God is in control. Nothing escapes him or happens without his knowledge. He is in charge of the universe and the little sparrow. How much more does he cherish and care for us! If our heavenly Father knows when one little bird falls from a tree, he can comfort us in our distress so that we don't have to be afraid.

What is the price of two sparrows—one copper coin? But not a single sparrow can fall to the ground without your Father knowing it. And the very hairs on your head are all numbered. So don't be afraid; you are more valuable to God than a whole flock of sparrows. MATTHEW 10:29-31

Husbands were made to be talked to. It helps them to concentrate their minds on what they're reading—like the sound of a weir.

CHAP. 4, I, P. 90

Lewis humorously painted Margaret Dimble (aka Mother Dimble) as a dithering, easily flustered woman who embarrasses Jane by kneeling at her bed and saying her prayers. She conjures up the proverbial picture of the woman whose ceaseless chatter numbs her husband's mind. Such a stereotypical portrayal, however, sharply contrasts the selfishness of Jane Studdock. Jane lives a carefully calculated life, one that measures out emotion so that she can avoid entanglements with people. Above all else she desires to live her own life and resents anyone—including her husband, Mark—who invades her space and tries to take over; she even takes this attitude to the extent of begrudging love itself.

After inviting herself to Jane's house to stay the night, Margaret pours out her immediate troubles to Jane, revealing her concern for others in similar distress and her melancholy longings for children she never had. Jane's reaction to all this soul searching? She yawns three times and begins to drop off to sleep. To divert this embarrassing moment from Jane, Mrs. Dimble excuses the younger woman's rudeness by making fun of herself. She apologizes that, after a thirty-year marriage, she has developed the habit of talking continuously to her husband, like the sound of a river running over a dam. But Jane yawns again.

Jane is so hardened by her self-absorption that she fails to show any genuine concern for the older lady. Her selfish actions are hurtful.

People matter. God brings all sorts of people across our paths to dispense his grace and love through us. They might not be of our social set or educational background. They may not even be of the same socioeconomic or ethnic group. Still, God desires that his people extend authentic empathy to all who come to us through a welcoming smile, listening ear, touch of the hand, cup of concern, or time spent. We need to receive God's mercy to have our eyes opened to the Mrs. Dimbles he brings across our path. And so seeing, let us give them a cup of ourselves to quench their thirst in the Lord's wisdom and strength.

If you give even a cup of cold water to one of the least of my followers, you will surely be rewarded. MATTHEW 10:42

6

This was the first thing Mark had been asked to do which he himself,
    before he did it, clearly knew to be criminal.   CHAP. 6, III, P. 158

Mark Studdock realizes that he is moving closer to acceptance in the inner circle of the N.I.C.E. when he is invited to the library. That is where confidential talks take place between key members of the organization: Lord Feverstone, Miss Fairy Hardcastle (head of the N.I.C.E. police force— aka *the Fairy*), physiologist Professor Filostrato, the Reverend Straik, and Professor Frost (one of two deputy directors). The names of these people reveal Lewis's satirical objective to suggest affliction and distortion. For instance, the Fairy and Filostrato illustrate a perversion of normal sexuality. When confronted by such characters, we realize that this is in a sense a contemporary fairy tale for adults and that these persons embodied the bad fairies endeavoring to control the Studdocks.

Mark had ignored his misgivings about the N.I.C.E. in favor of the sheer pleasure of being appreciated in the intimate circle. Now he finds himself further ensnared the day after Bill Hingest's funeral. Asked by Hardcastle to concoct two leading news articles concerning the engineered disturbances at Edgestow before they even happened (to produce a government-sanctioned state of emergency), Mark at first is shocked by the revelation, but he quickly mimics the tone of the group and embraces the notion without struggle. After continual conscience checks, beguiling sin has smiled at Studdock, who turns his head in collegial laughter and ignores his principles. That night, the more Mark works at the prefabrications, the more he justifies his actions and reconciles his recoiling reason.

Like Studdock, in the time of Jesus the Jewish people were lulled into a false security concerning their salvation because of an in-group mentality. Jesus taught his disciples to obey his teaching and the truth would set them free. In reaction, the wider Jewish audience declared that as a part of the Abrahamic family they never had been slaves and had no need of his freedom. Nonetheless, all people are ensnared in sin and need the Lord's liberation. Jesus wants to free us from the entanglement of our wrongdoings through our obedience to the truth of his teachings so that we might no longer be slaves of sin but permanent members of God's family.

Jesus replied, "I tell you the truth, everyone who sins is a slave of sin. A slave is not a permanent member of the family, but a son is part of the family forever."

JOHN 8:34-35

7

You do not fail in obedience through lack of love, but have lost love because you never attempted obedience. CHAP. 7, II, P. 178

The strange company of people at St. Anne's on the hill is led by their mysterious Director, a Cambridge philologist named Elwin Ransom, who had recently taken the name Mr. Fisher-King. The Director had traveled to other planets (Malacandra, or Mars, in *Out of the Silent Planet* and Perelandra, or Venus, in *Perelandra*) and talked to the bodiless eldila—the Oyéresu out of Deep Heaven, the guardian spirits of those planets. Because of the conspiracy against the human race by the N.I.C.E. at Belbury, Ransom is chosen by the planetary leaders to combat this enemy on Earth, the "silent planet." He is also the semidivine Pendragon of legendary Logres (present-day Edgestow)—which was the authentic Britain in the days of King Arthur—the essence of which survives in the remnant of St. Anne's.

The good, simple, and significantly *normal* world of St. Anne's turns on its head the anti-utopian world designed by the Macrobes—the dehumanizing demonic forces behind the N.I.C.E. and its "Head." Jane Studdock is connected with these happenings because her dreams foretold the enemy's actions at Belbury.

Upon meeting the space-traveling professor for the first time, Mrs. Studdock is invited to join the company at St. Anne's, and it is there that she learns her husband is working for the enemy. The conversation then focuses on marriage and her lost love for Mark. Jane had understood love as equality and free companionship, whereas the Director redefines it as obedience—submission in humility. Jane had lost her love for Mark because she did not attempt to serve him in obedience by humbling herself.

Fisher-King's explanation about love echoes the teachings of Christ. Indeed, in the midst of their dialogue Lewis has the Director eat a lunch—a small bottle of red wine and a bread roll—reminiscent of Communion. Jesus taught that to love him, his followers would need to obey his commandments. And because they love him by submission to his directives, the Father and he would love them and reveal themselves. If his followers do not do what Jesus said—obey the Father's message—they do not love him.

Do we love Jesus by yielding our lives to his teachings? Let us delight to obey the teachings of Christ and love God with our whole being.

Those who accept my commandments and obey them are the ones who love me. And because they love me, my Father will love them. And I will love them and reveal myself to each of them. JOHN 14:21

8 *Her [Margaret Dimble's] anxiety had reached that pitch at which almost every event, however small, threatens to become an irritation.*

CHAP. 12, V, P. 320

The battle begins. Elwin Ransom commissions Cecil Dimble and Arthur Denniston, with Jane Studdock as the guide, to find Merlin before the enemy does. The expedition is fraught with danger, not only from the N.I.C.E. but also the unknown eldilic powers of the magician. Now Margaret Dimble, left behind with Ransom and the others in the house of Logres to wait for news, sits in the kitchen isolated from the rest, unable to sleep and feverishly darning to divert her anxiety, all the while struggling to control her irritation over Ivy Maggs's frivolous chatter.

Perhaps we are not facing the same distressing circumstances as Mrs. Dimble, but we all experience stress and anxiety. Jesus taught his followers not to worry about the apprehensions of everyday life because human existence consists of far more than clothing and food. God looks after the flora and fauna of his world, and we are far more valuable to him than any of the plants and animals. Besides, worry can't change a thing about our situation (see Luke 12:22-26).

So let's stop worrying. Have faith in God. Trust him. He cares for us. God already knows our needs. As we make the Kingdom of God central in our lives, God will give us all that we need. The Father takes great pleasure in giving us daily the spiritual sustenance of his Kingdom. This is the essence of what Ransom says to Margaret Dimble on the eve of her husband's dangerous, potentially life-threatening mission.

Throughout this day, let's throw our anxieties and worries onto the broad shoulders of our heavenly Father to carry. In return, God will give us bundles of joy and packages of peace to unwrap that come from his deep love for us.

If God cares so wonderfully for flowers that are here today and thrown into the fire tomorrow, he will certainly care for you. LUKE 12:28

9

Previously failing to capture Jane, the N.I.C.E. members pressure Mark to entice his wife to their headquarters. He fails to do so and after being falsely accused of murder and imprisoned, he undergoes a dehumanizing practice to make him fit for the society of Macrobes. But he experiences a change of heart as he chooses "the Normal" against the scientific view for the first time, and then he meets an old tramp whom the enemy believes to be Merlin.

In the same chapter, Jane has a spiritual experience with the earthly fury of Venus and later changes her affection toward her husband as a result. In this mystical portrayal, the fairy story for adults is indirectly promoting the supernatural—an apologetic for Christian supernaturalism. Lewis desired his work to rise from allegory to myth and to affect the reader by shocking him or her into new, unexplored realms of experience and thought—an illumination of the human soul by the divine mystical reality. And at the very end of the chapter, Jane has an encounter with God in the garden—indicated by a paradoxical writing style—that is reminiscent of the Garden of Eden, and she experiences a change of allegiance to Christianity. Paraphrasing the words of William Hingest, Mark's inflexible colleague from his previous college, Bracton, you can't study God; you can only get to know him, which is quite a different thing.

Our lives are shaped by relationships. When we meet people, we experience various continuums of connection: from initial to continued, casual to intimate. Many are important in developing who we are as human beings. As Jane discovers, no encounter is greater than meeting God. Like Jane, the Samaritan woman at the well met the living God and was transformed. She then rushed to her people and told them to come and meet Jesus the Messiah. They came, recognizing that Jesus was the Savior of the world. Past ethnic animosities dissolved when the villagers were face-to-face with the holy God.

Jane represents the only possible change within the narrative. She chooses the good and natural beauty of St. Anne's and she meets real life in God. What happened to Jane could also happen to us. We need the Savior of the world to come and meet us. Through our faith he gives us the gift of real life.

Now we believe, not just because of what you told us, but because we have heard him ourselves. Now we know that he is indeed the Savior of the world. JOHN 4:42

10 *In fighting those who serve devils one always has this on one's side; their Masters hate them as much as they hate us.* CHAP. 14, V, PP. 392–393

It is the Director—Mr. Fisher-King, or Dr. Elwin Ransom—from the manor at St. Anne's who utters the words in the epigraph above. Just before Jane, Cecil, and Arthur leave to search for Merlin, the great magician of ancient Logres, the Director makes an explanation to Jane regarding her encounter with the terrestrial wrath of Venus. He unfolds the proportions of a cosmic battle: one taking place between heaven and hell (between Maleldil and the Bent Eldil) since the blockade of the Silent Planet was broken. On the very night he addresses the group, Ransom would bring the recently uncovered Merlin before his masters, the deep powers of heaven: Viritrilbia, Perelandra, Malacandra, Glund, and Lurga—Mercury, Venus, Mars, Jupiter, and Saturn. The magician would receive into himself the powers of the planetary spirits, and afterward he would go to Belbury as the interpreter for the man held at the N.I.C.E. and believed to be Merlin.

Ransom's prophecy comes to pass as Merlin follows the Director's orders and goes to the N.I.C.E. headquarters—the center of the Hideous Strength that desires to squeeze the earth in its grip. During an after-dinner speech by Horace Jules, the figurehead director of Belbury, the power given to Merlin turns the words of the N.I.C.E. crowd into nonsense, reminiscent of the biblical Babel. There, then, unravels a frenzy of destruction on such a scale that it sounds the clarion of Ransom's prediction. Thus begins the journey to save the world, Logres, and St. Anne's, as well as to bring Jane and Mark back together.

In Jesus' journey to save our world, he confronted the forces of the evil one. To bring the Kingdom of Heaven to earth, God in human form invaded our planet and attacked the ruling spiritual enemy. In doing so, Jesus turned the demonic world upside down, as we see in such encounters of his as with the demons in the Gadarene man. Screaming in torment, these demons pleaded to be sent into a herd of pigs feeding in the distance. Jesus complied with their request, and in a frenzied stampede, the swine plunged into the lake of Galilee and drowned. The man was free. But the townspeople reacted in fear, begging Jesus to leave.

Our all-powerful God is greater than he who is in the world. Through Christ, our God has delivered us from the evil one.

The demons came out of the man and entered the pigs, and the entire herd plunged down the steep hillside into the lake and drowned. LUKE 8:33

GOING DEEPER

The Bodleian Library at Oxford University has nearly 135 miles of bookshelves—who has read them all? Even the greatest scholars in the world are just scratching the surface when it comes to knowing what might be known. Baron von Hügel was a philosopher of religion and author whom Lewis enjoyed reading. In a letter to his niece, Gwendolyn Greene, von Hügel reminded her to beware of the first clarity, and to press on to the second clarity, and on again to the third and the fourth clarities. Like von Hügel, Lewis understood that there are always depths yet to explore. Perhaps one of the greatest things Lewis did for his readers was to make them mindful of the fact that life is far more complex than could ever be imagined.

We must be constantly reminded that any truth known can be plumbed more deeply and applied more widely; it can also be understood in coherent relation with other truths. And Lewis was always letting his readers know that one's current understanding must be dynamic and growing or it will calcify into misunderstanding. Whatever we know now, there is still so much more to know and to understand. Of course, this could be, for some, a matter of deep frustration. For others, it is the gateway to curiosity, wonder, awe, and eventually worship. So it was for Lewis. He was not afraid of honest questions or honest doubt.

Those who have no doubts or questions whatsoever must be in a terrible place, for they have deluded themselves into thinking they are all-knowing; that is, that they have become rivals of divine omniscience. Lewis wanted his readers to go deeper, to discover what is still hidden from their eyes, not because it cannot be known but because they have not yet grown to the place where they can see and grasp all that might be seen and understood.

This idea of pressing further in our understanding of God, ourselves, and the world where God has placed us is not unique to Lewis. The poets have always been calling their readers to attend to these things. Euripides, the Greek playwright Lewis was reading before his conversion, called these matters to mind. He ended *Alcestis* the way he ended many of his other plays: "Many are the shapes that fortune takes, and oft the gods bring things to pass beyond our expectation. That which we deemed so sure is not fulfilled, while for that we never thought would be, God finds out a way."[1]

Robert Browning, one of Lewis's favorite poets, exhorted readers of his "Rabbi ben Ezra" to "welcome each rebuff / that turns earth's smoothness rough." No matter how smooth our world may seem to us at times or how neatly we think we have it figured out, it has peaks and valleys and is full of texture and complexity. We should welcome even the troubling things that help us see the world with its contours as it is, rather than how we would have it be. Tennyson described such a perspective in his poem *In Memoriam A. H. H.*: "Our little systems have their day / They have their day and cease to be / They are but broken lights of Thee / And Thou O Lord art more than they." No one has plumbed the depths of God, or themselves, or this world; no one can say, "I understand all."

Furthermore, the whole maturation process reveals to us that there is more to grasp than is within our reach at any given moment. We know things today that we did not know ten years ago. This means we do not know things that we will probably know ten years hence. Our own development tells us we, too, are only scratching the surface of understanding. There are many mysteries of the faith, to be sure, but be careful not to play the mystery card too soon. Some things we consider to be mysteries now may yet reveal their secrets in the near future.

The search for knowledge and understanding may lead to an occasional detour, but fearing such things, we may miss out on much that is available with a little reflection. Lewis encouraged his readers to go deeper, and in that spirit the reflections that follow explore some of the depths that lie below the surface in some of his own best-known works.

CHAPTER 13

Prince Caspian

LUCY, EDMUND, SUSAN, AND PETER PEVENSIE are waiting for a train to take them to school when they are whisked back to Narnia. Only a year of earth time has passed since their adventures in the Wardrobe, but a thousand years of history have lapsed in Narnia. Evil seems to have triumphed, as Miraz usurps the throne while the rightful king, his nephew Caspian, is kept in youthful ignorance. It has been so long since Aslan's visit and "the good old days" that most are doubtful of the old stories and see no relevance or hope in Narnian history or prophecy for their own day. The reigning view of reality in Narnia is that the stories of Aslan and the Pevensies are only legend. The promise of Aslan's return, delayed so long, must be another part of the myth.

It's an old problem for us here on earth, dating from the promise to Adam and Eve of a coming deliverer (see Genesis 3:15). At least two thousand years passed after the first promise. And now, another two thousand years have passed since Jesus' promise to return. The first Christmas and Easter were a surprise to almost everyone, and the return of Jesus at the end of earth's history will be too.

The task for us all is to maintain the healthy tension between the unseen reality (past, present, and future) while making sense of what we do see. Caspian, though in virtual imprisonment by Miraz, believes the old stories and acts on them. The immediate outcome is his escape and the blowing of Susan's horn, which is what miraculously draws the Pevensies back to Narnia to help. Gradually, many of the characters adjust their thinking about Narnia's past and future and about the power and promise of Aslan. Even Lucy, who believes more than the others, must change her thinking about Aslan as she experiences more of him. Lucy had begun to know Aslan very well in *The Lion, the Witch and the Wardrobe.* But when she meets him again in *Prince Caspian,* he seems bigger. Aslan tells Lucy that every year will be like that: though he never changes, he will seem bigger.

In the same way, the writer of Hebrews encouraged us to leave the milk of basic belief for the meat of deeper spiritual nourishment (see Hebrews 5:12). God and his ways, though unchanging in character, are fresher and deeper to us every day if our faith is growing.

1   *They feel safer if no one in Narnia dares to go down to the coast and look out to the sea—toward Aslan's land and the morning and the eastern end of the world.*   CHAP. 4, P. 55

In his writings, Lewis used the German word *sehnsucht*, or "longing," to convey the most powerful sense of our deepest need. He saw this yearning as instrumental in drawing us closer to something more—a road that ultimately leads to God. The anticipation of greater, higher, and deeper wonders beyond the run-of-the-mill experiences in our everyday existence causes us to open our eyes, unplug our ears, and seek with our intellects truth that seems just beyond our grasp.

Buoyed by the stories of Old Narnia told to him by his nurse, Caspian longs to see the land as it had been. Sadly, he learns the awful truth: his own ancestors, the Telmarines, had driven out or killed the talking beasts, dwarfs, and other residents of Narnia. Worst of all, his uncle, Miraz, didn't want him to learn the truth.

Caspian's teacher, Doctor Cornelius the half-dwarf, also longs for glimpses of satyrs or dancing fauns, or for an echo of dwarf drums. But any glimpses are always just out of sight.

As Dr. Cornelius explains to Caspian in the above quote, the Telmarines want to suppress the truth of Old Narnia and the Golden Age of the kings and queens and Aslan. To speak of these stories is dangerous. But Cornelius can't help sharing them.

The Holy Spirit draws us and gives us hints. We feel the emptiness Augustine described as a God-shaped void in the depths of our souls, denying our illusion of wholeness and self-sufficiency apart from the giver of all good things.

The world cannot abide this. We're told "Be practical"; "Don't be such a dreamer—just do your job." Until we have had a taste of future glory, the bland flavor of the God-free gruel of everyday life will leave us rummaging about in the spice cabinet of life, wondering what we might add to it. Thank God that he has instilled this yearning in us. He would not have given it unless he was willing to satisfy it.

We, too, wait with eager hope for the day when God will give us our full rights as his adopted children, including the new bodies he has promised us. We were given this hope when we were saved.   ROMANS 8:23-24

2 *Wouldn't it be dreadful if some day in our own world . . . men started going wild inside, like animals here, and still looked like men, so that you'd never know which were which?* CHAP. 9, P. 122

In George MacDonald's classic children's book *The Princess and Curdie*, the young main character, Curdie, is sent on a dangerous mission to help save the kingdom from the influence of evil men. To aid him in his task, he is given a gift: he can tell by touch whether or not a person is becoming beastlike inside, even though he or she would retain the shape of a man or woman.

A fan of MacDonald's, Lewis was familiar with Curdie's story. In *Prince Caspian*, after Lucy survives an attack by a nontalking bear, she voices her fear of men turning into beasts. In this post–Golden Age Narnia, the Pevensies had yet to encounter one of the gentle talking beasts they had been used to. Encountering this wild bear was frightening enough; encountering people with a similar sort of wildness was too much of a nightmare to contemplate.

And yet, haven't we seen such a nightmare in reality? Watch almost any talk show or news program or click on your Internet news site and you'll see stories of abuse and activities so heinous you almost doubt their veracity. You'll also hear people bragging of their numerous adulteries; patting themselves on the back for how early in life they lost their innocence; and offering themselves absolution because they, at least, are *honest*. Sadly, when we are caught up in our actions, we are in danger of growing beast-like without even knowing it.

The apostle Paul warned of the destruction to which this path leads. Because "this life here on earth" is not the only life we'll have, there are consequences for our actions. We don't have to go the beast route, however. We can choose to be led by the Spirit (see Galatians 5:16-26).

They are headed for destruction. Their god is their appetite, they brag about shameful things, and they think only about this life here on earth.
PHILIPPIANS 3:19

3   *"Where did you think you saw him?" asked Susan.*
   "Don't talk like a grown-up," said Lucy, stamping her foot. "I didn't
   think I saw him. I saw him."   CHAP. 9, P. 125

Children sometimes exaggerate. You have only to listen to a child telling a story to know that. Well-meaning adults often remind them of that fact in order to teach an important lesson. But imagine the frustration a child feels when he or she isn't exaggerating but is, instead, telling a true story— one he or she wants desperately to be believed.

While making their way to Aslan's How—the Narnian army's command base—to join King Caspian and his army, Peter, Susan, Edmund, Lucy, and Trumpkin the Dwarf spend a frustrating time wandering in the woods, trying to get to the river that will take them to their destination. They are completely lost. But then something amazing happens: Lucy sees the long-absent Aslan! And she is sure that Aslan is trying to lead them in the right direction. Their problems are over, right? Wrong. Only Edmund chooses to believe Lucy. But Lucy and Edmund are outvoted by the others. By following Trumpkin's erroneous advice, they wind up going the wrong way and have to double back because they ignored what Lucy knew to be true. Not having seen Aslan themselves, they chose to believe what was not true.

Lucy was the one who first brought them to Narnia by stepping into the wardrobe in *The Lion, the Witch and the Wardrobe.* Edmund reminded Peter and Susan of that to no avail.

Isn't it interesting that Jesus told his disciples that the Kingdom of God had to be received "like a child"? The purity of a child's faith is quite remarkable. When children pray for something to happen, they believe it will happen. They don't rationalize; they simply believe.

I tell you the truth, anyone who doesn't receive the Kingdom of God like a child will never enter it.   MARK 10:15

4   *Lucy woke out of the deepest sleep you can imagine, with the feeling that the voice she liked best in the world had been calling her name.*

CHAP. 10, P. 137

In our day, as in the days of the Old Testament prophet Samuel, we sense that a word from the Lord is a rarity. We desire deeper connections with God but feel alone and separated from him—especially when our culture encourages us to compartmentalize our lives, explaining away God's voice when we do hear it. Samuel himself needed to be taught to overcome his initial naturalistic assumption. Three times God called to Samuel (see 1 Samuel 3); each time Samuel wondered whether Eli, the high priest, had called him.

After a frustrating time of claiming to see Aslan and not being believed, Lucy hears Aslan calling her one night. Why does Aslan call Lucy, the youngest of the Pevensies, instead of Peter, the High King? Because Lucy has always been the most sensitive of the four to Aslan. You have only to read of how she greets Aslan with joyful abandon to see how much she loves him. But more than that, Lucy takes the time to listen for Aslan's voice, to listen and to seek him.

Eli told Samuel how to answer God's voice. His advice was for Samuel to be a receptive, reverential listener. Listening to God is important, yes. But listening with a heart ready to obey is the most important thing.

The one who loves us more than anyone else and from whom our ability to love flows—the one who would make us most happy and content if we would open ourselves fully to him—constantly communicates with us. Are you listening?

The LORD called a third time, and once more Samuel got up and went to Eli. "Here I am. Did you call me?" Then Eli realized it was the LORD who was calling the boy. So he said to Samuel, "Go and lie down again, and if someone calls again, say, 'Speak, LORD, your servant is listening.'" 1 SAMUEL 3:8-9

5 *"Aslan . . . you're bigger."*
"That is because you are older, little one," answered he.
"Not because you are?"
"I am not. But every year you grow, you will find me bigger."

CHAP. 10, P. 141

If you've visited your old elementary school as an adult, you realize how much smaller everything seems. The water fountains are much lower than you remember, although they seemed just right when you were a child.

Good relationships go the opposite way—they get "bigger," meaning they grow more in depth. The more time we spend in relationship with anyone—learning the nuances of his personality, the depths of her knowledge and understanding, the lengths that he or she would go to in order to help us—the deeper the relationship grows. How much more is there to learn about an infinite being—the all-knowing, unending, all-powerful, omnipresent God who loves us passionately and never abandons us? This is what Aslan implies in his words to Lucy. The more we learn about God, the bigger he gets.

Our changing perspective of God is a theme Lewis returned to over and over in his writings. Often our view of God is directly tied to the growth in our spiritual lives, or lack thereof. Sometimes we are spiritual bonsai— trained, trimmed, and terrorized into living in a tiny pot of earth, fearful of a strenuous transplant into the great wide out-of-doors. At those times, God seems very small.

The Old Testament prophet Isaiah experienced God's mind-boggling and overpowering presence, which filled his senses, filled the Temple, and could be heard all around him. Whatever Isaiah's view of God, it certainly grew larger at the vision of the majestic God.

Note that God himself never *really* changes. We simply become more aware of how huge he is. We will never come to the end of our knowledge of him. Like Lucy, as we grow older we have the privilege of finding him bigger.

It was in the year King Uzziah died that I saw the Lord. He was sitting on a lofty throne, and the train of his robe filled the Temple. ISAIAH 6:1

6 *[Lucy said,] "How could I—I couldn't have left the others and come up to you alone, how could I? Don't look at me like that . . . oh well, I suppose I could."* CHAP. 10, P. 142

Excuses come easily sometimes. We don't want it to be our fault when trouble comes. And it's so much easier to blame someone else.

Lucy was all set to blame her siblings and Trumpkin the Dwarf for not believing her, which had resulted in their fruitless journey in search of the Great River. But one look into Aslan's patient eyes and she knows that she is without excuse. She could have chosen to obey Aslan and travel in the direction that he led, even if she had to travel alone.

Aslan refuses to debate what might have been or what might be the outcome of that obedience. Instead he again calls for her obedience. Now will come the hardest part of Lucy's journey. She has to wake everyone up in the middle of the night and tell them to follow Aslan, knowing that they will ridicule her. And they do.

Perhaps you've faced a similar situation after taking a stand of faith. Or perhaps you've failed to take a stand, fearing the same results that Lucy faced. Even now, you might be weighing the pros and cons of taking a stand. What might happen if you do? if you don't? The only realistic option, rather than worrying about the outcome, is to do what everyone can do: everyone can, as Aslan pointed out, discover the outcome of obedience by simply obeying. Decisive commitment, the conscious decision to do right despite the fear that others might judge our sanity, is the only way to learn how God intends to deal with a situation, whether or not he intends to vindicate us immediately.

It's never too late to do the right thing, but the right thing may change when we fail to obey quickly.

If you refuse to serve the LORD, then choose today whom you will serve. . . . But as for me and my family, we will serve the LORD. JOSHUA 24:15

7 *Lucy went first, biting her lip and trying not to say all the things she thought of saying to Susan. But she forgot them when she fixed her eyes on Aslan.* CHAP. 11, P. 149

What happens when you add fuel to a fire? That's easy. Depending on the type of fuel, the fire grows in strength and might even cause an explosion. What happens when you focus on the hurtful words or actions of another? Your anger grows in strength and might cause an explosion of a different sort.

When someone gives you a hard time, the temptation to "return the favor" increases. As you focus on your anger or on the hurtful words you've received, you fuel the fire of your anger until you're at the point where you're ready to lash out. But lashing out often leads to more trouble.

Lucy Pevensie is sorely tempted to give her sister, Susan, a piece of her mind. Susan's condescending and grumpy remarks when Lucy wakes up their group in the middle of the night at Aslan's command are very hurtful indeed. But fixing her eyes on Aslan causes Lucy's anger to dissipate. She makes a conscious decision not to lash out. This is grace in action.

Although Susan tries her best to sound like an adult, Lucy displays a mature self-control that Susan lacks. Lucy's trust in Aslan steels her against the jibes of Peter, Trumpkin, and even Edmund, and it eventually helps save Narnia. Her actions are a good example of a promise spoken through the prophet Isaiah (below). Note that the "perfect peace" described usually comes in times of trouble. Perhaps Lucy feels this peace as she follows Aslan, not knowing what will happen at the end.

Fixing your eyes on a goal usually helps you reach it. You don't veer off course. Keeping her eyes on Aslan, who was invisible to all but Lucy herself at one point, helped her and the others to surmount a difficult path and reach the goal—Aslan's How. What is your goal? On what or whom are your eyes fixed?

You will keep in perfect peace all who trust in you, all whose thoughts are fixed on you! ISAIAH 26:3

8   *"I wouldn't have felt safe with Bacchus and all his wild girls if we'd met them without Aslan."*
        "I should think not," said Lucy. CHAP. 11, P. 160

Hurricanes, tornadoes, blizzards, ferocious thunderstorms, earthquakes, and tsunamis show nature at its most untamed. We fear the devastation they cause and feel helpless when they're at full strength.

While with Aslan, Lucy and Susan meet up with characters out of Greek and Roman mythology—Bacchus, the Roman god of wine (the Greek Dionysus, also known as Bromios or Bassareus); Silenus, his tutor; and their followers. Once again, Lewis showed his extensive literary knowledge by weaving these characters in with his Narnian mythology. Bacchus is as untamed as a winter storm. And Aslan—son of the Emperor-beyond-the-Sea—does nothing to curb his enthusiasm. He allows Bacchus to do what he does best—provide helpful, healthful grapes. Yet even wild Bacchus is subservient to Aslan. Note that Bacchus doesn't appear until Aslan roars, and he seems to act within the boundaries set by Aslan. Note also that Lewis didn't change the nature of these characters. He didn't make Bacchus the quiet and shy god of lemonade simply because Bacchus happens to appear in this story. In this way, Lewis showed that Aslan is more powerful than even Lucy could have imagined.

Jesus' disciples felt helpless in the face of a squall. They were at their most vulnerable in a boat on the Sea of Galilee. And what's more, Jesus was asleep! But Jesus quickly demonstrated his authority by calming the storm. He didn't say, "Oh my, what a terrible, uncontrollable storm. You were right to fear it." He simply spoke to it and ended its fury.

Lucy and Susan could feel safe with Aslan, even among the untamed. We also can feel safe, even in untamed nature or in other situations that seem beyond our control, because God is our refuge (see Psalms 46:1; 59:16).

The disciples went and woke him up, shouting, "Lord, save us! We're going to drown!" Jesus responded, "Why are you afraid? You have so little faith!" Then he got up and rebuked the wind and waves, and suddenly there was a great calm. The disciples were amazed. "Who is this man?" they asked. "Even the winds and waves obey him!" MATTHEW 8:25-27

9

"But they also say that he came back to life again," said the Badger sharply.

"Yes, they say," answered Nikabrik, "but you'll notice that we hear precious little about anything he did afterward." CHAP. 12, P. 168

"What have you done for me lately?" We sometimes ask this of friends, family, and even God. Though people might have been extremely helpful to us, we might doubt their concern if years pass without our seeing or hearing from them.

In *The Lion, the Witch and the Wardrobe* Aslan had smashed the power of the White Witch and ended the tyranny of winter at a cost—his death. Even though he returned to life, for a thousand years afterward no one in Narnia had seen him. Within those years and up to the plotline of *Prince Caspian*, the Narnians had been conquered and oppressed by the Telmarines.

Nikabrik—the bitter, unbelieving dwarf—has a "what have you done for me lately" attitude. He is all for anyone who could rid the land of the accursed Telmarines. In his desperation—and lack of faith in the Old Narnian tales—he is even willing to bring back the White Witch in order to make that happen.

Ever know anyone willing to compromise that way? Nikabrik could not bring the White Witch back to the throne of Narnia any more than with his grumbling he could force the horn of Susan to work the way he thought it ought to.

Trufflehunter the badger tries to convince Nikabrik of the truth—Aslan returned to life and will return someday to aid the Narnians. You have only to read the rest of the story to see that Trufflehunter was right. But more important, everyone learns that belief in Aslan isn't enough. Aslan expects the Narnians to do their part—to act in ways pleasing to him. They could show their faith in Aslan by avoiding a partnership with evil and by fighting for what was good. And that's the message of James 2:26.

Just as the body is dead without breath, so also faith is dead without good works.
JAMES 2:26

10 *Not for the sake of your dignity, Reepicheep, but for the love that is between you and your people . . . still more for the kindness your people showed me . . . you shall have your tail again.* CHAP. 15, P. 209

We all have a little touch of the drama queen in us. Even the most humble and gracious of us can harbor a tiny corner of pride—whether in oneself, one's culture of origin, or in accomplishments. Sometimes life has a way of keeping our egos in check.

If you've seen the movie *The Chronicles of Narnia: Prince Caspian,* you might recognize at least the first line of the quote above. These are the words Aslan speaks in response to the request of Reepicheep, the valiant mouse warrior. In the war against the Telmarines, all Reepicheep's injuries are healed by Lucy, save one: most of his tail had been cut off, and Lucy's healing cordial could not regrow the tail. While Reepicheep worries that the loss will severely compromise his dignity, Aslan is more concerned about how tightly Reepicheep clings to that dignity. So what causes Aslan to say yes to Reepicheep's request? The love of Reepicheep's troop of mice—a love that extends to their willingness to cut off their own tails rather than allow Reepicheep to continue to bear the shame alone. That, along with Aslan's own love for those brave mice who had once aided him after he was put to death, moves him.

Jesus was touched by the love four friends bore for another when they carried their paralyzed friend to Jesus. One wonders if Lewis had the healing of the paralyzed man in mind when he wrote the scene of the mice carrying Reepicheep to Aslan. The fact that the man's friends went to such extraordinary lengths to bring him to Jesus prompted Jesus to declare the man's sins forgiven: his physical healing of the paralyzed man was the sign of his authority to forgive sins.

Reepicheep and the paralyzed man inspired the love and loyalty of their comrades. Do you?

Seeing their faith, Jesus said to the paralyzed man, "My child, your sins are forgiven." MARK 2:5

CHAPTER 14

An Experiment in Criticism
and *The Discarded Image*

THE TITLE *AN EXPERIMENT IN CRITICISM* may scare some potential readers. It needn't. This book is not hard to read. The sentences are short, the style simple, the ideas profound—vintage Lewis. It has, in fact, many delightful analogies and very useful, practical suggestions. Like the great Samuel Johnson, Lewis was a defender of the common reader against the perverse demands of modern elitists. Johnson said of a dull book, "To what use can the work be criticised that will not be read?" Here is common sense that Lewis would have approved.[1]

Lewis moved the discussion away from whether a book is good or bad to the kinds of readers it attracts and how it is read. Anticipating a movement called reader-response criticism, which focuses on the role of a reader in interpreting a text, Lewis suggested a simple principle: Good readers "receive" a text. They enter into the experience and world of ideas and values the author presents. Bad readers "use" a text. They demand only support for ways of feeling and believing that they already dogmatically hold. Worse, bad readers (including professional critics), twist authors' words to suit their favorite critical method. A good book attracts readers who receive; a bad book, only those who resist the possibility of change.

Along with breaking down the barrier between professionally trained and untrained readers, Lewis crashed through the wall between young and old, modern and ancient. For example, a taste for a particular book is not bad merely because it is appreciated by children. Lewis believed it a sign of his own maturity when he finally didn't care a fig if someone saw him reading a children's book. The only children's books or fairy tales that are good, in fact, are the ones you like to read again as an adult.

Lewis's *Experiment* doesn't just tell us how to read a text. It is also a great clue to the kinds of literature Lewis wrote himself. In it are wonderful chapters on myth, fantasy, realism, and poetry—all modes in which Lewis worked. What all his writings have in common is the ability to rearrange the landscape of our minds. We leave his books not less ourselves, but more. We see life with a new set of eyes. Small are the persons who see only through their own: this is the conclusion of the soaring last chapter and epilogue of *Experiment*. Anyone who likes to read should, at the very least, make a point of delighting in this section of the book.

We find a similar theme (expanding our view of reality) in a very different book, *The Discarded Image*. Except for its final chapter, most readers of Lewis—unless they are also serious theologians, philosophers, or literary critics—will not be very interested in this book of scholarship on the medieval worldview. Even a quick glance through it will reveal two things. First, it will be apparent that Lewis had read and digested in Greek or Latin every one of the huge number of ancient texts that he mentioned. Second, though not an apologetic book (a "defense"), *The Discarded Image* displays a thorough understanding of both pagan and Christian theology and philosophy and gives enough of the Christian gospel for someone under the conviction of the Holy Spirit to come to faith in Christ. It was no overstatement when Lewis said that all his books are evangelistic. Clearly, Lewis's main purpose in this volume was to provide a background for understanding medieval and renaissance literature shaped by the two great streams of thought called paganism and Christianity. And Lewis made no secret of his Christian position.

The next-to-last chapter ("The Influence of the Model") is accessible to anyone with an interest in literature. The final chapter ("Epilogue") is very readable and supremely useful to all who are interested in history and the way humanity gives a changing shape to its worldview—its understanding of reality as a whole. All worldview models get a great deal of reality in, though no one model captures reality fully. Lewis suggested that the questions asked by any generation are a stencil shaping the answers reality will give. Our experience of the world is always breaking the idol of our customary understanding, because the big picture—even our picture of the person closest to us in the world—is always bigger and more complicated than we can fully comprehend. In every generation, the way people understand the big picture most certainly changes, for better or worse.

The chapter unfolds some of the implications of Lewis's thoughts on worldview as follows: Our understanding of God is always too small and always in need of filling out; we must be humble about our understanding (be it ever so modern and scientific) of the meaning, purpose, and function of the universe; even our understanding of real people must be adjusted by our experience of them. But all this doesn't mean that anything goes. Our modern relativism is one of the things our experience of reality must correct.

1 *The process of growing up is to be valued for what we gain, not what we lose.* AN EXPERIMENT IN CRITICISM, CHAP. 7, P. 72

Lewis's *An Experiment in Criticism* is a book about reading and readers. This quotation, from his chapter on realism, is meant to encourage us not to reject fantasy or fairy tales simply because they are not realistic according to some limited standard; Lewis was especially concerned that we might reject them because they are thought of as children's books. Before the nineteenth century, all fictional books focused on the unusual; even fairy tales were originally written for adults, not children. In fact, the most deceptive books are those that seem real, that court the reader's identification with the characters, but have twisted values. No one expects to fly like Peter Pan or meet an ogre, children included. There are further implications of this principle.

Lewis said there was no greater proof of immaturity in a person or a time period than a disdain for things that appear to be associated with youth or an earlier era. He believed that an adult is more, not less, of a person if able to still understand the goodness inherent in the things of childhood and to keep its advantages, such as wonder and enthusiasm, while leaving its false fears and naivete. We can still enjoy the simple things while welcoming the new and more nuanced or complicated goods that grown-ups enjoy.

Our cynicism about adult politics, for example, can too easily spill over into cynicism about goodness in the design of God and hope in his ultimate plan. The value of good fictional books, like the kind Lewis wrote, is to nurture a healthy imagination. Without this gift, many will not be prepared to enter into the joys of this life or the one to come. Questions are good; unbelief is not. Never give up a childlike faith, but grow in your understanding of the complicated world with the expectation that the author of our faith knows how the story will end.

Let the children come to me. Don't stop them! For the Kingdom of Heaven belongs to those who are like these children. MATTHEW 19:14

2   *Next to a world in which there were no sorrows we should like one*
where sorrows were always significant and sublime.

AN EXPERIMENT IN CRITICISM, CHAP. 8, P. 79

In this section of *An Experiment in Criticism* Lewis discussed the way we misread tragedy. We can forget that literature (along with films or other art forms) is a patterning of events made from the material of life; it is not life itself. As a literary form, tragedy makes meaning of suffering, even if that meaning is a grand and heroic speech of the kind dying people seldom make or an unrealistically tidy sense of conclusion. The characters in real life, on the other hand, especially those who live on, must care for the mundane—like getting death certificates and paying funeral bills—in the midst of grief, which may not be part of a neat pattern we can figure out.

We live in a fallen world, in which bad things happen. Our natural reaction is to cry out, "Why, God, why? Why did you make this happen to me?" Even questions such as "What is it that God is trying to teach me through this?" may go unanswered. At the death of Lewis's wife, Joy, all sorts of possible meanings for the suffering and sorrow—or, worse, the possibility of a lack of meaning—flooded his mind. Was God a cosmic vivisectionist, conducting sinister experiments on us? If Lewis prayed "hard enough," could she be brought back? When people die, are they being punished, or are we who are left behind being punished?

Sometimes life just stinks, not because God wants that bad thing to happen, but because someone did something wrong, something wore out and broke, or someone made a mistake. The error Lewis was trying to help us avoid is the one that comes from our reading (or watching) the tragic as an art form. In artistic tragedy, we find pattern, finality, significance, and very often meaning. But these may not be apparent in our experience of real-life tragedy. Suffering is more often a crisis of faith than a crisis of understanding. We can expect the messiness of life. Jesus told his followers it would be that way, and he prayed not for their ease or rational understanding but for their endurance.

I'm not asking you to take them out of the world, but to keep them safe from the evil one. JOHN 17:15

3   *The real way of mending a man's taste is not to denigrate his present favourites but to teach him how to enjoy something better.*

AN EXPERIMENT IN CRITICISM, CHAP. II, P. 112

Both C. S. Lewis and the apostle Paul—great apologists, great defenders of the faith—understood the simple principle that you catch more flies with honey than you do with vinegar. Lewis himself came to faith in Christ not because anyone mocked his fascination with Norse mythology, but because his friends Hugo Dyson and J. R. R. Tolkien pointed out that those mythical elements, coupled with historical truth, ought to make the life of Jesus that much more appealing to him.

There are many people with whom we interact on a daily basis. God has put us into their lives not to shove our favorite bits of the truth down their throats but to love them. When we love people, we will learn to appreciate all the truly honorable and worthy things about them and learn from them the truths that they have learned.

As we have seen earlier in this book, Lewis used this technique when he wrote *The Abolition of Man*. In its appendix he quoted many great ideas from all around the world, from many different ages and cultures—quotes that conveyed the understanding that there is a moral bottom line, a code that is basically understood by all humanity—the concept of the *Tao*.

To have any kind of meaningful discussion, we must begin with areas of commonality, to find out what is agreed upon. Even a formal logical syllogism—the foundation of philosophical discourse—relies on the agreement that its premises are correct. If we cannot agree that Socrates is a man, for instance, or even that all people are mortal, it will be difficult to conclude that Socrates is mortal. It doesn't help to argue about whether he was a stonemason or a philosopher.

When we have been given the trust of other persons to the extent that they share their hearts with us, we will see clearly the ways in which they have already connected with or heard from God. We will be able to share with them the ways in which our experiences of God parallel theirs or little splashes of light they may be able to fit into their picture of the world.

As I was walking along I saw your many shrines. And one of your altars had this inscription on it: "To an Unknown God." This God, whom you worship without knowing, is the one I'm telling you about. ACTS 17:23

4

In the moral sphere, every act of justice or charity involves putting ourselves in the other person's place and thus transcending our own competitive particularity.

AN EXPERIMENT IN CRITICISM, EPILOGUE, P. 138

Lewis distinguished two kinds of readers in *An Experiment in Criticism*: those who *use* literature and those who *receive* literature. Those who use books value them only for what can be done with them; theirs is a purely pragmatic practice. But those who receive literature appreciate what the literature does to them: they receive the work, and their perspective and world are enlarged; they grow. Lewis recognized that when we receive literature our self-interest is diminished and our capacity to notice a wider world, glorious for its own sake, is increased. A good reader—that is, a receptive one—is always breaking out of the dungeon of self and discovering a wider world. Of course this kind of reading, Lewis believed, is consistent with the rhythms of life that meet the observant person on every side; the principles behind it are at work in justice and in charity (love) as well.

In justice we render to others their due, which is not merely punishment of the evildoer but also praise of those who do well. Justice awakens empathy; it causes us to go out from self and assist in seeking right for others. True justice is empathetic and, in that way, incarnation-like.

So, too, a true act of love allows the lover to enter into the world of the beloved as best as he or she is able. Self-interest is set aside in order to see the needs of that other and meet them. We receive another as a unique being, as not merely an extension of ourselves but also a holy object worthy of our service. Love gives of itself for the benefit of another.

To the degree that reading breaks us out of self-interest so we can receive what is set before us, reading allows us to grow in justice and love. The reader's world is one that leads to growth in the capacity to see a larger world and enter into it with empathy and grace.

Suppose someone comes into your meeting dressed in fancy clothes and expensive jewelry, and another comes in who is poor and dressed in dirty clothes. If you give special attention and a good seat to the rich person, but you say to the poor one, "You can stand over there, or else sit on the floor"—well, doesn't this discrimination show that your judgments are guided by evil motives?

JAMES 2:2-4

5 *In coming to understand anything we are rejecting the facts as they are for us in favour of the facts as they are.*

AN EXPERIMENT IN CRITICISM, EPILOGUE, P. 138

We cannot know a thing as it ought to be known if we apprehend only what value it has for us at any given moment. This kind of self-interest is too utilitarian; it shuts down understanding. To truly understand anything, we must seek to understand it as it truly is. Lewis believed good reading—the habit of reading well as receivers and not merely users of literature—can enable one to see the world with greater clarity. It is not a guarantee, but it is a start, and it can establish a lifetime habit of seeing all things as they are rather than how we want them to be.

The self-interested reader projects onto the text what he or she wants to find there. And the habit may have already been established in the daily routine of life's activities, so that self-interested reading is a mere extension of the bad habit. We fail to see with an objective eye and tend to notice only ourselves—our own likes and dislikes—wherever we go. But when reading is done at its best, according to Lewis, it becomes possible for a person to start seeing the world in its complexities. Good is not merely what *seems* good to us. Receptive reading allows us to see with new eyes, to see what is truly good in itself and to adjust our standard of good to a more objective appreciation. Likewise, bad is then not merely what offends us subjectively; we are offended by that which is objectively bad, and if we see well, we can say objectively why it is bad or else we will refrain from judgment.

There is authority in objectivity. While many demand to be listened to when they are only asserting their will or spewing their prejudices, the objective person can simply describe well what is so, letting reality itself convince and persuade. The greatest way to persuade another is to stand shoulder to shoulder with that person and describe the world as it is, not as we would have it be.

The people were amazed at his teaching, for he taught with real authority—quite unlike the teachers of religious law. MARK 1:22

6   *[In reading], as in worship, in love, in moral action, and in knowing,*
I transcend myself; and am never more myself than when I do.

AN EXPERIMENT IN CRITICISM, EPILOGUE, P. 141

To really know a thing, we must know it for what it is, not merely value it for its usefulness to us. To come to know anything requires a process of transcending self; that is, letting go of the urge to project onto things what we want them to be in favor of simply receiving them for what they are. While this is good in the realm of things, and especially in the realm of ideas, it is a necessity if one is to function in any kind of meaningful way in the realm of relationship. Love demands that we look beyond self to the welfare of another.

In moral activity, we must think beyond self-interest to what is right and good, not merely to what benefits us. If we are concerned only for our own benefit, we may compromise morality to get what we want. Laws, both civil and natural, have no hold on us if we are judging what is right or wrong merely from our own point of view. But an objective approach to morality allows us to respect a transcendent standard that clarifies what is good for us as well as for others. If we know that it is not good for another to steal from or lie to us, then we also know that it is wrong for *us* to steal or lie. The standard is objective, and its inexorable demands are for us as well as others.

In worship and in love, we also recognize the independent value of God and others; in this recognition we let go of any inflated sense of self. The Bible indicates that sin is when people play God over their own lives. Furthermore, playing God over the lives of others is sin compounded. Ironically, to act as God when we are not diminishes our humanity and that of others. On the other hand, to worship and love well, and to know and act well, is to break out of the dungeon of self and become true to our humanity.

Even perfection has its limits, but your commands have no limit. Oh, how I love your instructions! I think about them all day long. Your commands make me wiser than my enemies, for they are my constant guide. Yes, I have more insight than my teachers, for I am always thinking of your laws. PSALM 119:96-99

7 *The important thing is that sight begets philosophy. For "no man would seek God nor aspire to piety unless he had first seen the sky and the stars."*

THE DISCARDED IMAGE, CHAP. 4, P. 55

Romantic longing is born once we see something that transcends our particularity and personal interest; that is, romantic interest begins by looking beyond self. The Romantic poets were not concerned merely about that form of romance between a man and woman. They wrote of longing that could be tethered to a place and be called homesickness; it could be tethered to another person and be called love; it could also be tethered to nature or express a desire to recover lost innocence. Anything, therefore, that awakens one to a wider world is *romantic* in this sense.

For example, observing the patterned movement of the constellations; the constancy of the sun, moon, seasons; and the passing of days into nights and nights into days sets one's heart to wondering. This constancy, as opposed to randomness, that exists in the universe reveals its teleology. The universe reveals design and, if it has design, it must have a designer. If there is a design for the universe, then it is likely that humanity has a purpose. Thus the movements of the universe suggest to the observant eye things most profound.

When medieval observers looked at the heavens and contemplated the cosmology of the universe, they saw the movements of the heavens as a testimony to a Prime Mover: specifically, to God. But by what means did God move the universe? Lewis said it was essential to medieval cosmology that God moved the universe by love. Seen properly, everything testifies to God's love. He made the universe; therefore, his love is expressed in giving it design and purpose. He sustains the universe; therefore, his love is manifest in his providential care. And when God's creatures rebelled against him, in love he sent his Son to reconcile humanity to himself (see Ephesians 2:14-18).

On any starlit night, a heavenward gaze should set the heart to wondering. And wonder, properly followed and informed by God's revelation, will set one's heart in motion, for the Prime Mover is still in the business of moving us by his love.

The heavens proclaim the glory of God. The skies display his craftsmanship.

PSALM 19:1

Reason and appetite must not be left facing each other across a no-man's land. A trained sentiment of honour or chivalry must provide the "mean" that unites them and integrates the civilised man.

THE DISCARDED IMAGE, CHAP. 4, P. 58

According to the medieval worldview, humans have an amphibious nature. Not that we, like tadpoles that turn to frogs, are destined for both water and land. Rather, our amphibious nature is that we are both material and immaterial. We are like the animals in that we possess material bodies with appetite and need; we are like the angels in that we possess an immaterial nature with reason, will, and emotion. Every man and woman stands with a foot in two worlds. Much of life is lived in shifting our weight between the animal characteristics of our nature and the angelic. At times these characteristics of our humanity seem to be in conflict. We cannot live in denial of any feature of our complex and amphibious nature; but certainly, we must prioritize what part of us will be in charge and, in doing so, learn how to live in harmony with ourselves.

Our appetites in a material world (be it the appetite for food or the sexual appetite) must be reined in, lest we live lives of obesity or dissipation. On the other hand, our spiritual lives must be lived with our feet on the ground, lest our spirituality become devoid of substantive content. We are not materialists, nor are we Gnostics. We are both material beings and spiritual beings, and these "halves" of us can face off and be at war with each other. Yet how can they be reconciled?

Lewis reminded his readers that in the Middle Ages the means for keeping the material and immaterial in harmony was found through the trained and disciplined emotional life that led to chivalry. Chivalry concerned itself with the welfare of others. As we learn the life of empathy and compassion, we will seek to control those animal desires that put us in danger of taking advantage of another. In fact, we will harness bodily energy and strength in service of others to the glory of God. It is through emotional development and the capacity to feel for others that reason and appetite can find union and purpose.

You were cleansed from your sins when you obeyed the truth, so now you must show sincere love to each other as brothers and sisters. Love each other deeply with all your heart. I PETER I:22

9 *God is eternal, not perpetual. Strictly speaking, He never foresees;*
He simply sees. Your "future" is only an area . . . of His infinite Now.

THE DISCARDED IMAGE, CHAP. 4, P. 89

Medieval people, as all who have ever lived, sought to understand the ways of God relative to his sovereignty and their own free will. They sought to grasp the eternality of God and his dealings in time. They sought to understand God's infinity and his ability to confine himself in space and time. Furthermore, the medieval person wanted to know how God could know the future without deterministically affecting human choice.

Lewis observed that those in the Middle Ages understood God not as a perpetual being but an eternal one. On the one hand, if God were perpetual, he would progress and endure throughout time, making any kind of foreknowledge of future events impossible. On the other hand, if God is eternal, all times are always before him. Consequently, he does not need to acquire knowledge to grasp any subject or understand any future event. He is eternally present in all moments. He does not presuppose and then reason through a series of inferences to obtain a conclusion—an unnecessary exercise for someone whose knowledge is complete and immediate.

Undoubtedly, physicists would find something wrong with the following image, but it may have a limited value in making the point: the brightest star in the heavens (after our sun) is Sirius, the Dog Star, in the constellation Canis Major. When you see this star in the winter sky, you are looking at light that left that star eight years ago traveling at 186,000 miles per second (the speed of light). If an enormous man could straddle the distance between Earth and Sirius, he would be present in the time the light left the star as well as in the time the light arrived at Earth. Events that occurred in either place at either time would be immediate to him. Again, while the illustration has its weak points, it does show that enormity of this sort makes times at both Sirius and Earth present to a being who could straddle the distance between the two. If God is both eternal and infinite, then we can assume the events in time are for him eternally proximate—and that his loving care is immediate.

God replied to Moses, "I AM WHO I AM. Say this to the people of Israel: I AM has sent me to you." EXODUS 3:14

10 *The backward, like the upward, glance exhilarated him with a majestic spectacle, and humility was rewarded with the pleasures of admiration.*

THE DISCARDED IMAGE, CHAP. 7, P. 185

Lewis observed that medieval persons did not see themselves as living in a particularly noteworthy age. They could look back to the grandeur of Greece and Rome or forward to some spectacular age still to come; and because of this comparison, though comfortable in their own time, they did not put on airs. They could appreciate the accomplishments of those who went before and of those who would come after. There was a humility about medieval persons as Lewis describes their place in history.

The fourteenth-century author of the medieval work *The Cloud of Unknowing* said humility is caused by two things: an awareness of oneself as one truly is, for whoever truly knows himself would be humble, and awareness of God as he truly is, for who could stand before him without fear and trembling, awe and worship? These two things were then, as they are now, foundational for humility and honesty.

Envy and jealousy can destroy humility, leading to delusion—for they assume that the benefits received by others should have been given to us, and to misfortune—for envy steals joy and pleasure from our souls. If we can have pleasure only when things go our way, we will have a limited amount, for our capacities are relatively small. If we are jealous of the good that goes to another, we will live most of our lives in discontent. We will miss out on celebrating the welfare of others, for the corporate capacity for pleasure is enormous. There is a lot of good going around in this world; humility makes accessible the joy of it.

Lewis reminded his readers that there is a form of pleasure available in cultivating habits of admiration. If we can learn to take pleasure in the good that comes to others, we will never be at a loss. We can rejoice over the good things that others receive and take great pleasure in their happiness. The medieval person Lewis had in mind is someone who has figured out one of the great secrets of life; those who embrace a similar humility today can experience joy now even while admiring this medieval characteristic.

He gives us even more grace to stand against such evil desires. As the Scriptures say, "God opposes the proud but favors the humble." JAMES 4:6

CHAPTER 15

The Great Divorce

THE SIGN OF A GREAT BOOK is that you leave the experience of it changed forever. Old ideas are clearer, new ideas find a place, eternal truths come into focus and are held more deeply. For the spirit, intellect, and emotions, *The Great Divorce* is such a book. It may be the best of Lewis's books on the theme of choice. The nineteenth-century poet William Blake spoke of the marriage of heaven and hell, of contrary ideas uniting. Lewis maintained that no such marriage is possible: heaven and hell are divorced, and you can take nothing into one that belongs to the other. You must choose, and you are choosing every day, whether you know it or not.

Sidestepping our stereotypes of hell, the book's narrator finds himself in a "grey town" of empty buildings, always at twilight, always drippy and dreary. This is hell, though there is still time for its inhabitants to make a choice about staying there. The only people around are in line to board a bus, so the narrator joins them for company. Yet everyone is cranky and selfish. A bus finally arrives to take a couple dozen of them through space and into a world that is so much more real that they all appear as ghosts, and the grass pierces their feet.

These travelers are now at the outskirts of heaven, where it is perpetual predawn. The people who meet them are solid and bend the grass. All are filled with joy and love. They have come from deep heaven to meet the visitors and persuade them, if they can, to enter reality and meet Love and Truth himself. All but one choose to go back to hell for the same reason they went there in the first place: they prefer something else to God.

The people from the grey town are a sampling from every earthly vocation: working man, poet, painter, theologian, wife, mother, husband. Ten main scenes unfold as conversations between those from hell and counterparts whom they had known on earth and who had chosen heaven.

In some editions, a subtitle announces that the story is a dream. In others, we must wait until the end to learn that the narrator has been dreaming.

When darkness descends in the "grey town," it will be hell. When the dawn breaks in the solid place, it will be heaven. As the sun comes up at his back, the narrator realizes with horror that day has come, he is a ghost, and the time of choosing is over. Then he awakes to an air-raid siren and falling books to discover with sweet relief that he has been dreaming. He is still on earth, and the choice of his eternal destiny is still before him.

1   *I also was a phantom. Who will give me words to express the terror of that discovery?*   CHAP. 3, P. 126

Who would have thought that a walk in a world of abundant natural beauty could yield such ugly results? Having left the grey town and journeyed to the heavenly realm, the unnamed narrator of *The Great Divorce* quickly learns that there are two kinds of people in that realm: the solid people, or Spirits, who live there and the Ghosts who visit. He can't live in denial about his own status—it is too obvious with every step. The verdant grass and the flowers of heaven are more solid, more "real" than his phantom feet.

The Greek philosopher Plato would have agreed partially with the world Lewis depicted. It is a world of reason, redemption (key themes to which Plato often referred in his works), and a reality beyond the narrator's experience. The beauty and reality of this world provide a literally painful contrast to the narrator's limitations. Trying to pluck a flower or bend a blade of grass proves his powerlessness. He has yet to discover the solution heaven offers for his plight.

The apostle Paul probably felt just as trapped as he examined the horror of his own life, a life with a sin nature. Digging deeper into that nature was an expedition into a "heart of darkness" the likes of which writer Joseph Conrad could never have dreamed. Perhaps you understand Paul's despair as he realized his soul's true condition: that he was powerless to change. But there was a solution. Through Christ, Paul could be freed from his life of "sin and death." Through Christ's sacrificial death, God's forgiveness was extended.

Do you find yourself crying out like Paul? Perhaps a chronic temptation or fear you're having difficulty overcoming by sheer willpower is causing you to question whether you can ever change. Or perhaps you've even heard words of hopelessness saying there is nothing to be done, and you've taken them to heart. Consider the answer Paul discovered: God's strength begins as yours ends. He uses some of the most difficult situations of our lives to draw us closer and deeper.

Oh, what a miserable person I am! Who will free me from this life that is dominated by sin and death? Thank God! The answer is in Jesus Christ our Lord.

ROMANS 7:24-25

2   *[Dick said,] "Will you come with me to the mountains? It will hurt at first, until your feet are hardened. Reality is harsh to the feet of shadows. But will you come?"*   CHAP. 5, P. 136

One of the many conversations the narrator in *The Great Divorce* overhears involves a theological discussion between a Ghost and a Spirit named Dick—the Spirits being the inhabitants of this heavenly realm. Although the Ghost is a religious man, he is of the opinion that belief in God is one of the "childish things" to put away in favor of embracing works and intellectual ideas about religion. But Dick argues that belief in God is not an empty intellectual exercise. The only "works" required are repentance and belief—two often-painful ventures symbolized by the journey to the mountains.

Reality—seeing life for what it really is, beyond any fantasy—is a theme Lewis returned to often in his writings. Reality involves seeing God for who he is, not the fantasy god we might desire.

Perhaps you've had a conversation with someone who fails to believe in a God that he or she cannot discern intellectually. Or perhaps that person feels bitter toward God based on the harsh realities of life: the evils and disasters that befall people. Maybe you are that person.

The Ghost uses the verse below as a mantra of sorts—a justification for kicking God to the curb. But for Dick, belief in God is the fulfillment of that verse, not a justification for unbelief. Dick realizes that the struggle to believe in God, a struggle that comes through acknowledging the harsh realities of life, is necessary. One of these harsh realities is facing the fact that everyone is in need of repentance and forgiveness—walking the road to the mountains. The writer of 1 Corinthians, the often-persecuted apostle Paul, would certainly agree.

God invites us not to empty our minds of all reason but to come to terms with reality. Yes, life is painful at times. Yes, evil exists. Bad things happen to good people. But we "put away childish things" when we realize that the nature of God never changes. He is always good, even when life is bad. And he's more than capable of tackling the hard questions of life with you.

When I was a child, I spoke and thought and reasoned as a child. But when I grew up, I put away childish things.   1 CORINTHIANS 13:11

3

Fool. . . . There is not room for it in Hell.

CHAP. 6, P. 142

We're well familiar with the contrary sayings "You can't take it with you" and "He who dies with the most toys wins." One is true, and the other is part of a belief system that creates rapid consumerism in order to keep up with the Joneses and the ever-increasing demands of technology. Which one do you believe?

In *The Great Divorce*, a bright waterfall angel gives a Ghost named Ikey the warning quoted above as Ikey struggles to carry a golden apple. Yet one small apple there weighs a ton. Even the narrator has found to his chagrin that lifting a leaf is like lifting a heavy stone. Bringing an apple to the grey town is a forlorn hope, as the angel explains. Instead of staying and working toward residency in heaven, he has elected to bring a piece of heaven back to the grey town. As if anything in heaven could fit in hell! Ikey's greed causes him great pain and a lot of wasted effort.

In Jesus' parable quoted below, a wealthy farmer thought only of how much of his harvest he could store if he constructed larger barns. Little did he know that the harvest was the apple he would have to leave behind—that very night, in fact.

This parable is not a treatise against wealth or possessions, but against greed and the earthly mind-set that having things here on earth is really all that matters. As Jesus—and the waterfall angel—explained, the possessions we have here won't last through eternity. As the old saying goes, you can't take it with you. What we *can* take is a "rich relationship with God"—one in which our "roots grow down into him" (Colossians 2:7). This requires a far different labor than grasping and acquiring things. It involves peeling back the layers of our defenses and taking a hard look at our motives and attitudes.

[Jesus] said, "Beware! Guard against every kind of greed. Life is not measured by how much you own. . . . Yes, a person is a fool to store up earthly wealth but not have a rich relationship with God." LUKE 12:15, 21

4   *They say of some temporal suffering, "No future bliss can make up for it,"*
not knowing that Heaven, once attained, will work backwards and turn
even that agony into a glory.   CHAP. 9, P. 153

Some events in life are so painful that we can't imagine any good coming
out of them. Even if we're not wallowing in self-pity, we spurn trite "there,
there" offers of comfort. We want real comfort—real answers to life's suf-
ferings.

In a conversation between the narrator and George MacDonald in *The*
Great Divorce, MacDonald provides a perspective of eternity that helps
the narrator see the events of his life in a new way. Why would George
MacDonald make a "guest appearance" in one of Lewis's books? Lewis
made no secret of the fact that MacDonald's writings helped inspire him
on his own spiritual journey, so it's no wonder that MacDonald would
become a guide to the narrator just as Virgil was a guide for Dante Alighieri
in his *Divine Comedy*. Once a person accepts the righteousness of God,
MacDonald explained to the narrator, his or her life becomes a journey
toward heaven, with every event a stepping-stone on the road. Even the
hard times—the times of defeat and temptation—become paving stones
on the path to glory.

This is why the apostle Paul could write with relish a message that spells
out God's sovereignty. As horrible as some events of his life were, Paul
realized that God could bring ultimate good out of them. This is not to say
that the death of a child, a catastrophic illness, or the loss of a job is in itself
"good." But as Paul and the fictional George MacDonald would show us,
even these are part and parcel of citizenship in heaven. They draw us closer
to God and cause us to lean more heavily on him.

On the days when we struggle in agony, groping for the sense of it all,
we can rest assured that God can make something good out of even our
darkest days.

We know that God causes everything to work together for the good of those who
love God and are called according to his purpose for them.   ROMANS 8:28

5   *There are only two kinds of people in the end: those who say to God, "Thy will be done," and those to whom God says, in the end, "Thy will be done."*   CHAP. 9, P. 156

Watching someone suffer the consequences of his or her bad actions is never pleasant. Consider how you would feel if your child refused to study for a test, even after being nagged, and later received a failing mark. Perhaps you don't have to think about it—you've experienced those consequences firsthand!

Sometimes God allows his people to suffer their consequences. For years, the kingdom of Judah had received failing marks from God. Having spoken through such prophets as Isaiah and Jeremiah, God allowed them to reap the consequences of their actions. His seeming abandonment told them, in a sense, "Thy will be done."

The fictional George MacDonald uses this statement in reference to the narrator's concern that many Ghosts—his fellow citizens of the grey town—never make it onto the bus bound for heaven. His sentiments are a variation of the oft-asked question, "Why would a good God send people to hell?" MacDonald helps the narrator understand that hell is separation from God, freely chosen. God does not force anyone onto the road to hell—or to heaven.

But there is good news provided by the prophet Jeremiah: God never abandons his people. He's too compassionate for that. Even when we go our own way, "his unfailing love" causes him to act to save his people. But he can only make the offer of salvation. He won't force anyone to accept it. This places the responsibility squarely on our shoulders—just as it did on the people of the grey town. It's up to us to make the effort to accept not only his salvation but even our real need of it.

Are you saying to God, "Thy will be done," or are you sensing God's saying, "Thy will be done" in a decision you've made recently?

No one is abandoned by the Lord forever. Though he brings grief, he also shows compassion because of the greatness of his unfailing love.   LAMENTATIONS 3:31-32

6 *Then there will be no you left to criticise the mood, nor even to enjoy it,*
but just the grumble itself going on forever like a machine.

CHAP. 9, P. 158

Having observed a female Ghost grumbling to one of the solid people, the narrator wonders what is so wrong about the grumbler. Everyone grumbles now and then, right? Wasn't she essentially harmless? But as George MacDonald, his guide in heaven, reveals, the *attitude* behind the grumbling is the issue. An attitude of grumbling is all that is left of the Ghost. Ever know someone like that? She had chosen to embrace her own negative understanding of life rather than life itself. Consequently, she had no life left within her. She was merely a machine that grumbled.

This attitude was fully evident as the people of Israel wandered in the wilderness during the time of Moses. Their grumbling continually provoked the anger of Moses and caused even the long-suffering God to act—sometimes to the detriment of the people of Israel.

The danger of being in a cycle of grumbling involves a failure to recognize it for what it is. While we can readily point out the grumbling of others (especially in our spouse, children, or others close to us), sometimes our own bouts of grumbling fly beneath our radar. We don't always realize when we're caught in a cycle of complaints until a wise person points out the flaw.

Perhaps that's why the apostle Paul advised his readers to watch what they said. We are to critique our words, as MacDonald also discusses with the narrator, rooting out the bitter and the harsh. Instead of using speech to complain, why not use it to encourage or help in other ways? If you do, you will develop a habit of blessing rather than of grumbling.

Let everything you say be good and helpful, so that your words will be an
encouragement to those who hear them. . . . Get rid of all bitterness, rage, anger,
harsh words, and slander, as well as all types of evil behavior.

EPHESIANS 4:29, 31

7 *But, Pam, do think! Don't you see you are not beginning at all as long as you are in that state of mind? You're treating God only as a means to Michael.* CHAP. 11, P. 170

Can love ever be "bad"? That issue arises during an encounter between a Ghost named Pam and one of the solid people, named Reginald—her brother in life. Pam craves contact with her son, Michael, and cannot understand why she is not allowed to see him upon her arrival in the heavenly realm. She is even willing to go the route of "religion" in order to attain her goal—regaining her son.

The narrator is moved by the pain of that conversation as Pam rails against God and even against Reginald for the loss of her son. She ignores her brother's explanation that while Michael could not come to see her, *she* could journey to see him. This journey, however, would involve her embracing someone other than Michael: God.

Many have tried to bargain with God to attain a relationship or a longer life. "God, if you get me out of this/get this person for me, I will follow you," he or she prays in desperation. But even when God complies, the promise sometimes is forgotten. The temptation to use God as a means to an end is strongest when the object we seek is dear to us. But God wants to be sought for who he is, not for what he can give.

In a passage of Scripture known as the Shema (see Deuteronomy 6:4-9), Moses reminded the people of Israel to seek God not as a means to an end but as the end itself. He was to be the first priority in their lives. Jesus later repeated this commandment when challenged about the most important commandment in the law (see Matthew 22:34-40).

Putting God first provides a different perspective in our lives. Relationships, hopes, and desires are filtered through the lens of God's perspective. We no longer grasp at God as a means to an end.

You must love the LORD your God with all your heart, all your soul, and all your strength. DEUTERONOMY 6:5

8 *What sat on his shoulder was a little red lizard. . . .*
"Would you like me to make him quiet?" said the flaming
Spirit—an angel, as I now understood. CHAP. 11, PP. 174–175

Among the conversations that the narrator observes while walking with
George MacDonald, one of the most powerful involves a Ghost with a red
lizard on his shoulder and a shining angel by his side. The Ghost listens to
the lizard's whispering even as he tries to convince the angel that the lizard
has made him unfit for residence in heaven. The angel, however, never
veers from his desire to help the man by killing the lizard.

The Ghost can't at first bring himself to allow the angel to kill the
lizard. He tries to debate with the angel about the necessity of killing the
lizard. Finally, in the anguish of his soul, he submits. After a painful process, a death if you will, the man and the lizard are both transformed—the
man into the ideal of masculinity and the lizard into a remarkable horse.
No longer is the lizard a torment. It is now a tool the man can use.

The idea of a lizard perched on a man's shoulder might make some
laugh. But for many of us, this scenario is all too painfully real. We have our
own "lizard" to deal with—a besetting sin too obvious to deny: pornography or another sexual sin or addiction. Gossip. Lying. Our "lizard" teases
and torments us. We lie to others and ourselves about its effect on our lives.
We even cling to the "comfort" and familiarity we receive from it, like a
child sucking his or her thumb. We feel "divorced" from God, doubting his
ability or willingness to help or heal.

What is the lizard in your life? The first step is to admit that you are
powerless to change it without help. The next step is to cry for help like the
Ghost does in *The Great Divorce*—or like the desperate father who wasn't
quite sure if Jesus could do anything to help his son. "I do believe, but help
me overcome my unbelief!" You can't kill a lizard in your own strength.

"Have mercy on us and help us, if you can." "What do you mean, 'If I can'?" Jesus
asked. "Anything is possible if a person believes." The father instantly cried out,
"I do believe, but help me overcome my unbelief!" MARK 9:22-24

9   *The Dwarf and the Tragedian spoke in unison, not to her but one another. . . . I realised then that they were one person, or rather that both were remains of what had once been a person.*   CHAP.12, P. 183

One of the most tragic encounters witnessed by the narrator is the one between the Lady (Sarah Smith) and Frank, the Dwarf/Tragedian. Like the Green Lady in *Perelandra*, this Lady-Spirit has a majestic beauty that marks her as a citizen of heaven. The sweetness of her temperament draws others to God. By contrast, the Dwarf is a man closed in on himself. He mostly speaks through a puppet persona—the Tragedian. Every statement uttered is like a bad actor playing a role. He is not real. Even though Sarah tries to talk to Frank, rather than to the Tragedian, Frank clings to the phony persona.

Perhaps you've known people like that, who always seem to play a role as if an actor on a stage. Sadly, you're never quite sure who they are, since they're so engaged in the role. The hard part comes when you're in a close relationship with someone who clings to a role.

Even in the church you can find role-players. People talk about loving God without any actions to back up their words. Or, they cling to the role of a righteous believer while privately harboring unconfessed sin and doubt. That's why the apostle John encouraged believers to be real in their dealings with others. Instead of merely talking, we are to show love in tangible ways. This is the example set by Jesus when he walked the earth.

Those who claim to love God show their confidence in him by how real they are. Sometimes the most loving thing you can do is to admit your times of doubt and weakness. Admitting the reality of your situation can go a long way toward helping someone.

Dear children, let's not merely say that we love each other; let us show the truth by our actions. Our actions will show that we belong to the truth, so we will be confident when we stand before God.   1 JOHN 3:18-19

10 *The demand of the loveless and the self-imprisoned that they should be allowed to blackmail the universe: that till they consent to be happy (on their own terms) no one else shall taste joy.* CHAP. 13, P. 189

There are some conversations or stories that take time to process. The conversation between Sarah Smith and Frank, a man chained to a puppet called the Tragedian, is one that would take time and effort for the narrator to understand. Watching Frank the Dwarf shrink into the Tragedian role he prefers causes the narrator to question the fictional George MacDonald about the attitude of the Lady who claims to love Frank. How could she joyfully roam heaven while the Tragedian wanders alone and miserable?

But as MacDonald explains, the choice is always Frank's. He chooses to sink into a role, rather than release the chain and make the effort to be real. He chooses to blame the Lady for having embraced true love instead of the lifeless husk of love Frank claims to have.

Many a believer has been asked questions similar to those of the narrator. How can Christians be joyful when a place such as hell exists? How can there be joy in a world where there are hunger, pain, and other problems? Sometimes we find ourselves prisoners of the moods of those around us, especially if these people are significant to us. When they're unhappy, we're unhappy. But though happiness is based on certain conditions being met, joy can be found even in times of misery, because joy is not subject to the will of misery.

Joy starts with the choice to accept God's terms—salvation through Christ, obedience to his will. And because joy comes from God, it is out of our control. It exists even in the hardest times. David, a man known for his wholehearted devotion to God, boldly proclaimed to God why he was joyful—"because of you." Praise is the natural result of being filled with joy. Joy isn't a bury-your-head-in-the-sand denial. After all, some of the most joyful people have suffered much. Joy comes from the knowledge that a big God offers his protection and help in our biggest problems.

I will be filled with joy because of you. I will sing praises to your name, O Most High. PSALM 9:2

CHAPTER 16

"The Weight of Glory"

WORD FOR WORD, THIS SERMON may be the best thing Lewis ever wrote. Its language is stunningly poetic. Its subject, the golden theme in all of Lewis's work, is longing. One of the great appeals of Lewis's fiction is the power to awaken a longing for the thing that will connect us with something grand and eternal, something that transforms and enchants even the ordinary. In his spiritual autobiography, *Surprised by Joy*, Lewis described this longing as a piercing desire that is stronger than any earthly satisfaction. He concluded that since these desires have no fulfillment in our earthly experience, we must ultimately be made for something else. All desires, Lewis concluded elsewhere, are ultimately for heaven. The problem of the modern era is not the strength of our desires, but their object. In fact, in light of Scripture's promises, our desires are too weak. We settle for earthly ambitions and lusts when the glories of heaven are promised. We play in the slums when we could live in a mansion.

The mistake Lewis made for so long—the one made by many great poets, artists, and ourselves—is thinking that ultimate satisfaction can be found in the things that awaken desire. It is not *in* them; it is only mediated *by* them. Many earthly experiences awaken this greatest desire. We pursue them and find that fulfillment, like the horizon, recedes before us. Many things can awaken this deep desire, usually when we aren't looking for it—books, pictures, music, landscapes, memories of childhood—but none of them can satisfy it. If we look to *any* things to satisfy such a longing, we find them all "cheats," as Lewis said. We can see them as a foretaste of things to come, but they are not the thing itself.

What can we do with this understanding? We can lodge our hopes in our heavenly home and bear patiently with the burdens of our earthly journey as a necessary preparation. As the apostle Paul said, "The things we see now will soon be gone, but the things we cannot see will last forever" (2 Corinthians 4:18). We can also point others to the source of longing: to the Lord who made us for himself. Since we were all made for unimaginable eternal glory in Christ or else for unimaginable eternal horror apart from Christ, we must get busy about our neighbor's future glory, as well as our own. There are no "ordinary people." All have an eternal destiny. This fills every relationship, however casual, with significance. Viewed in this light, all of life is alive with adventure and meaning.

1 *If you asked twenty good men to-day what they thought the highest of the virtues, nineteen of them would reply, Unselfishness. But if you had asked almost any of the great Christians of old, he would have replied, Love.* P. 25

Duty. Responsibility. We probably heard these words in childhood as parents or guardians tried to instill within us the need to be good, responsible citizens. They tried to impart to us the need to be unselfish—to share with others, to play nicely with them, to pick up our toys, and to be helpful and kind. As we grew older, our consciences replaced our parents with reminders of what we need to do (pay taxes, return library books before they amass fines, obey traffic laws).

Therefore, we can readily relate to the quote with which Lewis began his sermon "The Weight of Glory." Unselfishness is a good deed we can check off easily on our to-do list. Our sense of duty is often tied up in the two words: *should* and *ought.* Thoughts of what we *should* or *ought* to do can be draining because both terms are negative, rather than positive. The virtue of unselfishness has a similar negative connotation, as Lewis explained. Not so with love.

Perhaps that's why the apostle Paul explained that love, rather than unselfishness, is the greatest virtue. Real love is the motivation behind any truly unselfish act. It keeps you going long after the sense of duty wears off. Consider the parent who sits up night after night with a sick child or the person who works two jobs to enable his or her spouse to return to school and fulfill a dream. Is it any wonder that Jesus told his disciples love is the most important commandment? (See Matthew 22:37-40.)

Love is what motivates a person to give his or her life for the gospel. A sense of duty could not have sustained the apostle Paul through beatings, shipwrecks, and other hazards of the missionary life.

Does love motivate you, or does duty?

Three things will last forever—faith, hope, and love—and the greatest of these is love. 1 CORINTHIANS 13:13

2   *We are . . . like an ignorant child who wants to go on making mud pies*
in a slum because he cannot imagine what is meant by the offer of a
holiday at the sea.   P. 26

What are your hopes or dreams? Sometimes we can't think beyond such dreams as winning the lottery or at least a free vacation, having peace on earth, or having our kids consistently behave. Though any of the above may seem like the answer to some of life's problems, each points to what C. S. Lewis described in "The Weight of Glory" as being too easily satisfied—in other words, settling too quickly.

Some bumper stickers and adages might lead one to believe that this life is all there is. So, grabbing all the gusto we can from buying the latest hyped beverage or going on the greatest vacation is highly advertised. But when the beverage is gone or the vacation ends, then what?

This easily satisfied mentality also affects our expectations of God and our lives as Christians. We have low expectations of the Christian life. Beyond the *shoulds* and *oughts*, we can't imagine the abundance Jesus describes in the Gospel of John. Or else we fear to imagine it, thinking that by doing so we would fall into the trap of the "prosperity doctrine." Lewis addressed this aspect a little further along in his sermon when he described unbelievers' accusing Christians of seeking rewards. But Jesus doesn't promise a dull and unsatisfying life. Instead, he invites us to go beyond complacency by seeking the cornucopia of spiritual riches God offers. This includes "knowledge of God" and a "confident hope" (Ephesians 1:17-18).

The life Jesus offers includes the living water that quenches thirst permanently (see John 4:13-14). But this promise of abundance doesn't mean we'll never suffer or doubt. It means, however, we have hope beyond the doubts and despair. Therefore, Jesus invites us out of the slums of our existence into the seaside of his love. Ready to take a swim?

The thief's purpose is to steal and kill and destroy. My purpose is to give them
a rich and satisfying life. JOHN 10:10

3 *These things—the beauty, the memory of our own past—are good images of what we really desire; but if they are mistaken for the thing itself, they turn into dumb idols, breaking the hearts of their worshippers.* P. 29

Ever find yourself moved to tears by a symphony, a poem, a heroic action, a particularly beautiful landscape, or the laughter of a baby? In the midst of the experience, we try to put what we long for into words. But the proper wording eludes us. Weeks after returning from a vacation spot, we can't quite recapture the magic of the experience even after looking at vacation videos or photographs. With a sense of nostalgia, we may try to capture in words or music the longing of our hearts, but the full experience remains elusive.

The desire for beauty, glory, and truth is programmed inside us; we're wired to seek these things, but only as signs that point to their Maker. Lewis returned to this longing again and again in many of his works. Yet this longing—this *sehnsucht*—cannot be completely captured in any experience we have on earth. Here, we can see only fleeting glimpses of beauty, which spur our longing for the real thing. So, what's the real thing? The Lord himself. He is the embodiment of beauty, glory, and truth. What we find beautiful here is only a poor reflection of the eternal beauty of God.

Yet how many of us fall into the trap of worshiping beauty or glory, easily satisfied with the shadow, rather than the Source? As Lewis warned, these "dumb idols"—these substitutes—wind up breaking our hearts.

David decided to seek beauty at its source by seeking the Lord. The sentiment below isn't just a "religious" notion that will fade with the passing of time or after the fulfillment of a dream. After all, David had everything: good looks, wives, children, wealth, military success, and a kingdom. But none of that could be compared with the Lord. That's why you don't find David asking for a better time on earth or more success. He knew that everything beautiful started with the Lord.

Where are you searching for satisfaction?

The one thing I ask of the LORD—the thing I seek most—is to live in the house of the LORD all the days of my life, delighting in the LORD's perfections and meditating in his Temple. PSALM 27:4

4 *Our sacred books give us some account of the object. It is, of course, a symbolical account. Heaven is, by definition, outside our experience, but all intelligible descriptions must be of things within our experience.*

PP. 30–31

If you've ever tried to describe an amazing place to someone who has never seen it, you know the frustration involved in making it seem as vivid to him or her as it is to you, especially if this place has a high value for you. Even if you had photographs to show, you'd find yourself tripping over adjectives such as *breathtaking, fascinating,* and *beautiful* in order to convey the full experience. Yet such descriptors can't quite convey such a sight.

Heaven is such a place, and one that can be described to us only through symbols. As the apostle John described his vision of the new Jerusalem (Revelation 21–22), he could describe what he saw based only on his own frame of reference. He thought in terms of precious metals and stones he knew, such as gold and jasper, to describe this shining, gated city. Undoubtedly he thought in terms of Jerusalem during his day—the city set on a hill.

This image of radiance has inspired writers through the centuries, including John Bunyan (*The Pilgrim's Progress*). Consider his shining Celestial City. Isn't it interesting that in neither of these descriptions of heaven do you find a war-torn city with dirty streets and hungry citizens? Instead, all is shining, fresh, and beautiful.

Reading a description of heaven like Bunyan's or the apostle John's causes us to long to be there. Such images sustain us when we feel soiled by the issues of earth. In heaven, where everything truly will be perfect, we will bask in the glory of God and share in the glory he promised us.

I saw a new heaven and a new earth, for the old heaven and the old earth had disappeared. And the sea was also gone. . . . So he took me in the Spirit to a great, high mountain, and he showed me the holy city, Jerusalem, descending out of heaven from God. It shone with the glory of God and sparkled like a precious stone—like jasper as clear as crystal. REVELATION 21:1, 10-11

5   *[W]e must never avert our eyes from those elements in [our religion] which seem puzzling or repellent; for it will be precisely the puzzling or the repellent which conceals what we do not yet know and need to know.*   P. 31

You're probably familiar with some doubts non-Christians have regarding the Christian life. Some nonbelievers are quite vocal with aspects of faith they hear about, especially if they don't see Christians living out their own beliefs. Many Christians also struggle with certain aspects of the faith life. Yet out of fear of being branded as a doubter or immature, we're reticent to admit to these struggles. We feel we should be past those doubts. But on this side of heaven, we will never be free of this battle.

In his discussion of heaven in "The Weight of Glory," Lewis explained that we can't expect to find answers in Christianity that will totally satisfy our questions and longings about heaven. If we could, then heaven would be a pretty shallow place. Instead, we will wrestle with them until we actually get there. Wrestling with spiritual truths is like exercising: it's good for the body and is something we will always need to do. This is all part of the training Paul described to his spiritual son, Timothy.

Lewis, the great apologist, was never one to shy away from a spiritual workout. He modeled for us the need to wrestle and keep wrestling even with those truths we find most "puzzling or repellent." Paul knew that in this life we will always be in a state of learning, growing, and longing. It's in the struggle that the pearl of wisdom or growth can develop.

"Physical training is good, but training for godliness is much better, promising benefits in this life and in the life to come." This is a trustworthy saying, and everyone should accept it. This is why we work hard and continue to struggle, for our hope is in the living God, who is the Savior of all people and particularly of all believers.   I TIMOTHY 4:8-10

6 *For glory means good report with God, acceptance by God, response, acknowledgment, and welcome into the heart of things. The door on which we have been knocking all our lives will open at last.* P. 36

Many of us probably wouldn't define *glory* as "acceptance." We think of honor, recognition, or fame. Lewis himself struggled with the notion of glory and its elusive definition. After studying the works of well-known Christians such as John Milton, Samuel Johnson, and Thomas Aquinas, Lewis came to the surprising conclusion described in the quote above.

We all long for acceptance, for inclusion. This is why we pledge to fraternities and sororities or join country clubs, social networks, and other organizations. Some exclusive clubs draw us because they include some people, but not all. Being accepted onto their membership rolls is a boost to the ego—at least for a time.

Although we become members of local churches in order to worship God there, that's also where we long to find inclusion and acceptance. We want church to be the place, as the old *Cheers* theme song says, "where everybody knows your name." Sometimes we don't find what we seek. Yet a warm welcome by God is part of the glory God promises believers. Being included in the family of God means we're ushered into "the heart of things," as Lewis described. According to the apostle John, we have the assurance that we're "children of God" when we believe in Christ. This is part of the rebirth described in John 1:12-13.

When you're born into a family, you're automatically included in the activities of that family. You have all the rights and privileges attached to being a family member. So it is with the family of God: you have the rights and the privileges of his fellowship, such as forgiveness, acceptance, and the Holy Spirit's presence.

Sadly, many people have a hard time imagining what it's like to be welcomed with joy into a family. Can you relate? Consider the fact that God also is "Father to the fatherless" (Psalm 68:5) and promises to "never fail you ... [and] never abandon you" (Hebrews 13:5).

To all who believed him and accepted him, he gave the right to become children of God. JOHN 1:12

7   *[O]ur longing to be reunited with something in the universe from which we now feel cut off . . . is no mere neurotic fancy, but the truest index of our real situation.*   P. 36

Holidays and summertime are usually the times for reunions—for getting the whole family together. We see friends or family members we haven't seen in years. Sometimes strained relationships can even be patched up as we gather at a park over grilled brats and watermelon.

When we're apart or estranged from others who are dear to us, we feel like the person who has lost a limb. This is what Lewis described here. We long for the wholeness a happy reunion entails. The longing he described, however, is for union with God. It's part of the desire for inclusion that defines glory. And this longing is a constant ache that won't heal on this side of heaven.

The pain of being excluded or rejected is one with which we're well acquainted. It has the power to plunge us to the depths of despair. But the ache of longing actually has the opposite effect because it signals our inclusion.

Writing years after Jesus ascended to heaven, the apostle Peter encouraged believers who had never seen Jesus. Although Peter had seen Jesus, he understood his readers' longing for the Lord he also missed. Since the Holy Spirit connected everyone in the body of Christ, the separation from Jesus was like that from a lost limb. But as Peter suggested, his readers could rejoice, knowing that someday they would be with Christ forever. This was a very encouraging message for a group of believers experiencing persecution and other unjust treatment.

Perhaps due to a sense of estrangement you're in need of the encouragement Peter and Lewis offered. If the estrangement is due to a past hurt you or someone else caused, consider the forgiveness God offers. Forgiveness links us to God in a tangible way and reminds us of what we have in him—a new beginning as well as the grace to forgive others.

You love him even though you have never seen him. Though you do not see him now, you trust him; and you rejoice with a glorious, inexpressible joy.

I PETER 1:8

8

The whole man is to drink joy from the fountain of joy.

P. 38

There's something about a fountain that brings joy to the heart. When you're thirsty, the humblest drinking fountain is like an oasis in a desert. And then there are the many beautiful fountains around the world built for visual refreshment—the Trevi Fountain in Rome, the fountains of Peterhof in St. Petersburg, and the two fountains at the Place de la Concorde are just a few outstanding examples. Even watching the creative ways water can be engineered through pipes and sculpture to overflow is a constant refreshment. Lewis talked about a symbolic fountain—one from which the thirsty can drink in all the joy they want.

Joy is a by-product of remaining in the love of Christ, as Jesus explained to his disciples. With his love constantly flowing through us, we will erupt in joy like any good fountain. Yet because of our sin nature, we sometimes can't imagine being such a fountain of joy. Other, less positive states, such as being filled with gloom or despair, come more easily to mind, and the invitation to become a fountain of joy awaits our acceptance.

Consider the fact that Jesus spoke to beleaguered disciples used to working hard for a living. They were part of a people conquered and oppressed by the Romans. Imagine how radical this promise might have seemed, especially as it was spoken in a hot, dry climate—Jesus's imagery must have really gripped his disciples. When you're thirsty, you can't wait to quench your thirst, to drink as much as you can hold. During the "dry" times of our lives, when we feel unable to spout the promises of God with any conviction, we can't imagine having our thirst quenched, let alone being filled to the point of overflowing. But that's exactly what Jesus promises here. He doesn't say your joy *might* overflow. He categorically states that it will. But first we must obey his commandments and remain in his love.

Feeling dry spiritually? Go to the fountain of joy and drink.

When you obey my commandments, you remain in my love, just as I obey my Father's commandments and remain in his love. I have told you these things so that you will be filled with my joy. Yes, your joy will overflow! JOHN 15:10-11

9 *[T]he dullest and most uninteresting person you talk to may one day be a creature which, if you saw it now, you would be strongly tempted to worship.* P. 39

If you're a fan of superhero graphic novels or movies, perhaps you feel a certain rush when the superhero sheds the everyday identity and emerges as the powerful being he or she is. Clark Kent whips off his glasses and outer clothes and swoops into the sky with cape flying. Diana Prince, aka Wonder Woman, clips on her bracelets and reveals her superhuman strength—the gift of her citizenship among the Amazons of Paradise Island. Even Batman, who has no superpowers, is considered a superhero because of his intelligence, skill, and cool gadgets.

Compared to them, Jimmy Olsen and Alfred the butler—the human sidekicks—seem pretty ordinary, don't they? We can relate to them more readily than we relate to Superman or Batman. Yet as Lewis explained in the quote above, even the "dullest and most uninteresting person" has a weight of glory that heaven will someday reveal in its splendor. Even Superman would be envious.

If you're a believer, you have a "super" identity, one that should not be kept secret. As citizens of heaven (see Philippians 3:20), we will someday have glorified bodies like that of the risen Christ. The apostle Paul wrote of the transformation believers will undergo "in the blink of an eye" (1 Corinthians 15:52). This is what Lewis hinted at. But there are some days when such a promise is hard to believe. Our weaknesses and insecurities make us feel as if we're just getting by. Instead, "overwhelming victory is ours" (Romans 8:37) in our trials today and through our hope of heaven. Believe it!

It will happen in a moment, in the blink of an eye, when the last trumpet is blown. For when the trumpet sounds, those who have died will be raised to live forever. And we who are living will also be transformed. I CORINTHIANS 15:52

10

[O]ur merriment must be of that kind (and it is, in fact, the merriest kind) which exists between people who have, from the outset, taken each other seriously—no flippancy, no superiority, no presumption. P. 39

Think about the last time you shared a laugh with someone—a sound of merriment not at anyone's expense, but out of pure joy and born out of a deep connection to the person. It's the kind of laugh babies and other young children utter all the time. It is the kind of soul-deep laughter with a seed of joy that makes you feel alive.

Isn't it interesting that many of the sound bites in the media most frequently mentioned are about something foolish a celebrity said or did? A feeling of superiority permeates some humor. During late-night talk shows we laugh at the sarcastic, caustic remarks, or we pass along videos we find on the Internet that showcase the talked-of behavior.

In a reminder of the glory we have through God, Lewis turned to the subject of humor. Since no one is just ordinary, we have no right to view ourselves as superior to anyone else. Instead, we are to give one another the gift of taking others seriously—ironically, by the way we use humor with one another. Consider the people you admire or love. The thought of ridiculing or telling a disparaging joke at their expense is repugnant, isn't it?

The apostle Paul was of a similar mind in his caution to believers concerning humor. We may not think that a joke we tell fits the category of "coarse." But if it involves treating someone with contempt, it falls in that category.

As citizens of heaven, we're not to treat one another—any other—with contempt. The more thankful we are, the less time we have to be contemptuous toward others. Being thankful means being filled with joy. When you're full, you can't help overflowing—and joy is the source of true merriment.

Obscene stories, foolish talk, and coarse jokes—these are not for you. Instead, let there be thankfulness to God. EPHESIANS 5:4

CHAPTER 17

The Horse and His Boy

EACH BOOK IN THE CHRONICLES OF NARNIA has many themes and fruitful approaches to it. Key themes in *The Horse and His Boy* are pride and humility and the often-unseen hand of a sovereign God guiding the events (even the traumas) of our lives for our good and his glory. All the key characters in this story undergo spiritual transformation. A proud, skeptical, talking horse becomes a content citizen and believer in Aslan; an ordinary boy is transformed into a king.

The story opens with Bree, a talking horse from Narnia, and Shasta, a foundling taken from Archenland who overhears that he is about to be sold by his fisherman master. Both decide to escape to the northern lands of their birth. They are joined by Aravis, a proud aristocratic girl, and her horse, Hwin, a very humble soul, who are on their way to warn Narnia and Archenland of an impending invasion from Calormen. On their way, the troop helps Queen Susan escape from an impending forced marriage. They are pursued by Susan's would-be husband, Rabadash, the cruel prince of Calormen and enemy of Narnia and Archenland.

A lion attack speeds the protagonists on, tests their character, and judges their sins. The lion, they later learn, is Aslan. The horse, Bree, decides he doesn't want to go to Narnia because as a talking horse he is special now, but in Narnia he will be only one of many. Furthermore, Bree gets lost in the lion attack and is ashamed. In the same attack, Aravis's back is clawed by Aslan, one scar for every stripe she caused to be lashed on a servant's back. All this is as necessary for these two as many unpleasant life experiences are for us because of what they must learn. Aravis learns justice and mercy. Both learn humility—simply having the proper view of oneself in relation to God and others.

Shasta is Bree's boy, as alluded to in the humorous title. His character is doubled in the humble horse, Hwin, just as Bree and Aravis are doubles. Hwin, like Queen Lucy and Shasta but unlike Bree, is quick to believe in Aslan. What the humble horse and boy must learn is courage. In Archenland, Shasta discovers that he is the slightly older lost twin son of King Lune and that his real name is Cor. He doesn't want to be king. Cor learns, along with everyone else, that we do not get to choose our roles— only how well or ill we will play them. When he grows up, Cor matures into a great and courageous leader.

As for Rabadash, who is bitter and scornful to the end, Aslan turns him into a ridiculous donkey and sends him back to Calormen. There he is turned again into a human but warned that if he ever ventures more than ten miles from the temple of the false god Tash, which he foolishly calls upon, he will be turned back into a donkey forever. By mercy or justice, all are transformed. Mercy is offered to all, though most are slow to see it and must be prodded by unpleasantness for their own good. Some reject mercy altogether, as does Rabadash the Ridiculous, and suffer the judgment of justice.

1

[I]f one is nervous there's nothing like having your face toward the danger and having something warm and solid at your back.

CHAP. 6, P. 92

As movies like *Monsters, Inc.* show, a warm blanket can be a formidable weapon in the fight against monsters! When you were a kid, perhaps you believed that. As you grew older, however, you realized that a blanket can't solve every problem in your path. Some dark nights of the soul require real comfort, as Shasta the orphan-slave learned in *The Horse and His Boy.*

After escaping from Calormen on the back of Bree, a talking horse from Narnia, Shasta faces a dark night—literally—as he waits at the Tombs for Bree and their fellow travelers: Aravis the Tarkheena and Hwin, another talking horse from Narnia. There are no blankets to hide under. So, imagine Shasta's initial terror and subsequent relief as a large cat comes and lies beside him. Although Shasta revels in the warmth of the cat at his back, little does he know that the large cat is Aslan the Lion.

David, the psalm writer and Israel's greatest king, wrote of a fearful time in his best-known psalm. As a shepherd, he knew by experience the need for a rod and staff in leading sheep. The rod helped a shepherd protect his flock from predators such as wolves. And the staff was used to guide the sheep or pull them to safety if they fell into trouble.

"The darkest valley" bears the face of any fearful experience we may have to deal with—a dreaded illness, the death of a loved one, a doubt that assails our faith. When you're cold or lonely, you need warmth of some kind—whether a blanket, a word or smile, or just the presence of a companion. But when you're afraid, you need to know that someone bigger and more powerful is with you. You need the warmth of the Shepherd's presence.

Even when I walk through the darkest valley, I will not be afraid, for you are close beside me. Your rod and your staff protect and comfort me. PSALM 23:4

2   *It hurt horribly and nearly winded him; but before he knew how it hurt him he was staggering back to help Aravis.*   CHAP. 10, P. 153

What's the biggest risk you've ever taken? Would you be willing to help someone even at the risk of being hurt yourself? Though we might risk life and limb if someone we love is involved, we might otherwise not act if there's any chance we'd be physically hurt or greatly inconvenienced. Yet occasionally we do hear stories of people who risked their lives to save total strangers from icy lakes or ferocious animals.

In the race to keep ahead of Prince Rabadash's invading Calormene forces, Shasta, Bree, Aravis, and Hwin find their strength flagging. Yet, seeing a lion bound after Aravis and Hwin, Shasta takes a daring leap off Bree's back to run to their rescue, though Bree the horse had refused to stop. Shasta doesn't really know either of them very well at this point. Yet he thinks more about their well-being than about the danger, his competence to help, or his own welfare.

The Old Testament prophet Isaiah talked of the Savior who would someday rescue others at great risk to himself. As with Shasta, it would "hurt horribly." In fact, Scripture says, he would be "crushed for our sins" and "whipped so we could be healed." In other words, he would assume the punishment—every cruel bit of it—that "our rebellion" deserved (Isaiah 53:5).

We have only to read the New Testament to know that Jesus was the Savior who staggered to the Cross after a grueling night of trials and brutality so that we wouldn't have to go. His sacrifice was one that would never have to be repeated. Yet it also inspires us to think beyond ourselves or our comfort zones in order to assist someone in need. It makes us willing to risk life and limb in order to honor the life he gave for us.

He was pierced for our rebellion, crushed for our sins. He was beaten so we could be whole. He was whipped so we could be healed.   ISAIAH 53:5

3

Shasta was marvelous. I'm just as bad as you, Bree. I've been snubbing him and looking down on him ever since you met us and now he turns out to be the best of us all. CHAP. 10, P. 161

Ever realize you were totally wrong about someone? Then perhaps an action or a word helped steer you to a deeper understanding of the person or convicted you about your attitude. The risk Shasta takes in trying to save Aravis and Hwin from the lion becomes a point of conviction for Bree and Aravis. Bree's status as a free horse of Narnia (an experienced war-horse, to boot) and Aravis's status as the daughter of the lord of the province of Calavar caused them to think themselves a cut above Shasta—a poor nobody from Calormen. But even before knowing his true identity, something they learn by the end of the story, they begin to think better of Shasta.

To stem the tide of judgmental thinking, the apostle Paul included the warning below in his letter to believers in Rome. One of the causes of disunity in a body is an attitude of superiority. It sets up a barrier between one person or group and another. This attitude must be weeded out in order for effective Kingdom work to be done.

Sometimes our upbringing or privileges cause us to believe that we're at least a little better than some others. But if we evaluate ourselves with God's measuring stick, we come up on the short end.

None of us can do anything apart from the grace of God. Even Paul with his vast accomplishments, Roman citizenship, and prestigious education knew that he owed everything to the one who met him on the Damascus Road (see Acts 9). An honest evaluation doesn't mean going the route of inferiority—an attitude God did not intend. Knowing that "I can do everything through Christ" (Philippians 4:13) is an honest evaluation.

Don't think you are better than you really are. Be honest in your evaluation of yourselves, measuring yourselves by the faith God has given us. ROMANS 12:3

4   *"I do think," said Shasta, "that I must be the most unfortunate boy that ever lived in the whole world. Everything goes right for everyone except me."* CHAP. 11, P. 172

Even the strong and the brave have moments of weakness. Consider the prophet Elijah, who ran from the threats of the murderous Queen Jezebel (see 1 Kings 19). Shasta, the orphan who escaped from Calormen, is in good company. After successfully warning King Lune of the impending army of Rabadash, Shasta finds himself on a wayward horse that refuses to follow his commands. All the men traveling with him have left him behind in the mad dash back to King Lune's castle. Subsequently he lands on another wayward horse—that of self-pity. And, like the physical horse he rides, Shasta believes he is powerless to stop it.

Ever have a day like that, when you think the world is against you? The toast burns, the kids squabble endlessly, your boss chews you out, and you get stopped for a speeding ticket. And then you invite yourself to a pity party for one.

The writer of Psalm 42 was no stranger to "woe is me" thinking. But he knew the dead end to which such thinking leads. That's why he prescribed his own medicine—"hope in God"—more than once in this psalm.

When you're downcast, the thought of hoping in God might seem impossible, especially if a feeling of being forgotten by God accompanies the thought. But there are some troubles of the soul that cause us to delve deeper into the well that is God himself. Only he has the power to take the reins of a wayward self-pity horse—as Aslan did for Shasta—and turn it around. As he provides a fresh vision for our situation, self-pity becomes praise and a reminder that God has a purpose for you and your situation.

Why am I discouraged? Why is my heart so sad? I will put my hope in God! I will praise him again—my Savior and my God! PSALM 42:5-6

5   *I was the lion who gave the Horses the new strength of fear for the last mile so that you should reach King Lune in time.*   CHAP. 11, P. 176

Would you ever believe that fear could be an advantage? Sometimes fear is a motivator that pushes us to the edge of ourselves toward help. As the great Lion Aslan explains to Shasta, an exhausted Bree and Hwin needed a little fear for the last lap of their journey. In our finite minds, we might be tempted to believe Aslan cruel for the terror inflicted on Bree and Hwin. Yet that terror spurred them to run faster than they would have thought possible. Subsequently, King Lune of Archenland is warned about the coming invaders and the kingdom saved.

Consider the times when fear pushed you beyond the limits you set for yourself. Perhaps the fear of losing a relationship caused you to work harder at the relationship, or the fear of getting a failing grade caused you to redouble your studying efforts.

The psalmist wrote of another kind of fear that is a motivator and strengthener: "fear of the LORD" (Psalm 111:10). This isn't the bone-chilling fear Bree and Hwin felt; it is, instead, reverence for God.

Mighty acts of God (calming storms, raising the dead, punishing wrong-doing) often inspire great fear. But even without those acts, God's character deserves respect. Reverence causes us to fear disappointing God or damaging our integrity as we live in the goldfish bowl that is life. Reverence is the fountain from which wisdom flows, and it pushes us to exert all efforts to please God and to help others.

Some might see reverence for God as old-fashioned in an age when many worship the irreverent attitudes and actions of celebrities. But when we have "fear of the LORD," we are always exactly where we should be.

Fear of the LORD is the foundation of true wisdom. All who obey his commandments will grow in wisdom. PSALM 111:10

6   *"Child," said the Voice, "I am telling you your story, not hers."*
CHAP. 11, P. 176

Do you ever compare your life with someone else's? that neighbor who always manages to keep his lawn trimmed, gets a new car every three years, and whose teens don't seem rebellious? that mom in your playgroup whose house always looks perfect and who seems to have the organizational skills of the White House chief of staff? that straight-A, dean's-list student whose trust fund pays for everything while you struggle with loans and a dismal work-study job? What do they know about life compared to you? Sometimes we're tempted to question God, wondering why our lives seem harder than another's. We want to know why the other story seems so much better than ours.

Having seen the great lion rake his claws along Aravis's back, Shasta can't help questioning the unseen being (Aslan) about Aravis's wounding. How could Aslan do such a thing? What is the story behind that? But Aslan refuses to explain the details of someone else's story.

Peter, one of Jesus' disciples, also expressed curiosity about the story of another. While talking with Jesus, Peter wanted to know what would happen to John. But Jesus refused to be drawn out about John. His business was with Peter at the moment. Peter, like Shasta, would have to be content with an unsatisfied curiosity.

Sometimes our wanting to know what will happen to another stems from fear that God somehow favors that person more. But as the experiences of Shasta and Peter show, not only is God amazingly discreet—our secrets and sorrows are safe with him—but he is also personal. He knows our individual stories and is seeing each one through.

Peter turned around and saw behind them the disciple Jesus loved—the one who had leaned over to Jesus during supper and asked, "Lord, who will betray you?" Peter asked Jesus, "What about him, Lord?" Jesus replied, "If I want him to remain alive until I return, what is that to you? As for you, follow me."
JOHN 21:20-22

7

That is why the Lion kept on my left. He was between me and the edge all the time. CHAP. 13, P. 196

Traveling along mountain roads can seem hazardous. Even with guard-rails that help motorists avoid driving off cliffs, it can be dangerous to take to the hills, especially at certain times of the year or at night when icy or poorly maintained roads are particularly hazardous. But sometimes you have no choice, especially if your destination lies at the other end of a mountain pass.

When Shasta sees in broad daylight the treacherous cliff path he had innocently taken one night during his trip to Anvard, he realizes the narrowness of his escape from death. His escape had been due entirely to Aslan's walking on the cliff side to prevent him from falling. Aslan hadn't announced his intent to preserve Shasta's life. He simply did it out of love.

Before he was king of Israel, David managed more split-second escapes than the fictional James Bond or Jason Bourne could ever dream of, thanks to the help of the Lord. Writing Psalm 18 helped David reflect on God's continual deliverance from the hand of a jealous Saul. God's intervention also kept him from acting rashly when he was tempted to take the life of Saul, not once but twice (see 1 Samuel 24; 26). Ironically, neither time did Saul realize his narrow escape from death until David told him.

Sometimes we have little idea of just how narrowly we escaped pain or death. But sometimes God allows us glimpses of what we avoided. We can see the evidence of wrecked lives all around us. These sad glimpses remind us of how far we've come or where we would be without the Lord's intervention. May we sing like David, "You have given me your shield of victory."

You have given me your shield of victory. Your right hand supports me; your help has made me great. You have made a wide path for my feet to keep them from slipping. PSALM 18:35-36

8   *"Please," she said, "you're so beautiful. You may eat me if you like. I'd sooner be eaten by you than fed by anyone else."* CHAP. 14, P. 215

What's the most beautiful thing you've seen recently? Your child's gap-toothed smile? The ocean at sunset? Beauty always attracts, doesn't it? A beautiful person, sunset, or song strikes us at the heart. While some standards of beauty change with the era, others are eternal. What you love is always beautiful, regardless of what society might say.

Having been chased by a lion, Hwin, the talking Narnian horse, decides to surrender when the lion suddenly appears again. Imagine her courage as she approaches him. Although he had frightened her beyond measure, she is struck to the core by his beauty and majesty. The Lion—Aslan—rewards her humility with affection and knowledge of himself. He shows his delight in her coming to him.

Although King David wrote about the beauty of the Lord (see Psalm 27:4, NIV), the prophet Isaiah painted a different picture of the Messiah to come. He would not have the flashy, look-at-me countenance of a movie star, nor would he seem at all royal. Instead, his transparency would appeal to the eyes of faith. Those who sought him would see him for the King he truly is.

Jesus is that Messiah. He willingly set aside his majesty and glory to take on the troubles of our world. But approaching him always requires an act of faith and humility. After all, "the LORD . . . keeps his distance from the proud" (Psalm 138:6). But out of love for people, he "humbles the proud" (Isaiah 26:5).

Beauty attracts us. But humility attracts God. It is more than beautiful to him.

My servant grew up in the LORD's presence like a tender green shoot, like a root in dry ground. There was nothing beautiful or majestic about his appearance, nothing to attract us to him. ISAIAH 53:2

9   *The scratches on your back, tear for tear, throb for throb, blood for blood, were equal to the stripes laid on the back of your stepmother's slave. . . . You needed to know what it felt like.*   CHAP. 14, P. 216

Have you ever heard someone make a cutting remark to someone else and then react in surprise when the recipient of the remark responds in hurt or anger? Not being in that person's shoes, the offender can't imagine how the other feels. Lacking this insight, sometimes we hurt others, knowingly or unknowingly.

Remember how Shasta questioned Aslan about the attack on Aravis (meditation six of this chapter)? Now the truth of that incident would be made known. Escaping from her land, Aravis had drugged her slave to avoid detection. Sadly, the slave was later beaten, as Aravis had surmised when telling the story to Shasta, Bree, and Hwin earlier in the story. But during an encounter with a mysterious lion, Aravis found herself scratched by its claws. Now she learns this Lion was Aslan, who had a lesson to impart: you reap what you sow. Aravis needed to know the cost of her cavalier attitude toward the slave.

The apostle Paul was pretty blunt as he wrote to the Christians in Galatia. A person's behavior paves the way for like behavior to happen in his or her life. Though we may not experience exactly what some-one else experiences, sometimes God allows just that in order to temper characteristics in us that keep us anchored to the same harmful attitudes. Ever the skilled gardener, the Lord continually prunes away our ungainly attitudes to make us useful, wise, and loving. Being thrust into someone else's shoes makes us more aware of the feelings of others and less likely to be cavalier.

What have you reaped recently? How has God made you aware of the feelings of another?

Don't be misled—you cannot mock the justice of God. You will always harvest what you plant. Those who live only to satisfy their own sinful nature will harvest decay and death from that sinful nature. But those who live to please the Spirit will harvest everlasting life from the Spirit.   GALATIANS 6:7-8

10

[E]ven a traitor may mend. I have known one that did.

CHAP. 15, P. 230

Judas. Brutus. Benedict Arnold. Julius and Ethel Rosenberg. You have only to glance at this list to know that these individuals have lived long in infamy because of their betrayal of others. In fact, some of those names are synonymous with the word *traitor*.

Edmund Pevensie would have added his own name to the list. Having betrayed his family in *The Lion, the Witch and the Wardrobe*, he later repents and becomes a friend of Aslan. Having experienced Aslan's grace in allowing him to become king of Narnia along with his brother, Peter, King Edmund realizes that even a traitor like Rabadash—the hot-tempered, warring prince of the Calormenes—could change.

Peter the apostle would also add his name to the list, having experienced the pain of denying Christ three times. He couldn't help squirming later as Jesus asked him three times if he loved him. But what better way to reinstate Peter than by having him declare three times that he loved Jesus—the same number as his denials?

Each of us could also add our name to such a list. Even though we may not think we're as bad as the people in the first paragraph, as people born in sin we're just as culpable. That's why God's offered love is known as grace. It wouldn't be grace if we deserved it. As we receive his grace, we become, in a way, like rechargeable batteries: as he fills us, we're charged to become useful again. The key is to receive his grace, rather than giving up or wallowing in self-pity or pride. This is a lesson that Judas and Rabadash failed to learn. But Edmund and the apostle Peter passed with flying colors. How about you?

A third time he asked him, "Simon son of John, do you love me?" Peter was hurt that Jesus asked the question a third time. He said, "Lord, you know everything. You know that I love you." Jesus said, "Then feed my sheep." JOHN 21:17

CHAPTER 18

A Grief Observed

LEWIS WAS A BACHELOR for most of his adult life. After marrying American Helen Joy Davidman Gresham, he discovered a happiness and richness in life he had not anticipated.

When the British government declined permission for Joy's continued stay in England, Lewis married her, in name only, at the Oxford Registry Office in 1956. Then terminal cancer took Joy to the hospital the following year, and Lewis and Joy had what was in his mind a true marriage, in the hospital in 1957, with Anglican minister Peter Bide officiating, so he could take Joy home to care for her. Bide, who had a healing gift, prayed for Joy's recovery, which miraculously came, and the leg bone that had been eaten through by cancer healed. Joy lived until 1960, when the cancer returned to take her. When she died, Lewis knew from her life and her own last words that she had peace with God. His pain was not tinged with doubts about what had happened to Joy. This book is about personal sense of loss, the fundamental change in life as Lewis had come to live it.

Because the book is so intensely personal, Lewis originally published it under the pseudonym N. W. Clerk. He referred to Joy only as "H.," after her little-known first name. The four numbered parts of this short book correspond to the four exercise books he used as diaries. Its frequent displays of raw emotion serve as the starting point for the more theological and rational reflections—the combined effect being a rather detailed picture of his internal conflict, understanding, growth, and final resolution of grief. As Lewis recorded his sorrow, the process unfolds around the well-known sequence of grief: shock, denial, anger, depression, and acceptance. At his lowest point, Lewis said, he never doubted God's existence but did wonder if God were not a cosmic sadist.

Part of the book's value is in the keen observation and clarifying analogies quite typical of Lewis. For example, he compared pain to fear, not only because of the way both alarm us but because both are always surprising us: a hundred ordinary life experiences and common expressions unexpectedly remind the bereaved Lewis of how Joy would have reacted or what she might have said. Throughout the book, his initially unchecked emotion was examined and even refined by more rational and theological perspectives. The pain subsided, though it never completely left, and a better understanding of life and death and a deeper faith remained.

1 *[G]o to Him when your need is desperate . . . and what do you find? A door slammed in your face, and a sound of bolting and double bolting on the inside.* CHAP. 1, P. 6

Philip Yancey took a whole book to answer the question, Where is God when it hurts? In the aftermath of the death of his wife, Joy, C. S. Lewis did the same. But as he struggled through the agony of grief, Lewis couldn't help thinking that God was to be found only behind a locked door—one that left Lewis on the outside in the cold. This was a far different door from the ones the devils of *Paradise Lost* locked and bolted, having refused to repent. This was a door God himself seemed to bar.

Job expressed a similar agony before his friends and God. After hearing about the deaths of all his children and the destruction of his crops and livestock, Job chose to talk out his grief instead of cursing God, as his wife suggested (see Job 2:9). His words were real and raw. But he found what Lewis, King David, and many others in grief also discovered—that some responses of God are a mystery.

Perhaps you can relate. The locked door seems contrary to God's promise in the book of Jeremiah that God will be found in our seeking (see Jeremiah 29:13-14), or to any other promises that God is near (see Psalm 34:18). When God remains silent, some are deterred from seeking him further.

But though in this life we may never understand why certain things happen or why God responds the way that he does, Job's and Lewis's experiences remind us to keep the lines of communication open between us and God. In this relationship, even words spoken in anger or ignorance are better than no words spoken at all. God would prefer his children to bang on the door rather than walk away from it.

I cry to you, O God, but you don't answer. I stand before you, but you don't even look. JOB 30:20

2   *Already, less than a month after her death, I can feel the slow, insidious beginning of a process that will make the H. I think of into a more and more imaginary woman.*   CHAP. 2, P. 18

"I'm starting to forget." Many who have spent years in grief know the panic of believing they've begun to forget tiny details of their loved ones' lives. *Were his eyes really as brown as I remember? Do I really remember her laugh? Was he wearing a blue sweater when we traveled that day?* Losing these precious details means losing him or her all over again.

Having to rely only on his memories of Joy after her death from bone cancer, Lewis feared the second loss of the "actual" Joy—the fading of the vibrancy of her image, like a photograph fading over time. If he had to sketch a portrait of her—including her laughter, her eyes, her sensibilities—would he get the details exactly right? If he continued to forget key details, would she become a woman of his imagination over time?

As painful a part of the grieving process as this is, the principle can also serve as a reminder of another image. Sometimes our image of God can seem just as imaginary. What's even more frightening is that we're often not even aware of this distorted image. Times of disappointment or disillusionment can rob our image of God of its vibrancy, especially if we're out of fellowship with God. Seeing him as anything other than he really is seems like viewing a badly out-of-focus photograph.

Even though we don't always see him clearly, God's image never changes. As the writer of Hebrews declared, God remains the same no matter how much time elapses. We change, but God never does. When people and circumstances change, knowing that God never does can be truly comforting.

Jesus Christ is the same yesterday, today, and forever.   HEBREWS 13:8

3   *The grave and the image are equally links with the irrecoverable and symbols for the unimaginable. But the image has the added disadvantage that it will do whatever you want.*   CHAP. 2, P. 21

Graveyards are filled with minimonuments of people and relationships. You see wreaths, carefully tended plots, mausoleums, tombstones, and other items dedicated to the memory of loved ones and given by those left behind.

Yearly visits to the cemetery on birthdays, anniversaries, or Memorial Day can be comforting for many mourners. These visits make them feel connected to the lost loved one. But of course the grave isn't the actual person. As Lewis explains, it can only be a symbol. Yet being able to tend the grass over a grave or place flowers there provides the illusion of control that death strips from life.

Lewis recalled his horror from long ago as he once heard a man cheerfully refer to the plot he was about to visit as being his mother: How could he think of that plot as his mother? Yet after Joy's death, Lewis could understand the need to cling to at least some aspect of the lost loved one, if not to go that far.

Death seems unconquerable, since sooner or later everyone will succumb to it. It's one of the guarantees of life—you know, like taxes. Those who have no hope might spend their time building up monuments to the dead, believing that the grave is truly the end of that person. Like the people described in Ecclesiastes 9:3, they believe that hope ends at the grave. But a grave doesn't represent the final state of a person, thanks to the sacrifice of Jesus Christ! Although we will suffer the sting of death, death will eventually give way to the eternal life offered by God. Like the apostle Paul, we can declare, "O death, where is your victory?" The victory lies with Jesus. Is that what you believe?

"Death is swallowed up in victory. O death, where is your victory? O death, where is your sting?" . . . But thank God! He gives us victory over sin and death through our Lord Jesus Christ.   I CORINTHIANS 15:54-55, 57

4 *Only a real risk tests the reality of a belief.*

CHAP. 2, P. 23

"Put your money where your mouth is." We've all heard that phrase. In a sense, it invites us to show what we believe, rather than simply talking about it. But sometimes, when our lives are shaken by grief or pain, we find ourselves questioning what we believe.

In *A Grief Observed*, the window to his grieving process, Lewis found himself in this position as he contemplated the final destination of his deceased wife. Did she still exist with God somewhere? If so, what did existing with God really mean? Now that she was dead, the challenge for Lewis was to sort through what he actually believed about life after death and even his habit of praying for the dead. He discovered that death is the ultimate risk of belief.

Some people consult psychics or other occult sources in a desperate attempt to reconnect with loved ones or to prove that life exists after death. They're willing to build a foundation on whatever alleged proof they're offered concerning the loved ones' existence. Of course, it's not much of a foundation.

You can't stand on ground you're not sure exists. The apostle Paul chose to stand not on hearsay, but on the promises in God's Word. While some people in his day refused to believe in a bodily resurrection, Paul argued that a physical resurrection would take place after death. His proof was the life of Christ (see 1 Corinthians 15:12-28). Having experienced the risen Christ on the Damascus Road (see Acts 9), Paul fully believed that Jesus rose from the dead. And if Jesus rose from the dead, we will too.

What I am saying, dear brothers and sisters, is that our physical bodies cannot inherit the Kingdom of God. These dying bodies cannot inherit what will last forever. But let me reveal to you a wonderful secret. We will not all die, but we will all be transformed! 1 CORINTHIANS 15:50-51

Talk to me about the truth of religion and I'll listen gladly. . . . But don't come talking to me about the consolations of religion or I shall suspect that you don't understand.   CHAP. 2, P. 25

In a grieving situation, well-meaning people who aren't sure what to say sometimes offer "consolations" that grate, rather than heal. A widow who is asked, "Aren't you glad your husband's with the Lord?" isn't sure what to think. More than likely, she would rather have him by her side just then instead of "away from these earthly bodies" (2 Corinthians 5:8). The exhortation "Stand on the promises of God" seems empty when you're grieving.

In his grief over Joy's death, Lewis wrestled with the attempts at consolation offered by others—words that did not take away the sting of her absence or take into account his feelings on the matter. Even the notion of being reunited with Joy in heaven offered little comfort. Sadly, pat answers given by those who "don't understand" have that effect. These sentiments become merely "religious" and rote, rather than consoling.

James, the brother of Jesus, had an apt definition of religion, one that involves action rather than parroted statements. Caring for widows and orphans is the kind of religion that *really* consoles. Practical action takes into account the needs of the person and meets that person where he or she is.

The apostle Paul put this sentiment in another way: "Weep with those who weep" (Romans 12:15). Instead of talking, cry with that person—*be* with that person in his or her distress. After all, a time of grief is a time to cry.

Pure and genuine religion in the sight of God the Father means caring for orphans and widows in their distress and refusing to let the world corrupt you.
JAMES 1:27

6 *If my house has collapsed at one blow, that is because it was a house of cards. The faith which "took these things into account" was not faith but imagination.* CHAP. 3, P. 37

If you own a home, you know the importance of checking the foundation periodically. In this way, you stem the tide of problems such as termites, widening cracks, and water leakage, which could lead to serious damage to your home. If you can't do the work of repair or preventive maintenance yourself, you call in an expert. Some things are too important to put off.

Some situations in life affect another kind of foundation: the foundation of your faith. Grief is like an earthquake that rocks the foundation of the ones who mourn. As he continued to wrestle in the aftermath of Joy's death, Lewis discovered holes in his spiritual foundation—holes that needed patching before further damage could occur. He could only patch them by wrestling with hard faith questions.

Lewis was not content to have the type of faith that was merely a "house of cards"—a flimsy type of faith that one breath could knock down. Instead, strong faith required wrestling through those times that cause the severest blows to faith.

No stranger to spiritual doubt, the apostle Peter also advocated wrestling with these issues (see 1 Peter 5:9). But with the wrestling, he provided a promise that God would fulfill—the promise of support, restoration, and a firm foundation.

Like good home owners care for the foundation of their homes, we must care for the foundation of our faith. But remember that the Spirit in residence within you will shore up any cracks in the foundation caused by suffering and pain. This might require assessing the weak spots—doubts— in order to properly patch the foundation.

If you are having work done to the foundation, communication with the subcontractor is a must. So is communication with God during your own restoration process.

In his kindness God called you to share in his eternal glory by means of Christ Jesus. So after you have suffered a little while, he will restore, support, and strengthen you, and he will place you on a firm foundation. I PETER 5:10

7   *[S]uppose that what you are up against is a surgeon whose intentions are wholly good. The kinder and more conscientious he is, the more inexorably he will go on cutting.*   CHAP. 3, P. 43

Do you know anyone who likes going to the dentist or to any other doctor? Few of us relish sitting in the chair and listening to the whine of the drill as the dentist works on a cavity or the hygienist cleans our teeth. We don't long for checkups or surgery. Yet any of the above actions help in the long run. Surgery corrects problems and saves lives. Still, in the middle of a painful dental procedure, some of us might be tempted to tap the dentist on the shoulder and demand that he or she stop.

Lewis compared the actions of our good God to those of a surgeon. As Lewis explained, a good surgeon would not stop a procedure simply because a patient dislikes being operated upon. A good surgeon works to make sure all the diseased elements are removed and the patient thoroughly treated. Not only is God a surgeon, he is also a gardener—one concerned about the growth of his people. Good gardeners know when to prune in order to help the plant produce. Every leaf is examined and diseased limbs cut away to ensure the health of the plant.

Pruning often occurs during some of life's hardest times. God prunes away diseased images of himself as well as surface-level ideas of faith. Grief is sometimes God's way of helping us go deeper in our faith. As with surgery, pruning doesn't feel comfortable and is often not welcomed. But the results are worth the hassle.

Where have you seen God's work of pruning in your life? Are you more tempted to help or hinder his progress?

[Jesus said,] "I am the true grapevine, and my Father is the gardener. . . .
He prunes the branches that do bear fruit so they will produce even more."
JOHN 15:1-2

8 *You can't see anything properly while your eyes are blurred with tears.*
CHAP. 3, P. 45

Ever wonder if someone is really mourning a loss if he or she doesn't dissolve into tears? To hear a widow speak casually of her dead husband, or a parent of a child, sometimes causes others to react with suspicion. "Perhaps she didn't miss him (or her) as much as she professed," some might say. Yet how often do we remain at a loss for words when someone expresses inconsolable grief?

Lewis realized that he saw his deceased wife more clearly once the tide of tear-filled grief had ebbed. That's the irony of grief. This did not mean that he missed her less. Instead, he no longer grieved as one without hope, as 1 Thessalonians 4:13 explains. He was coming to terms with her loss—his mind was no longer quite as numb. This is the stage of acceptance—one of the five stages of grief, according to Swiss psychiatrist Elisabeth Kübler-Ross.

Lewis even acknowledged his own assumptions of whether others were over their grief or had forgotten loved ones. Now he realized that coming to terms with grief is not such a bad thing.

Paul had a similar message for the believers in and around Thessalonica. Some were fearful that those who died would never be seen again: they died, and that was the end of them. Paul provided a clearer perspective to cut through their hopelessness. One day, those who died would return to life again, just as Jesus returned to life after his crucifixion and burial.

Coming to a place of acceptance after a loss doesn't mean that you have ceased to care for your loved one. It simply means you no longer grieve as one without hope.

Dear brothers and sisters, we want you to know what will happen to the believers who have died so you will not grieve like people who have no hope.
I THESSALONIANS 4:13

9   *For in grief nothing "stays put." One keeps on emerging from a phase, but it always recurs.*   CHAP. 3, P. 56

Swiss psychiatrist Elisabeth Kübler-Ross is best known for her book *On Death and Dying*, particularly the five stages of grief outlined in it. The first stage is denial, in which the grieving person either shuts down emotionally or is in denial about the grief itself. The second is anger, sometimes directed toward God or the deceased. The third, negotiation/bargaining, involves making promises to God in exchange for a postponement to grief. The fourth, depression, is when anger and grief meld together into a ball of hopelessness until finally the last stage, acceptance, is reached. A grieving person might go back and forth between the stages or experience only some of them.

Lewis could relate, having found himself plunged back into the morass of tears and anger after thinking that he was finally coming to terms with his loss. Why couldn't grief be like a car—remaining where it was parked? Instead, his mood continued to shift. Feeling better one day and crying the next was a source of frustration. The cycle of grief raised more questions for which he had no answers. This is the problem of grief. There is no set pattern to how long it lasts or how long it takes to go from one stage to another. The process is not "one size fits all."

Solomon, believed to be the writer of Ecclesiastes, explored the cyclical nature of life. While the statements in the verse below might seem pat or obvious, they reveal an undeniable fact: there is a season for everything. But as humans we don't often know when these seasons will end. Therefore, we find ourselves frustrated when we think we're over something only to fall back into despair. Only God knows when we will be finished with the time to grieve.

But like the darkness of a long, hard winter, during which we might endure several dark cloudy days without once seeing the sun, this, too, will pass.

A time to cry and a time to laugh. A time to grieve and a time to dance.
ECCLESIASTES 3:4

10 *My idea of God is not a divine idea. It has to be shattered time after time. He shatters it Himself.* CHAP. 4, P. 66

What happens when you keep stretching a rubber band? If stretched beyond its capacity, it will break instead of bouncing back. Sometimes we feel like that—stretched to the breaking point—because of circumstances in life that leave us feeling overwhelmed. The death of a spouse is one such circumstance, one in which Lewis felt himself stretched beyond his limits.

As he wrestled with the pain of that loss, he also found his view of God stretching and ultimately being shattered by God. You don't expect to find God in the shattering business. That's the province of the careless, isn't it? Yet the dissolution of God's image allowed God to remake the image—fashioning it to his own specifications, like an expert glassblower shaping molten glass.

Such a shattering is often a deal-breaker for those who view suspiciously a God who can allow evil in the world. But to demonstrate his sovereignty, God sometimes uses unusual means. For example, he spoke through a prophet who specialized in divination. Balaam was not a prophet called by God. In fact, he was asked by a foreign king to curse the people of Israel as they wandered in the wilderness toward the Promised Land (see Numbers 22). Yet God not only spoke truth through Balaam, thus preventing him from cursing Israel, but also spoke through his donkey! God's words are a reminder of his constancy.

Perhaps, like Lewis, you're going through a time in which God is shattering your view of him. Consider the words below, spoken through Balaam. Even though our view of God may shift from time to time, it's comforting to know that God's qualities never change.

God is not a man, so he does not lie. He is not human, so he does not change his mind. Has he ever spoken and failed to act? Has he ever promised and not carried it through? NUMBERS 23:19

WORDS OF GRACE

Lewis's strength as a communicator was due in part to his masterful use of words. He had an education in the classics and was highly proficient in Greek and Latin. Furthermore, he knew Anglo-Saxon as well as French, Italian, and a smattering of German—and there is plenty of evidence that he even knew some Turkish. For instance, *Aslan* is the Turkish and Persian word for "lion," and *Jadis*—the name of the queen of Charn, later the White Witch of Narnia—can be traced to a word meaning "witch." Lewis's wide-ranging grasp of language allowed him to use just the right words to say things precisely. His descriptions minimized the risk of ambiguity; furthermore, his clarity of expression encouraged his readers' own imaginative embodiments of Lewis's depictions. Whether or not one agrees with Lewis, one can *see* exactly what he meant, from the description of an expression on the face of his characters to the reasons and inferences supporting an argument in his Christian apologetics. Lewis was a master when it came to words and descriptions.

Words, of course, carry more than clarity for the mind. When something is described well, we find ourselves inclining toward the thing itself. It invites us to respond. With our minds we respond with intellectual grasp and understanding. Sometimes we respond with the will, for truly, to understand a thing may require us to make choices commensurate with that understanding: a description of the dangerous may lead to a willful response of fight or flight. A description of beauty may lead one to choose to linger long and drink in all that is offered for view. Furthermore, descriptions may invite an emotional response: words of hatred breed hatred; words of love awaken the heart to adoration. Words appeal to the whole person. Lewis understood this, and his words, measured as they were, seek to win a response from his readers that opens them up to a wider world where grace can be known and experienced.

Perhaps no topic appeals more to the deep need of the soul than words of grace. There is something in Lewis that seems to appeal to that part of each man, woman, and child who longs to be loved. This theme of Lewis's, though expressed throughout his work, finds one of its most endearing expressions in *The Lion, the Witch and the Wardrobe*. Aslan, the Christ figure, incarnates himself into Narnia: "the Word became flesh" (John 1:14, NKJV) in that world as it did in ours. Aslan, as an act of grace, gives himself to save Edmund and all Narnia. So great is the expression of this love that it is not conditioned on Edmund's performance or capacity to earn it; in fact Edmund can do nothing to save himself from peril—nothing of merit. His neediness is met by Aslan's love and sacrifice; nothing else will do.

Of course, Lewis was well aware that in a fallen world, good may become perverted. As God can use words of grace, his creatures can compromise those words and pollute them through selfish desire. In *The Magician's Nephew*, Jadis, the queen of Charn, is evil. The inhabitants of her world seek to depose her and have mounted a civil war against her. She speaks the "Deplorable Word," a magical word that saves her only by destroying her world. In this act she becomes an anti-Aslan. Her word reminds us of all the self-centered words that have ever been spoken and of all the hurt that has ever followed in their wake. She underscores by her act how desperate each of us is for a word of grace and mercy to set us free from the destructive power of self-reference.

In Lewis's first science fiction novel, *Out of the Silent Planet*, one cannot help but think he was underscoring the idea that Earth, the "silent planet," has lost its voice; having fallen from grace, it is the planet where words of grace need to be spoken and its people liberated to become more like the unfallen Malacandra (Mars). Of course, Lewis was quick to remind his readers that wherever one acknowledges the need for grace, it will be given.

In *Studies in Words*, Lewis highlighted again how important words and their meanings are and gave definitions that allow his readers to think and reflect more deeply about a host of concepts and ideas. Nevertheless, as has been mentioned, the word *definition* means "of the finite"; we define things by their limitation and their function. So how do we define the infinite God? Even at the climax of time—a theme Lewis wrote about in "The World's Last Night" and in his essay "Historicism," as well as in the Narnian book *The Last Battle*—we will not come to a full understanding of the ways of grace. More words will yet be spoken, and all eternity will not exhaust the themes of God's great love and grace toward us. There is more to be spoken as we go "further up and further in."

CHAPTER 19

The Lion, the Witch and the Wardrobe

The Lion, the Witch and the Wardrobe is Lewis's most enduringly popular and best-loved book and is the introduction for many to the writing of C. S. Lewis. It is frequently required reading in schools; it has been turned into movies, plays, and songs; and it is the subject of scholarly research. This book is the first of the seven Narnia stories written and published and was the first of the Narnia films produced by Disney and Walden Media. It is significant that it should be first, for here Lewis created the essential characters and circumstances for understanding Narnia while at the same time symbolizing the most important elements of Christian theology in fresh and unforgettable form. Here is the essence of the gospel: sin, sacrifice, forgiveness, and new life. It is at once a retelling of the central story of human history and the story of every individual conversion.

Lewis said that in his fiction he hoped to sneak past the "watchful dragons" of readers' prejudices about Christianity. Having read the gospel in a fictionalized form, our imaginations are prepared to receive the straightforward truth when we meet it in the Bible or hear it in a sermon. We can easily see the advantage for the person who is skeptical about Christianity, as Lewis himself had been as a teenager and young adult. But the watchful dragons are there in another form for longtime believers. They take the form of the routine—the familiar, the traditional—and become dull and perhaps even uninteresting. But as these readers enter into the adventures of the four Pevensie children—the big mysterious house of the professor and the magical wardrobe—and slip into the enchanted world of Narnia, all this is as new as it was for Lucy, Edmund, Susan, and Peter. The dragons are asleep, and our imaginations are wide awake. The wonder, the shock, and the joy of the gospel can wash over us like a mighty cleansing wave.

Many have tried to account for the unusual hold this book places on the imagination. Among the best explanations are that it enchants, it makes goodness real and desirable, and it sets us longing for our true destiny. And it does this for children and adults alike.

1 *Always winter and never Christmas; think of that!*

CHAP. 2, P. 16

One of the first things Lucy learns upon entering Narnia is that the White Witch has usurped Aslan's rule and cursed Narnia. As Tumnus the Faun tells Lucy, for a hundred years it has been winter, but always without Christmas. This symbol is one of Lewis's most powerful and memorable. The appeal is immediate, even for those who associate Christmas only with Santa Claus and presents, when even cold and snow can become beautiful with the anticipation of the season. But what if it were endless cold and snow with no hope of spring or Christmas?

It is just one step further to the real meaning of Christmas that makes this symbol of unrelieved cold explode with meaning. Christmas, of course, celebrates the birth of Jesus—the gift of God that brings forgiveness and eternal life, the very hinge that opens the door to the meaning of human history. When Aslan comes, as when Jesus does, the curse on both the environment and human nature can be lifted. The coming of Aslan is greatly anticipated and is preceded by the appearance of Father Christmas, who gives gifts, and the spring thaw.

All this anticipates the supreme gift, the one that will break all curses and restore everything to its rightful order. That gift is Aslan himself, whose willing sacrifice of his innocent life will free Edmund and all Narnia. The icy grip of winter, with dormant plants and hibernating animals, aptly symbolizes the soul-numbing effect of sin and rebellion before liberating forgiveness recommences the flow of life and joy. And as with the birth of Jesus at Christmas, the initiative must come from beyond our world. Until Aslan begins to move, winter will never break.

The creation looks forward to the day when it will join God's children in glorious freedom from death and decay. For we know that all creation has been groaning as in the pains of childbirth right up to the present time. ROMANS 8:21-22

2 *[T]his was enchanted Turkish Delight and . . . anyone who had once tasted it would want more and more of it, and would even, if they were allowed, go on eating it till they killed themselves.* CHAP. 4, P. 33

One sin leads to another. Edmund makes fun of Lucy and resents Peter's efforts to make him stop grumbling and picking on Lucy. Edmund's pride and selfishness have taught him to hate. When the queen offers him Turkish Delight, he takes it as a foretaste of other "pleasures": getting even with Peter and proving the others wrong, lording it over them as the White Witch's prince and king. The White Witch is expert at drawing Edmund further in. To get more Turkish Delight, he must first bring his brother and sisters to her castle. Gluttony leads to lies, desertion, treachery, betrayal, and death—even, very nearly, his own.

Sin is addictive. Once Edmund tastes Turkish Delight, he craves more. The devil's biggest lie is to try something just once; his second biggest lie is that since you have done it once, you may as well do it again. When we have already broken the barrier of conscience and formulated an excuse, the way is clear for more sin. Even when Edmund knows deep down that he has made a series of huge mistakes, he still treasures the idea of Turkish Delight. At the Beavers' house, he has no desire for the nourishing food on the table before him. His appetite for the good has been destroyed by eating the unhealthy candy. Now, he wants only more candy and more pleasures.

As we learned from Screwtape in *The Screwtape Letters*, the pattern of addiction is ever-increasing desire along with ever-diminishing pleasure. Though Edmund had overeaten the very first time the witch gave him Turkish Delight and had felt sick and looked awful, still he wants more. We see clearly that Edmund has been a fool and a dupe. Is it possible that we ourselves gobble evil in a hundred forms a day, inviting our own destruction and thus destroying our appetite for the wholesome?

Temptation comes from our own desires, which entice us and drag us away. These desires give birth to sinful actions. And when sin is allowed to grow, it gives birth to death. JAMES 1:14-15

3 *"But do you really mean, sir," said Peter, "that there could be other worlds—all over the place, just round the corner—like that?"*

CHAP. 5, P. 54

The professor answers Peter's question about the existence of other worlds with a confident affirmative. The professor may not be speaking "common" sense, but he certainly makes good sense. Lewis often and readily conceded that there may be other forms of intelligent life in our universe or even other universes unknown to us. It requires no great stretch of imagination to think that the God who made this universe, and will unmake and remake it, could do the same as many times as he wishes. Most of reality is unseen by any one of us. Besides the relatively great amount of activity in our lifetimes that we will never see, there are vast tracts of time before we were born and after we die that will remain unknown to us finite mortals. Even much about our very selves is opaque to our rational minds. And beyond the reaches of interstellar space, in which a million lifetimes is insufficient for sending and receiving a message at the speed of light, there is the unseen reality of the spiritual world, which is durable and permanent.

Lucy walks unwittingly through an ordinary wardrobe into Narnia. In *The Magician's Nephew*, Digory (the boy in that story but the professor in *The Lion, the Witch and the Wardrobe*) and Polly chance into Charn, a dying world, and then into Narnia as Aslan is making it. Having been to other worlds, the professor now knows that what is unseen is more real than what is seen. God, who is an unseen Spirit, created the unseen angelic hosts, who have appeared to humanity on rare occasions. God, through Christ, also created the vast universe. Instead of being bewildered by the vastness of our own universe or the existence of possible others, we are invited—even blessedly commanded—to put our faith in the author of it all, who has taken the initiative to enter the smallness of our world that he may take us into his vast, eternal cosmic home.

This world is not our permanent home; we are looking forward to a home yet to come. HEBREWS 13:14

4   *It was like that now. At the name of Aslan each one of the children felt something jump in its inside.*   CHAP. 7, P. 64

All four Pevensie children come into the Narnian world for the first time. After the initial surprise and delight, they see that it is also a hostile world of coldness, intrigue, and danger. Hope is announced by a strange messenger: a talking beaver who announces that Aslan has landed and is "on the move." With the mention of Aslan's name, the world is no longer the same. The children have an experience of what Lewis called the *numinous*: an encounter with something utterly different or "other" from ourselves. To explain the feeling, Lewis said it's like having a dream about something that you don't understand but know to be the key to something really important. You have the feeling that when you understand the meaning, it will turn the whole dream to either a nightmare or something like a fairy tale you never want to end.

Everyone whose spirit has sensed something of God's transcendence has felt this phenomenon. Whether or not fear is a part of it, the important thing is that it moves us to worship, which is our normal, healthy relationship to the transcendent God. Our reaction to such a God tells more about us than it does about him. An encounter with even the name Aslan reveals the character of every child at the Beavers' table and foreshadows his or her response as the children get closer and closer to meeting the Lion in person.

Edmund has already chosen evil—though thankfully that is not the end of his story—and he has a nightmarish experience of the numinous: in this case, the horror of being found out in something he knows deep down is very wrong. But the other three have the fairy-tale dream experience. Lucy feels a holiday excitement, Peter feels the rush of a new adventure, and Susan feels the enchantment that comes from music. These experiences for the three who love and want goodness draw them to Aslan. When they hear his name, something deep within tells them that Aslan is at the center of their experience both in Narnia and beyond.

God elevated him [Jesus] to the place of highest honor and gave him the name above all other names, that at the name of Jesus every knee should bow, in heaven and on earth and under the earth, and every tongue confess that Jesus Christ is Lord, to the glory of God the Father. PHILIPPIANS 2:9-11

5

Wrong will be right, when Aslan comes in sight,
At the sound of his roar, sorrows will be no more.

CHAP. 8, P. 74

This is the prophecy that comforted the Narnians during the hundred years of winter and cruelty under the curse of the usurping White Witch. We hear it for the first time—along with Peter, Susan, Edmund, and Lucy—from Mr. Beaver. What a welcome and needed word of hope. Edmund, as his siblings will soon discover, has turned traitor and seems to be lost to the White Witch. Mr. Tumnus has fallen, too, and has surely been turned to stone. Everyone else has suffered under the evil queen's oppression as well. On top of this, the children are powerless before her wand—they'd be turned to stone in an instant—and the monstrous creatures under her command, such as ogres, hags, and other horrors who delight in evil and seem to have all the power. Nothing seems right. Into this waking nightmare the name *Aslan* comes like the sound of a trumpet at the head of a delivering army. It is he who will save Mr. Tumnus, Edmund, the other children and their new friends, and all of Narnia.

It is Aslan's roar that silences the White Witch when she questions his promise to die in Edmund's place. Aslan roars again when he is resurrected from cruel death, and Peter, Susan, and Lucy see his face turn "terrible" in righteous anger as he prepares to pour out judgment on the witch and all her minions. Aslan's roar, as the prophecy has foretold, is the sign that sorrows will soon be over and right will reign secure. Hearing that Aslan has come to Narnia is like hearing "King of kings and Lord of lords" in the "Hallelujah" chorus of Handel's oratorio *Messiah*, announcing that the goodness, love, glory, and wisdom that made our world has come to put it right.

Everything around us is going to be destroyed. . . . But we are looking forward to the new heavens and new earth he has promised, a world filled with God's righteousness. 2 PETER 3:11, 13

6 *'Course he isn't safe. But he's good.*

CHAP. 8, PP. 75–76

The Pevensies have a lot to learn in Narnia about the battle between goodness and evil and about Aslan and the White Witch, who are keys in the struggle. It seems that every turn in the conversation at the Beavers' house is a shock or surprise. Nearly every assumption about themselves and their circumstances is wrong. This includes the complex nature of Aslan. When Susan and Lucy hear that Aslan is a lion, they wonder, naturally enough, if he would be safe. Mr. Beaver then presents them and us with a now-famous paradox: Aslan is not safe, but he is good.

The paradox is one we all encounter. We assume that any goodness in the world would advance our agendas and make us happy. We often glibly pray to God as though he is a genie who must grant our wishes, whatever they are. We want to be in control, and when we can't be, our next wish is for God to control things for us after our liking. That is not reality. We learn with maturity that a wise God, for our own good, would never grant all we ask, no more than good parents who must often say no to the foolish requests of their children. This is one way in which God, like Aslan, is not safe.

We discover another way he is not safe when we finally understand something of God's holiness and our own shortcomings. Isaiah lamented that his very righteousness was like dirty rags by comparison to God's goodness (Isaiah 64:6). Sinful humanity is not safe in the presence of goodness. Sin must be eliminated and the sinner cleansed; the alternative is separation from goodness forever. Edmund is safe only when Aslan's goodness is substituted for his own evil; and in the same way, before Jesus' sacrifice is ours in faith, Jesus' goodness is actually our doom. But when his goodness becomes our undeserved gift, his goodness is our deliverance, and we are safe.

Since we have been made right in God's sight by the blood of Christ, he will certainly save us from God's condemnation. For since our friendship with God was restored by the death of his Son while we were still his enemies, we will certainly be saved through the life of his Son. ROMANS 5:9-10

7

"Only Aslan," said Mr. Beaver, "we must go and meet him. That's our only chance now." CHAP. 8, P. 82

Most of us are brought up to be independent. We see it as a virtue that we need no help from anyone else. Among their first words, children seem to learn "I do it." But we are all born utterly dependent on someone else for every need. Without outside help, we would soon die. This images exactly our need for salvation from sin and God's guidance in our daily lives. Insistence on independence from God is certain spiritual death, as surely as physical death follows independence for a newborn.

When Peter, Susan, and Lucy learn that Mr. Tumnus has been captured by the White Witch, they think it is their job to find a scheme to free him. When Edmund is found to be a traitor, they all feel duty bound to save their brother. They are right in wanting their friend's and relative's deliverance. They couldn't be more wrong on how to go about it, however. The fastest way (and the only one that will work) is to find Aslan. In the end, they and others will be in the middle of the big battle to free not only Mr. Tumnus and Edmund but all of Narnia.

First, Aslan must work the deep magic put into the world from before the dawn of time. He, like Jesus, must be the sacrifice for the world he made—a sacrifice that releases the power to everything inside and out. With his victory over death and evil, Aslan's ultimate victory is certain. Only by taking our place in his army can we do any good against the otherwise overwhelming odds. The best advice Peter, Susan, and Lucy ever receive is Mr. Beaver's solemn warning that Aslan is their only hope. What they would learn from meeting Aslan is that they need no other help than his and that in following him they would find the freedom to live out the destiny for which they were born.

There is salvation in no one else! God has given no other name under heaven by which we must be saved. ACTS 4:12

8

Aslan is on the move. The Witch's magic is weakening.

CHAP. 10, P. 103

In a run for their lives, the Beavers and three of the Pevensie children narrowly escape capture by the snarling wolves of the White Witch's secret police. They slog through the snow at night and take shelter in a cave, hoping to avoid the witch and make it to Aslan and deliverance at the Stone Table. While hiding in the cave, they hear a sledge and reindeer bells and are afraid the White Witch has found them. Mr. Beaver bravely goes out to see which way the witch will go. To their surprise, Mr. Beaver calls them out to stand face-to-face with Father Christmas.

The Narnians have had a hundred years of winter with no Christmas. When Father Christmas shows up when the witch herself had been expected, we can imagine the celebration that follows. Father Christmas himself announces the significance of his coming: "Aslan is on the move. The Witch's magic is weakening." It's as though John the Baptist, the angel announcing Jesus' incarnation, and the gift-giving Holy Spirit were rolled into one for the moment. Christmas marks the beginning of the end of evil's domination over both worlds—Narnia and our own. When the scene shifts back to the witch, she is struggling to move her sledge through the melting snow, which gives the humans and the Beavers the chance to find Aslan. Signs of spring are everywhere: snow melting, grass greening, flowers blooming, birds singing.

There will still be battles and setbacks, but with Aslan personally in Narnia, the victory is assured. We are in exactly the same position—we await our deliverance. Our ransom has been paid as surely as Edmund's, but we are charged to fight on with courage and hope. Like Aslan, the Savior of our world did what he came to do: in love and with great humiliation he paid the price for our betrayal of his just law, established his Kingdom on a sure foundation, and proved his power over death by coming back to life. He enlists us in his army and delays his final return to give us the chance to choose his side.

I have told you all this so that you may have peace in me. Here on earth you will have many trials and sorrows. But take heart, because I have overcome the world.

JOHN 16:33

9

[W]hen a willing victim who had committed no treachery was killed in a traitor's stead, the Table would crack and Death itself would start working backwards. CHAP. 15, P. 160

As Susan and Lucy look on from a place of hiding, Aslan is tied, shaved, muzzled, beaten, jeered, and finally killed. As soon as they can, they release his body from the muzzle, while kind mice chew off the ropes. They awake from a cruel night of cold and sorrow to dawn and the sound of a great noise, as the Stone Table on which Aslan had been killed cracks in two. When the children, expecting the worst, wonder aloud if this is more magic, Aslan's voice booms in affirmation. He is alive! And what a wonderful romp they have in celebration! Aslan explains the "deeper magic" that he and his father the Emperor knew but the witch did not: when a willing but innocent victim was killed for a traitor, the Table would crack and Death itself would work backward.

The symbolism is very close to the Bible's account of Jesus' death and resurrection. When Jesus died, rocks cracked and the heavy curtain in the Temple, separating the Holy Place from the Most Holy Place, was torn in two from top to bottom. This was to show that all people, not just the high priest once a year, could come into the presence of God. In Narnia, the Table, with ancient writing all around it, symbolizes the Old Testament law. God himself wrote the Ten Commandments on stone tablets (see Exodus 31:18). Now the power of the law, which demands death for the sin of not keeping the commandments, has been broken by Jesus' willing sacrifice, the innocent for the guilty.

When Jesus came back to life and left the tomb, death really did work backward, and many graves gave up the righteous dead, who were then also resurrected. Death worked backward in freeing those who had died before the coming of Jesus, but who died in faith that God would send a redeemer to take away the penalty of sin. The only imaginable response to this is Susan's and Lucy's: they celebrate with Aslan.

The earth shook, rocks split apart, and tombs opened. The bodies of many godly men and women who had died were raised from the dead . . . after Jesus' resurrection. MATTHEW 27:51-53

10 *Once a king or queen in Narnia, always a king or queen. Bear it well,*
Sons of Adam! Bear it well, Daughters of Eve! CHAP. 17, P. 179

Some who have read *The Last Battle* may see this quote and remember that Susan does not end up in the new Narnia, having in the interim between the books become a friend of this world instead of Narnia. It certainly seems like a contradiction. One young reader wrote to Lewis about it, and he tried to comfort him by pointing out that Susan is still in this world in our time (which is different from Narnian time) and may still make the right choices and ultimately end up in Narnia. We must remember that Narnia is not heaven; otherwise, why would the White Witch be there, along with her followers, and even the still-sinful humans?

We meet the same apparent contradiction in the Bible when Paul laments some who have left the faith or when Jesus says, "Anyone who puts a hand to the plow and then looks back is not fit for the Kingdom of God" (Luke 9:62). As with Susan's possibly temporary desertion of Narnia, these are clearly warnings. But are they really contradictions? They can't be. We must reconcile such statements with the host of assurances that the life Jesus gives is eternal—it never ends. The problem comes with thinking that someone is truly a child of God and joint heir with Jesus when he or she is not. It is helpful to remember that we are never saved by our own initiative anyway, but by God's, and that he will not contradict himself. Similarly, it is Aslan who decides when people from our world will be called into Narnia and which of them will be kings and queens. If we doubt his promises, we risk his roar.

[Jesus says,] "My sheep listen to my voice; I know them, and they follow me. I give them eternal life, and they will never perish. No one can snatch them away from me, for my Father has given them to me, and he is more powerful than anyone else. No one can snatch them from the Father's hand. The Father and I are one."

JOHN 10:27-30

CHAPTER 20

The Magician's Nephew

THIS BOOK ABOUT THE CREATION OF NARNIA, which comes first in more recent publications of the seven-book series, was the last to be written. Lewis began writing it immediately after he finished writing *The Lion, the Witch and the Wardrobe*, in 1949—though that book was published in 1950. But the writing didn't go well, so he went on to write *Prince Caspian*, *The Voyage of the* Dawn Treader, *The Horse and His Boy*, and *The Silver Chair*. Then he tried *The Magician's Nephew* again, giving it up to write *The Last Battle*. He finally completed the book on the beginning of Narnia last of all in 1954 (published 1955), after he had written of its destruction and re-creation in *The Last Battle*.

This prequel tells of Narnia's creation as Aslan sings it into existence. It also lets us know that Jadis comes into Narnia from a world named Charn, which she had destroyed by a secret, evil power. Through the foolishness of Digory, she escapes Charn and follows Digory and his friend Polly (via rings belonging to Digory's "magician" uncle, Andrew) to London and then to Narnia, while it is still a dark and unformed world. There they witness Aslan singing the sun and stars, plants and animals into existence, giving to some of his creation language and reason. While the land is yet in its infancy, evil is loose in Narnia. Aslan acts to protect Narnia, allowing Digory to be a part of the solution, though the ultimate salvation must come by Aslan's death. In obeying Aslan, Digory is also allowed to take back to our world a fruit that will heal his dying mother.

In this book, the consequences of evil and the costliness of grace to counter it come together with the destructiveness of evil and creativity of love in all its grandeur. Like the chronicles as a whole, *The Magician's Nephew* presents the archetypal struggle of good and evil: God and Satan, Aslan and Jadis, Digory and Uncle Andrew. We are captivated by goodness and repelled by evil. Lewis helped us in the same enterprise so consciously undertaken long ago by the Puritans: training the affections so we love and hate the right things. In so doing, we will learn not only to *know* goodness when we see it but also to *love* it. As we are reminded so often in the Bible, evil seems to prosper in this world. In this book we get to take the long view into the future, where all accounts are settled in justice and mercy.

1   *Men like me, who possess hidden wisdom, are freed from common rules just as we are cut off from common pleasures. Ours, my boy, is a high and lonely destiny.*   CHAP. 2, P. 21

Uncle Andrew has traded his soul for the illusion of power. He has just sent Polly out of this world to an unknown destination, and Digory has rebuked him for cowardice in not going himself and for tricking Polly into going against her will. Now Uncle Andrew is appealing to Digory's sense of common decency in going as the only means of her return. Uncle Andrew takes pride in secret knowledge as something that sets him apart from the "common rules" of ordinary mortals like Digory and Polly.

Rationalization and pride are recognizable in Uncle Andrew's words. We cannot live with a belief that is contrary to our behavior. If we choose a course of action that violates our conscience, as a psychological principle and spiritual consequence we are compelled either to repent of it or make an excuse—to rationalize or give a reason why the behavior is acceptable. If this becomes habitual, we so abuse our sense of reason that we confuse good and evil, which Paul warned against in Romans 1. This is why Lewis called pride the deepest of all sins. It puts the self in charge, and thus we make our own rules of morality. It is the path to all other vices.

True morality, by contrast, flows from the very character of God. We can't be at the center and have God at the center at the same time. Uncle Andrew's rationalization is that he can use the children just as he used guinea pigs before them. His supposed high aim of exploring other worlds comes at a devastatingly high price: his soul. What is worse, he does not see that he is about to transport earthly evil to worlds unknown. The power of deciding other people's destiny is a demonic power, and the beginning of all such evil choices as this one by Uncle Andrew is in our minds.

To pursue God's goals in God's way is the only recipe for a "high destiny." The battle is won or lost by the thoughts we entertain. We make our thoughts captive to Christ (see 2 Corinthians 10:5, NIV) or else to "empty philosophy": there are no other alternatives.

Don't let anyone capture you with empty philosophies and high-sounding nonsense that come from human thinking and from the spiritual powers of this world, rather than from Christ. COLOSSIANS 2:8

2 *Then I spoke the Deplorable Word. A moment later I was the only living thing beneath the sun.* CHAP. 5, P. 71

These words from Jadis, the White Witch—the Satan figure in the Narnia stories—explain for Digory and Polly why Charn, the world they have "chanced" upon, is full of death, decay, and finally nothing at all. Paralleling Uncle Andrew but on a larger scale and at the cost of her own soul and those of many others, Jadis has learned a very powerful magic. Aslan's magic (and, in our world, God's miraculous power) is always for ultimate good and is always creative except in righteous judgment. "Dark magic" like that of Andrew and Jadis (supernatural power from the demonic world) is always destructive. Dark magic is always pursued to gain personal domination at great cost to the soul of the seeker, as Andrew and Jadis illustrate. There is perhaps no more powerful example of satanic pride in fiction than this. Jadis is so full of herself that she cannot bear the thought of anyone else being in control. She would rather destroy the world than let her sister or anyone else reign over it.

Except for the hand of God holding evil in check, such would be the fate of our world in Satan's destructive spite—or even on a comparable scale if a madman got control of nuclear weapons. But we don't have to look far from home to find the same spirit of destructive pride. We see the same spirit in the child who wrecks the game rather than let someone else win, or in the corporate bureaucrat who would rather sink a deal or even a company than allow someone else due credit because the achievement is not his or her own. When this spirit becomes a habitual state of mind and soul, Paul told us, this is the result: "new ways of sinning" without mercy or any cry from a conscience long since dead to God's moral reality.

The only mercy Aslan can extend to Andrew in the new world is to put him to sleep, for life without self at the center has become miserable for him. So it is with Jadis. And so, warned Paul, may it be for any who fail to keep a devouring pride in check.

Since they thought it foolish to acknowledge God, he abandoned them to their foolish thinking and let them do things that should never be done. . . . They are backstabbers, haters of God, insolent, proud, and boastful. They invent new ways of sinning . . . and have no mercy. ROMANS 1:28, 30-31

3 *Well, you know how it feels if you begin hoping for something that you want desperately badly; you almost fight against the hope because it is too good to be true; you've been disappointed so often before.*

CHAP. 7, P. 100

Feeling that he is losing his mother, Digory represents Lewis's own feelings at the loss of his mother to cancer when he was only nine years old. As he explained in *Surprised by Joy*, Lewis had a toothache and headache and wanted his mother, but she was too ill to come. He prayed for her healing, but she died. So the boy quickly gave up on God. Looking back, Lewis could see that he thought of God not as someone to be obeyed but simply as a "magician" who could and should grant one's wishes. Once again, in boarding school, Lewis worked at prayer, painfully requiring of himself a certain nameless emotion confused with faith, then abandoned the effort and declared himself an atheist until he was nearly thirty.

Digory's persistent quest is to find a cure for his mother in one of the new worlds. When he looks to Aslan, he is on the right path, but it is not until he learns to place obedience to Aslan before his own deepest earthly desire that he can safely be given that desire.

We have all prayed and longed for some good thing until we face the prospect of despair. This happens frequently, even in the midst of trying very hard to serve God. We throw ourselves into some work we are convinced God does or should approve of and get discouraged when the effort falters or fails. If God is not going to show up (in ways we can recognize), then why continue? So hope itself begins to die. We must, like Digory, learn that it is not for us to dictate terms to God, either for ourselves or for those we love. Another form of pride thinks, without actually saying so, that we know better than God what we or another person needs.

Aslan sheds tears at Digory's pain, even though he knows he will heal Digory's mother. But in love Aslan first gives Digory what he needs more—the faith to follow, no matter what.

[Jesus said,] "If you love your father or mother more than you love me, you are not worthy of being mine. . . . If you cling to your life, you will lose it; but if you give up your life for me, you will find it." MATTHEW 10:37, 39

4 *The earth was of many colors: they were fresh, hot and vivid. They made you feel excited; until you saw the Singer himself, and then you forgot everything else. It was a Lion.* CHAP. 8, P. 118

After witnessing the death of Charn at Jadis's Deplorable Word and after escaping the madness of Jadis at a destruction derby in London, Digory and Polly are carried by their magic rings to another dark world. But this world is not dying; it is waiting to be born.

There is a precedent for associating music with Creation. In Job "the morning stars sang together" at Creation (38:7). In Psalm 65, all creation shouts and sings for joy. So in *The Magician's Nephew*, Aslan sings the stars into existence and then, Digory is certain, the stars themselves begin to sing. From the ground, plants and animals and other wonders emerge to life at the sound of Aslan's voice. But what draws Digory, Polly, and the cabby and his horse (while repelling Jadis and Uncle Andrew) is Aslan himself.

This scene shows that heaven is not a bribe. Heaven's essence is not the place itself or the things in it or even the resurrected saints—it is Christ himself. As many have wisely said in one form or another, the person who has Christ plus all there is has no more than the person who has Christ and nothing more. Throughout the Narnian Chronicles, Lewis gave us scenes of characters meeting Aslan—in a sense, Jesus. They see him either as the answer to their hearts' desire (the beatific vision) or else as their final doom because of their choice of evil instead of him (a vision of "the Satanic face of doom," or the "miserific" vision—see chapter 9 of *Perelandra*). All our desires, rightly understood, are for Christ. And in the end, what he gives us is himself.

Christ . . . existed before anything was created and is supreme over all creation, for through him God created everything in the heavenly realms and on earth. He made the things we can see and the things we can't see . . . and he holds all creation together. COLOSSIANS 1:15-17

5 *"Hail, Aslan. We hear and obey. We are awake. We love. We think.
We speak. We know."*

[Strawberry said,] "But please, we don't know very much yet."

CHAP. 10, P. 138

After Narnia is filled with living beings, the rational ones turn instinctively in praise to Aslan. Turning to the Creator in worship and thanksgiving is the proper and healthy response of every created being—human, beast, or angel. In Narnia, many animals are elected for rationality, including the ability to speak and praise. Making literal the metaphorical language of Psalm 65, even trees can "shout and sing" in Aslan's praise. This is much, indeed. But there is a further healthy response to Aslan, a response to the infinite Christ and Creator.

There is so much to learn about Aslan and living life in Narnia as he intended it to be lived. This lesson comes from Strawberry, the cab horse—soon to become the glorious winged horse, Fledge, who will carry Digory and Polly on a mission for Aslan that will bless all in Narnia and many in our world too. Strawberry, in saying, "we don't know very much yet," has it right. In his case, only moments have passed since gaining rationality. But even all eternity will not exhaust the riches of knowledge in Christ Jesus, let alone earthly lives that are quickly gone "like spring flowers, they soon wither" (Psalm 37:2).

As one pastor often said, the most common expression in heaven will be, "Oh, I didn't know that!" We will forever be learning and exploring. Christ is, after all, infinite. We are, and forever will be, finite. We will never through all eternity get to the end of Jesus. There will always be more to discover and more to praise. And here, in *The Magician's Nephew*, we have that truth "straight from the horse's mouth."

In him [Jesus] lie hidden all the treasures of wisdom and knowledge.

COLOSSIANS 2:3

6   *I give to you forever this land of Narnia. I give you the woods, the fruits, the rivers. I give you the stars and I give you myself.*   CHAP. 10, P. 138

These are Aslan's first words to the gathered rational creatures of Narnia at the end of his creative acts. These words granting them Narnia as an inheritance are, like the act of Creation itself, a gift. At the creation of Eden, Adam and Eve were given rule over all the plants and animals and given the presence of God as he came to them daily in the cool of the evening (see Genesis 3:8). To Abraham and his descendants came the promise of Canaan, a land flowing with milk and honey (see Exodus 3:8). And in the Tabernacle and eventually the Temple, God gave his own presence. All this is a preparation for the coming of God in Christ, who not only gave a world to enjoy but also gave himself.

At the end of human history, when God has destroyed all that is evil and preserved all that is good, he will give everything to Jesus. It is rightfully his, as Paul wrote in Romans, "for everything comes from him and exists by his power and is intended for his glory" (Romans 11:36). Then, Jesus will turn to us and say, "All that is mine is yours." Astonishingly, we are heirs with him.

But that is only the beginning of wonders. The wonder of wonders is that he gives us himself, that where he is we may be (see John 14:3). All the glory we behold in creation and all the good in others made in his image are only reflections of the glory that is in Christ, the glory he invites us to share.

Aslan delights in giving away himself and all he has made. In this gift of love we glimpse the deep character of our Creator.

Since we are his children, we are his heirs. In fact, together with Christ we are heirs of God's glory.   ROMANS 8:17

7   *Now the trouble about trying to make yourself stupider than you really are is that you very often succeed. Uncle Andrew did. He soon did hear nothing but roaring in Aslan's song. . . . And when at last the Lion spoke and said, "Narnia awake," he didn't hear any words: he heard only a snarl.*   CHAP. 10, P. 148

Contrary to the popular saying, seeing is not believing. Rather, as Lewis showed in many of his books, believing is seeing. Orual can't see Psyche's castle or taste her heavenly food (*Till We Have Faces*); the dwarfs can't see Aslan's country or taste the feast right under their noses (*The Last Battle*). Similarly, Uncle Andrew, knowing that lions can't sing, convinces himself that Aslan's magnificent creative song, which makes Narnia green and blooming and suddenly full of animal life, is only an ugly roar. He makes himself stupid by his refusal to believe. Uncle Andrew fancies himself a scientist and magician, when he is really just a pseudoscientist with preconceived ideas, no ethical virtue, and nothing but a few inherited rings into which another had put the magic.

The mind makes a more effective prison than barred doors do. We meet this type in every walk of life: those who are closed to truth, interpreting everything in doctrinaire terms.

Andrew is blind to Jadis's powerful evil and its dangers (until too late) and to Aslan's greater power and goodness. That Andrew has paid a high price for secret, destructive knowledge he already knows. Just how high a price is beyond his knowing—but not beyond ours. As Lewis often said, good can understand evil, but evil cannot understand good. The warning that comes through Uncle Andrew's story is this: We reject God's truth, including the truth that he exists, at great peril. Paul said in Romans 1 that all can see from Creation that God exists and has "eternal power and divine nature" (v. 20). Denying this, as Uncle Andrew does, results in minds that are "dark and confused," in which singing is heard as growling and beauty is seen as repulsive. We can make ourselves more stupid than we really are.

Yes, they knew God, but they wouldn't worship him as God or even give him thanks. And they began to think up foolish ideas of what God was like. As a result, their minds became dark and confused. Claiming to be wise, they instead became utter fools.   ROMANS 1:21-22

8 *And as Adam's race has done the harm, Adam's race shall help to heal it.*
CHAP. 11, P. 160

Digory, against Polly's wise advice and then by forcing past her, has rung the bell in Charn that awakens the witch Jadis. Though Digory sees his error (and eventually asks Polly's forgiveness, as well as Aslan's), he is not strong enough or smart enough to escape Jadis. She wreaks havoc in London before Digory and Polly manage by their magic rings to get her out. Hoping to take her back to Charn, they bring her instead to Narnia before its creation. After singing Narnia and all its inhabitants into existence, Aslan informs the rational creatures that even before this new world is hours old, evil is loose in it. Though Digory is ashamed to admit his role in bringing evil, he cannot tell a lie to Aslan. But after confession and repentance comes forgiveness. And after that comes grace. Aslan will give Digory, son of Adam, the privilege of being the means Aslan will use to bring protection to Narnia.

Of course, this is the exact parallel of the grace God gave to Adam and Eve after their sin and fall. His promise in Genesis 3:15 is that he would bring into the world through their offspring one who would defeat evil forever. Adam and Eve had the privilege of participating in the healing of the Curse that came by their sin. The promise was fulfilled in Christ, who is called "the second man" or the second Adam (1 Corinthians 15:47).

Digory is not the solution to the consequences of his sin, any more than Adam was. Digory's role only foreshadows what will be accomplished at great cost by Aslan himself.

Just as death came into the world through a man [Adam], now the resurrection from the dead has begun through another man [Jesus]. 1 CORINTHIANS 15:21

9   *Come in by the gold gates or not at all,*
Take of my fruit for others or forbear,
For those who steal or those who climb my wall
Shall find their heart's desire and find despair.

CHAP. 13, P. 185

Jesus put all the righteousness of the moral law into two related principles: love God and "love your neighbor as yourself" (Mark 12:28-31). These are the very principles Digory must learn in Narnia. Digory has the second command partly down in that he wants desperately to see his mother healed. In love, Aslan must see to it that Digory gets the commands in their right order and loves Aslan (God) most of all.

To protect Narnia from the evil Jadis for hundreds of years, Aslan sends Digory to a faraway garden to get an apple from the tree of life and youth. He is to bring the apple to Aslan. When Digory arrives at the garden, he sees that it has a wall running around it and the poem quoted above written in silver on its golden gates. The evil witch Jadis meets Digory in the garden and tempts him, as Satan did Eve, with eating the fruit. She has climbed over the wall and has just eaten one of the great silver apples. Jadis tries, by many subtle arguments, to get Digory to eat an apple himself or to at least, if he really loves his mother, take one directly to her. Digory must put first things first. Though certain reasonable arguments and his own emotions tempt him to take control, Digory obeys. When God commands, it is better to obey than to understand. Digory eventually learns that there are things worse than losing someone you love in death.

Digory flees the garden, bringing the apple to Aslan. Having put Aslan first, Digory now has the opportunity to apply the second command, to love others as himself. He is permitted to plant the apple from which grows the tree that will protect Narnia. From that very tree, Aslan permits Digory to take an apple that will bring healing to his mother.

Before we are of any use to others, we must love God first and demonstrate it by our obedience.

[Jesus said,] "I am the gate. Those who come in through me will be saved."
JOHN 10:9

10 *But length of days with an evil heart is only length of misery and already she begins to know it. All get what they want; they do not always like it.*

CHAP. 14, P. 205

Digory has seen Jadis eat the forbidden fruit from the tree of life and youth. Everything about her actions is wrong—from the manner of entering the garden to the eating itself and tempting Digory to do so. She is one of those the Bible so often warns about: she not only does evil but delights in leading others to do it. Though she stole the apple from Aslan's garden for selfish reasons, Aslan explains that the fruit still works and that Jadis will have what she thought she wanted: endless youthful days. But her days will only add to her bitterness, frustration, and final punishment. Isaiah warned, "What sorrow for those who say that evil is good and good is evil. . . . What sorrow for those who are wise in their own eyes and think themselves so clever" (Isaiah 5:20-21).

Jadis has chosen to do things her way for her own reasons. There is an old saying that when the gods want to punish us, they give us what we pray for. In the Christian context, we may say that God's "no" answers to our prayers are always for our good. God knows us far better than we know ourselves. He also knows that we need him most of all. Lewis said in *The Problem of Pain* that when we live for ourselves, we get what we want, but what we find in that coffin of the self is hell.

But we often fall into the same trap as Jadis, on a smaller scale. We think we know what will make us happy, though God might have forbidden it. On a subtler level, we may think God should act in a certain way—perhaps even for his glory in our service for him—but when he "fails," we take matters into our own hands. We may get what we think we want or even what we think God needs from us, but if God is not the author of it, in the end we won't even like it. Why? Because, quite apart from other consequences, we won't like what we have become.

The wicked are too proud to seek God. They seem to think that God is dead. Yet they succeed in everything they do. They do not see your [God's] punishment awaiting them. PSALM 10:4-5

CHAPTER 21

Out of the Silent Planet

LEWIS AND TOLKIEN LAMENTED that no one was writing the kinds of books they wanted to read, so they undertook to write such books themselves. The first fruit of this resolve was Lewis's *Out of the Silent Planet* (1938), the initial book in what would become the Space Trilogy, or the Ransom Trilogy as it is sometimes called, along with *Perelandra* (1943) and *That Hideous Strength* (1945). All three feature Elwin Ransom (who has many of the qualities of Tolkien and even of Lewis himself) as the central figure. Ransom travels to Malacandra (Mars) in the first book, Perelandra (Venus) in the second, but stays on Earth (Thulcandra) in the final volume, in which he is an important though less central character.

Out of the Silent Planet introduced two new elements into science fiction. First, Lewis reversed the view of inhabitants of other planets as horrible (as in the science fiction of H. G. Wells). Before his conversion, Lewis, too, saw the universe as a desert of wasted space, with no apparent use, and Earth as an infinitesimally small dot lost within cosmic vastness. *Out of the Silent Planet* recovered the medieval view of space as "the heavens," a place teeming with angelic life. The second element new to science fiction was a thoroughly integrated Christian theme. We could even say that, with this book, Lewis inaugurated Christian myth—"myth" as a method of truth telling. Its theology was so thoroughly integrated that most secular critics missed the Christian element altogether when the book first came out. It is hard to imagine how any reader of the Bible could miss it, however.

As the story opens, Ransom is kidnapped by an evil scientist, Edward Weston, and his partner, Dick Devine. They think, mistakenly projecting their own evil mind-set, that the ruler of Malacandra wants a human sacrifice. Their mission is to settle space for the propagation of the human race when human inhabitants have made Earth unlivable. Weston cares nothing for the three species of rational inhabitants of Malacandra: the *Pfifltriggi*, who love to dig and are skilled in crafts; the *Hrossa*, who live in valleys just below the planet's crust and excel in poetry and song; and the *Sorns*, who occupy the mountainous regions and are the philosophers. Though each race has a special function and all three live in harmony and interdependence, Weston is intent on wiping them out to make room for earthlings, whom he views as the top of evolutionary "progress."

Ransom comes to understand and accept his providentially guided role to deliver the planet from the evil human invaders, who embody the philosophical ideal of human survival at all costs that dominated the science fiction of Lewis's day. Ransom learns from the Malacandrian inhabitants that ruling spirits travel and communicate freely throughout the universe but that no communication has come from his planet, Thulcandra—the "silent planet" that has been quarantined by God to contain its evil. There are many delights and insights in this series, but a special contribution of the trilogy's first two books is to show us the beauty of an unfallen world. We get an idea of what has been lost to us through sin and what Christ has recovered—ransomed—for us in the coming new creation.

1 *The mere presence of a human being, with its offer of at least some companionship, broke down the tension in which his nerves had long been resisting a bottomless dismay.* CHAP. 3, P. 26

Despair is the natural destination of the isolated. Any pain, loss, or difficulty is materially magnified by the belief—true or false—that one is alone in experiencing it. The desperation that fear and isolation breed is so great that even the appearance of Weston, one of the men who had drugged and abducted Ransom and forced him onto the ship bound for Malacandra, is a tremendous relief and cause for hope. After all, Weston is another human presence in the unbearably vast, frightening outer space in which Ransom awakes. The value of a peer in the midst of the unknown and terrifying is almost inestimable.

The church silently bears witness to this abyss with its scores of believers who struggle quietly with shame, believing the lie that their repeated sins and failures are evidence of some unnatural moral deficit, some singular defect that no one else can understand, let alone help them to escape. Their shame deepens, their failures mount, and hopelessness reigns.

Our discipleship is crippled by the distillation of the spiritual life to a single dyadic relationship: "me" and "Jesus." When this kind of exclusive pairing is marred by sin, the believer is cast adrift at sea, bereft of any peer aid. Lost to the castaway is the invaluable gift of the wisdom of more experienced, wiser Christians who have lived through and learned from the very same struggles. What struggling believers need is the companionship of these mature Christians, who would provide words of encouragement, empathetic prayers, and practical advice to bear them above "a bottomless dismay."

Dear brothers and sisters, if another believer is overcome by some sin, you who are godly should gently and humbly help that person back onto the right path. . . . Share each other's burdens, and in this way obey the law of Christ.

GALATIANS 6:1-2

2

Ransom's abductors, Weston and Devine, have the awesome privilege of being the first humans to interact with life on Malacandra, but because its inhabitants do not appear to serve any obvious purpose in their plans, the men never truly recognize them or their greater wisdom. Weston and Devine remain incapable of Ransom's achievement of genuine communication with the inhabitants of Malacandra.

We can find similar utilitarianism creeping into the work of the church today as the bond between strategies and stewardship grows. In the recognition that God's commands and values are to be prioritized, there can come ever-increasing pressure to maximize our investments (time, money, interest, energy) into God's work by restricting them to those ventures that promise the greatest results with the least amount of expenditure. Unbeknownst to many who engage in such ventures, utilitarianism and mechanism subtly but strongly shift the value of resources, plans, and even people, boiling everything down to quantifiable usefulness. Under the strain of strategy, ministry vision once sharpened to further God's work becomes myopic; anyone and anything without visible potential for achieving the stated goals is not merely valueless but not even noticed. With no obvious utility, God-given gifts and potential breakthroughs may never be employed because they are never seen in the first place.

The church cannot fall into the same pattern of failure as those who do not know God; our vision cannot be limited to what directly and obviously serves our purposes. Surely the most strategic way to join in God's work is by cultivating his vision, so that we are able to see and value all gifts, even without being able to map out their future application in detail. With God's vision we will be able to speak the encouraging, hopeful words that will strike the motivating spark in the unlikely someone through whom God has planned to do great things.

We have stopped evaluating others from a human point of view. At one time we thought of Christ merely from a human point of view. How differently we know him now! 2 CORINTHIANS 5:16

3

He was quite aware of the danger of madness, and applied himself vigorously to his devotions and his toilet. CHAP. 9, P. 52

The panic of being abducted to Malacandra, being forcibly taken before the *Sorns*, and narrowly escaping his captors has strained Ransom's mind to its limits. Although he cannot make sense of where he is, he does know to care for his mind by caring for his body. It is the balance of flesh and spirit together that maintains sanity.

God never intended human life to be compartmentalized into a severe ethereal spirituality that denigrates the physical. God's plan is instead for a whole life—wholly integrated and wholly healthy.

This is illustrated beautifully in the life of Elijah (see 1 Kings 18–19). Following a public manifestation of God's power over false gods, a royal death threat plunged Elijah into a panicked flight into the desert, where he begged God for death. His emotional and spiritual despair was acute, but God saw beyond that. God's immediate response was not another display of his power or theological words but, instead, sleep. God let Elijah rest after the adrenaline high of the Mt. Carmel sacrifices, the race down the mountain with King Ahab's chariot, and the frenzied journey into the desert. Then God provided Elijah with water, meals, and more rest. Only after seeing to those provisions did God direct Elijah to embark on the journey that would end forty days later in an intimate spiritual encounter. But long before that, God had already begun to alleviate Elijah's maddening stress by providing for his physical needs.

Following God should involve proper care—not obsessive, but proper care—of the bodies that he designed for us. The physical state does not determine the spiritual state, but does influence it. We can work with God to maintain the health of both.

Seek his will in all you do, and he will show you which path to take. Don't be impressed with your own wisdom. Instead, fear the LORD and turn away from evil. Then you will have healing for your body and strength for your bones.

PROVERBS 3:6-8

4   *Then something happened which completely altered his state of mind. . . .*
The creature was talking. It had a language.   CHAP. 9, P. 56

In this moment Ransom rockets from terror to curiosity, all because of unexpected words. On the run and totally at the mercy of any creature he might meet, Ransom expects an attack when he discovers a seal-like creature (one of the *Hrossa*). Instead, he hears the creature talking. The introduction of language, even this unintelligible language, is transformative.

Words imply understanding, intelligence, perhaps even empathy. The Malacandrian creature's language is unknown, but not terrifying because it offers the potential of true communication in time. And a philologist like Ransom welcomes the opportunity to learn a new language.

A man tortured by demons experienced the same release when Jesus spoke to him. When Jesus first reached the region of the Gerasenes and called out to the demoniac, the man responded with a cry, so great was his terror of torture. But his screams did not drown out Jesus' next words: "What is your name?" (Mark 5:9).

Jesus saw through the demons' attempted diversions—the shrieks and the fury—to the man who, in everyone else's estimation, had disappeared long ago. Jesus did not seize him or yell back at the demons. There was no sensational display of the Son of the Most High's power against a legion of dark angels. Instead, Jesus rescued the man with words. His simple acknowledgment of the man he had created began to unravel the demonic power. Though the demons answered for the man in defiance, their reign was ended. Jesus dismissed them and remained with the newly freed, sane man. When the townspeople came upon them later, they were sitting, presumably talking—what about, we are not told. Based on Jesus' manifestation of himself as the Lord, with the power and words necessary to free the man, we can trust that every word Jesus spoke was a morsel of grace, nourishing a soul that had been emaciated by fear and demons far too long.

We, too, can dispense grace with our words.

Let the message about Christ, in all its richness, fill your lives. Teach and counsel each other with all the wisdom he gives.   COLOSSIANS 3:16

5

Hedonism is, by its nature, exhausting. It drives one to pursue, devour, and renew the pursuit. The very process tramples the pleasure because it affords no opportunity to enjoy what has been sought so voraciously. The pleasure is gobbled up and tossed aside without another thought as the pursuer seeks a new quarry to provide an equally ephemeral pleasure.

Hyoi, the *Hross* Ransom first meets, has an understanding of pleasure that is more aligned with the biblical presentation of it. The Old Testament festivals appointed by God for his people to observe were designed, perhaps, to obviate the hedonistic cycle of empty pursuit. In addition to affirming their dependence on him, renewing their commitment to him, and teaching new generations his faithfulness and power, the festivals also served to prolong the collective pleasure of Israel's blessings. Even today, we can appreciate how thousands of years of history have imparted a vast richness to the Passover by renewing and sustaining the pleasure of centuries of celebrations.

Perhaps because our culture values efficiency, or perhaps because we are growing accustomed to watching so much of our technology and traditions grow obsolete within our life spans, we are not apt to memorialize. "What has God done for you this week?" is a question we can answer well, but what about a year ago? five years ago? The memories are foggy, for they have not been cultivated. Without that cultivation, the pleasures of marveling at God's provision, of joyfully weeping at his renewed forgiveness, and of rejoicing at his miracles are lost.

Sit down. Pray and think over the past season or year. Ask God to remind you of what he has taught you and done for you. Write it down, and thank him for each item. Keep the list and pray over it periodically. Prolong the blessings and strengthen your faith by keeping God's works and words vibrant in your memory.

Remember the wonders he has performed, his miracles, and the rulings he has given.   I CHRONICLES 16:12

6 *His speech died away into the inarticulate. He did not know the words for "forgive," or "shame," or "fault," hardly the word for "sorry." He could only stare . . . in speechless guilt.* CHAP. 13, P. 82

Language is rich, vibrant, and colorful, but at times terribly frail. There are losses and hurts that cut too deep for words to heal, and experiences and emotions that exceed what words can express. Ransom's speech is silenced by grief over the loss of Hyoi, his first friend in Malacandra, and by guilt. The guilt is both relational, because fellow humans have brought murder to a world where it was unknown, and personal, because his individual choices have brought this Malacandrian creature into the path of Weston and Devine's weapons. In such moments we, too, stand aghast, insecure, shifting and shifted. It is then that words seem more urgent than ever—and less accessible than ever.

But instinct can direct us to the choice that is simplest and wisest: silence. To the inexperienced it feels like surrender, but it can be the most articulate expression of which humans are capable. Unlike the more common silences that isolate, judge, marginalize, or reject, those silences that are sensitive and empathetic can transmit healing. When grief is sudden and deep, silence can communicate the likeness of our shared shock and disorientation. Companionship is what is necessary in those moments—not well-crafted answers or lengthy discourses, but another human who shares the experience deeply enough to recognize the intensity of the pain.

Our words *fault* and *sorry* don't always have the power to heal, and their pale utterances may only intensify feelings of betrayal and failure. In such cases silence can express knowledge of guilt better than any shallow, flippant acceptance.

Silence allows for nonverbal balms to settle and to begin their long, slow work of healing. Silence wears the edge off shock and helps people resettle their feet after they've toppled on the ground. And silence, led by the Spirit of God, can prepare people for the right words, given in the right time.

Understand this, my dear brothers and sisters: You must all be quick to listen, slow to speak. JAMES 1:19

7 *And once you are on your way to him, I do not think he will let the bent ones stop you.* CHAP. 13, P. 84

Even when you acknowledge your fears, you have confirmed God's goodness and authority, and you have resolved to obey, there still is no promise that all will go well. Other formidable obstacles may come. In what seems to be an inverse formula, those who have persevered most in their dedication to God can best attest to the reality of a persistent enemy. They know that commitment to God is precisely what will wake the enemy's interest and make a believer the target of attacks.

Ransom's commitment to finally seek out Oyarsa does not relieve him of the danger of Weston and Devine's enmity; however, as Whin, another *Hross*, explains here, Ransom is not alone in resisting them.

Acknowledging the reality of the enemy is not a matter of fear or faith, but of wisdom. It is wise to know that attacks are coming and to prepare for them. Not anticipating spiritual opposition leaves believers vulnerable so that when an attack does come it is all the more acute. But neither the attacks nor the enemy is the focal point; Christ is. Jesus himself endured Satan's most intense and violent opposition and emerged in a victory that casts itself over eternity. Satan is already defeated.

If you have made the commitment to follow God, he is not unaware of what you will face from Satan. God knows what is ahead just as well as he knows what is behind. God will not abandon you or leave you without the resources to walk through the pressure without falling. He will not allow you to be so overwhelmed that you will be forced to concede defeat. Step forward in faith and confidence, believing that Jesus has indeed overcome the "bent one" of our universe. God has prepared the path for you to walk forward without fear of being thwarted.

Despite all these things, overwhelming victory is ours through Christ, who loved us. ROMANS 8:37

8 *Thulcandra is the world we do not know. It alone is outside the heaven, and no message comes from it.* CHAP. 19, P. 119

Sorrow overwhelms Ransom when he comes to see his home, Earth, as it truly is: Thulcandra is the "silent" planet, which alone is marred by sin and is estranged from all other worlds. The eldila (guardian spirits) of Thulcandra remain out of communication with the eldila of other worlds.

Lewis's image is not exaggerated. Thulcandra illustrates sin's immense power to alienate, which it must do in order to thrive. The choice to sin is always a choice to reject God's directives, and the easiest way to do that is by estranging yourself from God so that his words are almost inaudible. But sin seeks to fracture not just one, but *every* plane of relationships. Sin falsely woos us into believing that our desires are the obvious priority. It makes us believe that other people can be stepped on as we sacrifice their good for our own.

Each successive sin draws us more and more inward into a tighter and darker knot of distortion and loneliness. But the sin is so encompassing and the self-focus so intense that we become oblivious to the repercussions. Like Lewis's Thulcandrians, those trapped in sin and apart from Christ have no conception of the gravity of their loss and isolation.

Given another vantage point, as Ransom is, can you see your true position? What sins, if any, are you guarding? How are they leading you away from family, neighbors, and other believers? You can start taking steps back to see, hear, and reconnect with God and his creation.

Finally, I confessed all my sins to you and stopped trying to hide my guilt. I said to myself, "I will confess my rebellion to the LORD.*" And you forgave me! All my guilt is gone.* PSALM 32:5

9 *"[Y]ou have taken many vain troubles to avoid standing where you stand now."*

[Ransom said,] "That is true, Oyarsa. Bent creatures are full of fears."

CHAP. 18, P. 121

For several chapters of *Out of the Silent Planet*, Ransom avoids appearing before Oyarsa, Malacandra's guardian. The evil actions of others and his own fears keep Ransom away. Now he stands before Oyarsa at last and is asked to give an account of his avoidance. Ransom speaks a truth that only the most honest believers will admit about their own discipleship: obedience is often a struggle not so much because God's will is unclear as because his motives are—which makes his will undesirable and, therefore, frightening.

Oyarsa is equally unclear about Ransom's fear. Once he comes to understand Ransom better, he realizes that Ransom was completely unaware of the eldil's motives in sending for Ransom.

When God's directive carries with it a potential cost—loss of comfort, of position, of pride, of life—fear can overshadow doctrine. We forget our tiny stature in light of God's power and sovereignty, and we run. Fear supplies us with an underlying bravado so that we think we are clever enough, fast enough, or simply desperate enough to squeak past God's notice and commands.

Fear then becomes the compass point that we follow; it only disorients, however. Lost, we stumble and spin in our folly, multiplying errors but never straying entirely from what we are seeking to avoid. Fears motivate us to flee a calling that we cannot understand or accept, to board a ship to take us as far from God's direction as Jonah's Tarshish was from Nineveh. But like Jonah's and Ransom's, those flight endeavors will fail. Fears brought distress and danger to them and to others whose lives they touched, but in the end, both men planted their feet at the epicenter of their fear: Jonah marched through the heart of his enemies' capital city (see Jonah 3), and Ransom presented himself to the unpredictable Oyarsa. Both still bore their fears, and both ended up exactly where they were called to be. But their fears and their resigned obedience were not the ends of their stories.

The LORD of Heaven's Armies has spoken—who can change his plans? When his hand is raised, who can stop him? ISAIAH 14:27

10 *You are guilty of no evil, Ransom of Thulcandra, except a little*
fearfulness. For that, the journey you go on is your pain, and perhaps
your cure. CHAP. 21, P. 142

Bent creatures—even redeemed bent creatures—are indeed full of fears, which misdirect, bring harm to, and fracture the church. But the glory of faith in Christ is our matchless hope. The hope and regeneration that we receive through Christ mean that our fears, even the fears that have brought us to our most dismal failures, do not determine our futures. Yet another wondrous gem of grace is that God has designed the life of a disciple as a journey. It is ongoing as well as incapable in itself of exhausting hope.

The future is never wholly revealed to us, but we can be certain that in the future, and probably sooner than we would wish, we will again experience the call of God intersecting with personal risks in our lives. We are continually offered the opportunity to choose better than we did before and to leave fearfulness behind us as a lesson instead of a pattern. We can choose to walk ahead obediently, but not in ignorance or in illusion that the next steps will be easier or safer in some way; loss and danger and facing the undesirable are ever possible. The journey Ransom faces at the end of his time on Malacandra presents him with the same danger that has terrified him ever since his arrival—that of his likely death—this time as a result of being charged with keeping a watch on the evil in his world. The circumstances have not changed, but Ransom has.

We can choose, as Ransom does, to recognize the dangers, to remember our past, and to still obey, trusting in the superiority of the goodness of God and his purposes. We can turn away from our past error of giving in to fear and, instead, transform that former impediment into a tool of our cure.

We can rejoice, too, when we run into problems and trials, for we know that they
help us develop endurance. And endurance develops strength of character, and
character strengthens our confident hope of salvation. And this hope will not lead
to disappointment. ROMANS 5:3-5

CHAPTER 22

Studies in Words

WHEN GOD MADE US IN HIS IMAGE, he gave us words. And with words, he commanded obedience and spoke judgment on disobedience.

Who can deny the centrality of words to what it means to be human? Like all other gifts, this one can be used for good or for evil. Who has not been deeply hurt by words? Who has not been healed or reconciled by words well spoken? Words are a gift, and they require careful and faithful stewardship. It is not surprising that Lewis, a man who lived by words in his vocation and avocation, would write about their history and meaning. *Studies in Words*, like a few other books reflected on in this volume, is the fruit of Lewis's professional labor and grew out of lectures given at Cambridge University in the later years of his career. Most of the book is of mainly scholarly interest, tracing the meaning of ten key words (and others in their family) over time: *nature, sad, wit, free, sense, simple, conscience* and *conscious, world,* and *life*—with a few pages on the phrase *I dare say.* Because not everyone has the talent to do this work, we can take advantage of the work of those like Lewis who do, though only serious students of the medieval and Renaissance periods will likely want the help.

But there are a few items of general interest and importance, too. Most of these will be found in Lewis's introduction to the book and in the final chapter, "At the Fringe of Language." Because we can be either faithful or unfaithful stewards of our language, in his introduction Lewis taught us how to be involved practically in preserving our legacy. For example, we commit "verbicide" or "word murder" by using evaluative words instead of descriptive ones. Rather than laboring to understand and describe, we resort to words such as *good* and *bad,* never bothering to say why. Lewis was not so naive as to think that language could or should be frozen. Words change meanings, along with culture and habits of use. But from this fact two general principles emerge.

First, Lewis said that if we pay attention, we can help ensure that our language remains serviceable for effective communication as long as possible. Second, by studying words in their historical context, we may know what important texts from the past have to tell us. The problem comes with words that seem to fit the text with a common modern meaning but that have actually changed to the point of making misreading the norm. The final chapter is about what language can and cannot do and how it changes. Lewis observed that language is poor at describing complex shapes or movements—diagram and gesture are better for these things. On the other hand, language does a good job at communicating emotion. Lewis showed us how poetic language does this successfully.

Studies in Words is not difficult reading and repays the effort by making us better readers.

1   *[K]nowledge is necessary. Intelligence and sensibility by themselves are not enough.*   CHAP. 1, P. 4

The type of knowledge that Lewis was describing here is exegesis—the process of investigative scholarship that accurately uncovers an author's original meaning. This is no casual understanding, no easy comprehension that keeps the concept at a distance. It is deep and experiential and completely unlike an "intelligent" but shallow cognitive understanding.

And so we come to the parallel: *knowing God.* Those two simple words encompass the complex whole of the Christian life. They denote both intimacy and increasing profundity. True interpersonal *knowledge* is the core of spiritual life. The Bible tells us that through his natural creation God has made visible "his invisible qualities—his eternal power and divine nature" (Romans 1:20). But deductions from general revelation alone are not true knowledge. Such recognition falls far short of what God desires for us and from us. He does not want a distant club of weak, uncommitted admirers who nod their intellectual heads at his existence and continue their lives without any alteration. He offers instead familial relationships, adoption as children, and acceptance as co-heirs with his Son. He promises the bond of marriage between himself—the Lord of the universe—and his bride, the church.

These are images of relationships of extreme intimacy, demanding extreme investments. To know God as he condescends to let us know him requires our all. It is not only a question of *knowing* what is right, of vaguely worshiping God because we cognitively accept who he is. Knowing God means reordering our lives to line up with his purposes, becoming who he desires us to be.

Everything else is worthless when compared with the infinite value of knowing Christ Jesus my Lord. For his sake I have discarded everything else, counting it all as garbage, so that I could gain Christ. . . . I want to know Christ and experience the mighty power that raised him from the dead. PHILIPPIANS 3:8, 10

2   *But it is not enough to make sense. We want to find the sense the author intended.*   CHAP. I, P. 5

In this passage Lewis was addressing the laughable work of scholars who draw seemingly "brilliant" interpretations of literature that have not the faintest connection with the author's original purpose. Unfortunately, that kind of arrogance and error is not limited to the world of literature.

One aspect of the Bible's beauty is its timelessness: the perpetuity of its messages and the universality that makes it vital to every culture, time, and individual. But the Bible is not so universal that it has abandoned definite meaning. We have wearisome examples of those who fail to uncover those truly biblical messages and instead warp Scripture to match their predetermined agendas as they claim support for ungodly rhetoric and actions.

Less reprehensible, but more common, is the individualistic devotional treasure hunt of seeking what the Bible has to say to *me*, for *me*, which can result in the same type of twisting. Those who narrow their reading to that lens can easily find "support" for decisions they've already made, "guidance" that matches their prized wishes, and "values" that replicate their pet interests. They can dismiss all that is uncomfortable and challenging by ignoring other passages or crafting an interpretation to make the words parrot their desired message.

But that is not truly reading God's Word, and it involves no communion with its author. Instead, it is a ludicrous approach. Think of God's nature, his unfathomable goodness and wisdom. What self-fabricated message could exceed the meaning that God has already embedded in his words? God's Word is worth our devotion, study, meditation, and memorization only when we are disciplined to approach it with integrity and with an eagerness to uncover what God is saying through it. But to do so, we have to put ourselves and our agendas aside, consciously and humbly giving up our filters and allowing ourselves to perceive God's true intention, which in the end is the only sense that matters.

Open my eyes to see the wonderful truths in your instructions.   PSALM 119:18

3   *Verbicide, the murder of a word, happens in many ways. Inflation is one of the commonest.*   CHAP. 1, P. 7

Through language we can be used by God as his means of healing in the world, to bring hope, light, freedom, comfort, encouragement, joy. But we can also dull language's capacity to be used for God's purposes by stretching words beyond true meaning. Lewis had cause to critique this misapplication. What strength or truth is there in the description "God is *love*," when the same descriptor is lazily parceled out to describe not only relationships but also our affinities for clothes, desserts, and sports? *Awesome* has long since been worn out from common overuse and underapplication, so that it no longer approaches an accurate description of God.

In speech and in print, divergent meanings are crowded into one word without thought, resulting not in the communication of ideas or truth but merely in noisy air. Words are "puffed up" until they have no substance and have lost any power to heal or impart grace. With such flabby language, how can we hope to communicate God's message to the world, a message that is truly awesome and incredible, literally *unbelievable* apart from his Spirit?

Perhaps this seems an esoteric point, something to be reserved for grammarians and English professors. But God clearly values meaning and precision in language. Think of God's careful preservation of his Holy Word. Think of Jesus' pronouncement that not a letter of the law would be eliminated or lost (see Matthew 5:18). Consider also his condemnation of elaborate vows: "Just say a simple, 'Yes, I will' or 'No, I won't'" (Matthew 5:37).

Above all, think of God's painstaking sacrifice of living and suffering as the Word made flesh in order to communicate the gospel in a way that his human creation could understand. View your words as a gift and a tool, and ask God to help you sharpen them so that you will be better equipped to speak truth to those around you.

I tell you this, you must give an account on judgment day for every idle word you speak.   MATTHEW 12:36

4   *[T]he greatest cause of verbicide is the fact that most people are obviously far more anxious to express their approval and disapproval of things than to describe them.*   CHAP. I, P. 7

When did we grow so quick to label? To use Lewis's imagery, dozens of terms have been recklessly murdered in the crush to publicize to the world that others are not like us. So often the labels never address meaning but become potent shorthand for more pejorative terms.

It's easier to dismiss others and their ideas when they bear labels—deserved or otherwise—that signify their place in a separate, more misguided camp. From our more secure ground, where little is questioned or evaluated, true understanding of any outsiders is unnecessary. We have no need to communicate with or understand them, because we know the simple facts of our rightness and their error. Or so we think.

Thus the labels are forced further from any proximity to their true sense. This sort of labeling, though, shines as poor a light on the labeler as on the judged. Those who unjustly judge magnify their own disproportionate anger, disdain, and lack of love. They unwittingly become advertisements of attitudes and behaviors that are as ungodly as what they are condemning—if not more so. They cannot know that, though, because they are too filled with opposition to truly see what they are opposing.

This is why the Bible warns us not to speak in hasty wrath. We cannot see things as they are, and we certainly are in no position to truly engage those who have encountered us when we are blinded with anger. There may indeed be points of contention, but the real issues of importance will never be reached because of the swelling anger that shrouds them.

Take time to pray and calm yourself before judging others. If you cannot speak or write of them without tripping over words overladen with your own exaggerated feelings and judgments, then take care; you may be committing *verbicide*, murdering your own words as well as another's character.

Look beneath the surface so you can judge correctly.   JOHN 7:24

5

[A]ll studies end in doubts.

CHAP. I, P. 9

One of the paradoxes of the Christian life is that the more believers learn and grow, the more sensitive they become to how much they do not know. Maturity brings humility—a better appreciation of God's perfection and of our distance from it. Faith becomes deeper, though not necessarily more solid. It is less rigid than in its first days, often because believers have come to experience the unique power of doubt.

Those young in their faith often dismiss doubt as a shameful lack of faith. But doubt is not unbelief; they are quite distinct. Lewis and his fellow Oxford writers knew that. They were men of impressive scholarship and faith, but they were also men who welcomed doubt and the work that it did in their lives. Doubt recognizes the tensions and the ambiguities of life and, most important, our inability to grasp truth with the same timing and depth as God does. Doubt can herald the perseverance of the desire to believe despite circumstances, mentalities, and feelings that work precisely against belief. With the foundation of a commitment to Christ, doubt becomes the cry of belief in the dark and the starting point of new, deeper insight.

Learning is critical to this kind of faith-building doubt. More study of God's Word, more interactions with believers from other life experiences, more principles gained from other cultures can stretch our vision of God and the church and can leave us with more questions than before. This should not be avoided but welcomed. One cannot entrench oneself in pride when a doubt is pushing for further examination. Doubt can motivate us to continually seek God's perspective and guidance and to reaffirm our submission to his guidance, as doubt reminds us that none of us have perfect vision.

Now our knowledge is partial and incomplete. . . . Now we see things imperfectly, like puzzling reflections in a mirror, but then we will see everything with perfect clarity. All that I know now is partial and incomplete, but then I will know everything completely, just as God now knows me completely.

I CORINTHIANS 13:9, 12

6   *We are not born with all the virtues, they don't come of their own accord. We have to work at them.*   CHAP. 2, P. 47

Lewis offered the above words as a possible, but not definitive, translation of Seneca's Latin. However accurate that translation is, it certainly resounds with biblical truth. Resolve must follow understanding, and effort follow resolve, in order for lasting changes to come. Christians are to be new creations (see 2 Corinthians 5:17, NIV), and this renovation is a process of time and effort. It seems axiomatic to say that change comes over time, but its simplicity belies the intensity of the challenge. Natural paths are worn deep, and that which is habitual is not readily supplanted.

Desiring virtue is fairly simple; achieving it is the much more trying work of prayer, tears, and grinding dedication. The effort to imitate Christ is so contrary to the natural way of life that discouragement is a ready by-product. It is one that can skew perspective until we ask, with sincere bafflement, *why* we ever attempted to involve ourselves in such an unnatural struggle in the first place. If virtues are so good, why should attaining them be such a battle?

We must not forget our origins. We do not come into the world as creatures of virtuous perfection. The Holy Spirit changes our nature, yes, but does not instantly endow us with every good quality. Sometimes the word of encouragement that we need in the midst of the challenge is the simple reminder that we are aiming for what is contrary to our entire lives up until this point, and turning such a tide is a work of resistance but, above all, it is a *work*.

The sinful nature wants to do evil, which is just the opposite of what the Spirit wants. And the Spirit gives us desires that are the opposite of what the sinful nature desires. . . . Those who belong to Christ Jesus have nailed the passions and desires of their sinful nature to his cross and crucified them there. Since we are living by the Spirit, let us follow the Spirit's leading in every part of our lives.

GALATIANS 5:17, 24-25

7

The distinction between having had enough and having had too much is, as we all know, a fine one. CHAP. 3, P. 77

The truth of this statement by Lewis rings clear far beyond the world of etymology. Gross consumerism is so pervasive around the globe that it has almost lost its power to stun. Consumption is stoked by professional ads and by acquaintances who urge us to "get more" because "you deserve it" and who chide us to "never settle for less." The underlying presuppositions about instant satisfaction and the inherent superiority of "more" are rarely examined.

There is no question of limits and no caution about the gradual passing from being satisfied to sated to gorged. The sickening weight of this kind of overindulgence is never acknowledged. Decadence is no longer a critique, but a flavor. Simplicity is synonymous with stupid, and lack of ambition with folly. Like the foolish man in Luke 12, we tear down our barns day and night to make room for new, larger, and assuredly better ones to stuff with the excess that is not needed but hoarded with disturbing passion. Our needs are abundantly met, but not in the manner God designed. The result is not satisfaction but further hunger, further drive to consume, further self-focus—a cycle that perpetually distracts us from the work of God.

Temperance, the discipline that frees us from this cycle, teaches us to say, and to mean, "No, I am content" to others and to self. It weans us from the overstimulation of all that can be had and reacclimates us to the subtle tug within that quietly signals satisfaction.

Changing this mentality will be difficult. It will entail turning our values and perspectives around to be completely opposite of the force of the surrounding culture. It means retraining ourselves to understand that "enough" is not unattainable, that it is in fact our true definition of satisfaction. But the joy is that the shift will bring us in line with God's good, pleasing, and perfect standards (see Romans 12:2). Ask for his power to replace the slogans of consumerism with his gracious word: *contentment.* That is our true treasure.

Not that I was ever in need, for I have learned how to be content with whatever I have. I know how to live on almost nothing or with everything. I have learned the secret of living in every situation, whether it is with a full stomach or empty, with plenty or little. PHILIPPIANS 4:11-12

8 *I read some unusually violent reviews lately which were all by the same man. . . . When we get to the end we find that the critic has told us everything about himself and nothing about the book.* CHAP. 12, P. 330

So what if this critic did write his critique with more venom than objectivity? Doesn't the man have a right to his opinion? Yes, but Lewis was not critiquing the *man* for his opinion, but the *critic*. The critic holds a position of some influence. He purports to have education, background, and taste superior to those of the average person, which endow him with the ability to make expert judgments. His careless, self-centered critiques misuse this position and betray his claims.

The same danger exists in churches, where leaders claim something—maturity, experience, calling, education—that elevates them to positions of respect and authority. These leaders often fall into divisiveness and criticisms in which they allow their personal judgments to override all else. They mislead others by their own uncontrolled emotions.

This is why the Bible does not portray the role of leader as one to be taken up lightly. It cautions Christians against seeking leadership blithely and warns leaders that they are subject to more severe punishments for sins. To have the care of others' souls and the power to shape them and their faith is a solemn, holy charge. Those who accept it and then abuse the privilege in order to imprint their self-serving, untrue opinions on followers do a terrible thing. Their personal agenda replaces God's message, and if listeners are not as acute as Lewis was to recognize the overwrought individual supplanting truth, personal agendas become points of contention, sects form, and the church fragments.

Believers are at times called to judge, but to judge righteously, not through the filter of personal motives. Be cautious about thoughtlessly absorbing the words of leaders, but even more so, of leading without care.

Dear brothers and sisters, not many of you should become teachers in the church, for we who teach will be judged more strictly. JAMES 3:1

9 *The strength of our dislike is itself a probable symptom that all is not well within; that some raw place in our psychology has been touched, or else that some personal or partisan motive is secretly at work.*

CHAP. 12, P. 331

Nearly all of us know a person like the critic Lewis has described—one who slices at others without warning, maiming all with criticisms and cruel words before they can assert themselves as enemies. This is the critic whose words have driven all others away, but who still clings to sharpened words, waiting furtively to strike preemptively.

"All is not well within" by any means. Our focus naturally settles on the injustice of the attack and the sting of the words. Our inclination is to avoid the critic, but this inclination is not the answer.

Lives built around a core of pain and anger will bear the architecture of isolation, ugliness, and withdrawal—the opposite of God's design. These are persons in pain, as much pain as victims of abuse or natural disaster. Yes, critics have created a bitter cell by personal choices, but ultimately they are suffering from sin and are as much in need of God's words as "innocent victims."

Bitter critics are unattractive, and they promise us pain. But if God has placed one or more in your life, perhaps they are there to be touched by you. See an aggressive front for what it is—an inadequate attempt at protection that only exacerbates inner misery. Ask God to steel you against their cutting words and to use you to break through their bitter shell and lead them through the frightening but blessed process of releasing their hoarded pain. Reject the offense that rises at being rebuffed and reviled, and allow God to use you to speak and lead the hurting critics away from their perversion of words into healing and release.

The hearts of these people are hardened . . . so their eyes cannot see, and their ears cannot hear, and their hearts cannot understand, and they cannot turn to me and let me heal them. ACTS 28:27

10

If we were simply exercising judgment we should be calmer; less anxious to speak. And if we do speak, we shall almost certainly make fools of ourselves. CHAP. 12, P. 331

After reflecting on the tendency of critics to fall into acerbic ranting, C. S. Lewis did not conclude as you might expect. Rather than giving a detailed outline of what criticism should entail, he concluded with a general caution about any unevaluated speech. We should indeed be cautious about speaking too quickly, making fools of ourselves and hindering God's work. That is a proper starting place. But it is only a starting place. The Bible proclaims that there are times appointed for speech as well as for silence (see Ecclesiastes 3:7). Our quandary is differentiating between the two.

In their awesome personal encounters with God, several prophets had protested their inability to speak: Moses appealed to his inadequacy (Exodus 4:10), Isaiah quaked in dread over his sinfulness (Isaiah 6:5), and Jeremiah cited his youth (Jeremiah 1:6). But significantly, God did not dismiss any of them for resisting or for lack of faith. Instead, he affirmed the divine provenance of the message he gave Moses and granted him the partnership of Aaron (Exodus 4:14-16). Isaiah received the consecration of an angelic coal on his lips (Isaiah 6:6-7), and God himself touched Jeremiah's mouth to impart his words to him (Jeremiah 1:9-10). All of them then obeyed and became national trumpets of God's messages.

Perhaps God did not harshly condemn the hesitancy of Moses, Isaiah, and Jeremiah because it fueled their reliance on him. The three knew the enormity of the tasks given to them and their utter dependence on God to say anything that would have an impact on his people.

Anxiety that leads to deeper dependence on God is not a failing but a potential door to miracles. If we seek to speak with humble caution and dependence, we can be assured that God will direct us to speak, and he will provide the right words at the right time.

May the words of my mouth and the meditation of my heart be pleasing to you, O LORD, my rock and my redeemer. PSALM 19:14

CHAPTER 23

"The World's Last Night" and "Historicism"

BORROWING AN ANALOGY FROM LUTHER, Lewis reminded us in his essay "The World's Last Night" that we can fall off a horse on either side. In the past many made the matter of Christ's return almost their only interest in Jesus' teaching, to the point of making charts and predictions—failed predictions. Because of the quacks and the embarrassments, most Christians now shy away from it—a fall off the other side of the horse. The healthy view is the one recognizing that all of Jesus' teaching must be fully embraced. This includes Jesus' promise and warning that he could come at any time and that no one but the Father knows that time (see Matthew 24:36). Lewis believed that Jesus meant exactly what he said: that he did not know the time. In his incarnation, he submitted to the limitation of not knowing.

A more important reason for modern reluctance to embrace the doctrine of the Second Coming is that it stands in opposition to the great myth of progress our culture has accepted: that just as life emerged from nonlife and human emerged from animal, so the world will keep improving toward some unknown perfectibility. We have trouble accepting an abrupt end, an intervention from outside our world. But as it was in the beginning, so it shall be at the end. Neither the world as a whole nor we as individuals are independent. The doctrine of Christ's return is the medicine our sick culture needs.

The implications of this doctrine are as follows: (1) We must be ready, since he has assured us that his return will come at a time when we are not looking; and (2) we must stay faithfully at our work, since we don't know when he will come. Both hope and fear are emotions, and as such will come and go; an excess of either is unhealthy. The key is to remember that civilizations, government, charity hospitals, our lives . . . and even Earth itself will have an end. We obediently do our work with eternity in view. The most useful approach, Lewis advised, is to develop the habit of asking how an action (or lack thereof) will stand up under the final righteous judgment of the Lord. Instead of impatience or dread, we must view whatever time we have as a gift to be used. This essay gives a way of thinking "Christianly" (biblically) about the way we approach history itself. It applies to all of us, because we all live in a present moment of time that takes its meaning from what we think about the past and the future. Therefore, the placement of these reflections in proximity to those of *The Last Battle* should be clear.

The essay "Historicism" is founded on a word Lewis invented, like *scientism* elsewhere, to describe a false view or bad practice of a worthy discipline: respectively, historical and scientific research. Regarding historicism, Lewis's foundational idea was this: we cannot know the meaning of history from within history. Until we have some report from an observer who sees the way it all fits together, we will always get it wrong. Viewed ahead of time, "the lessons of history" turn out to be the meaning we place on events from our own set of values, not what was, in some objective way, really there. Even in small events, we bring our values to bear on whether they are worth including or were right or wrong, good or bad, helpful or harmful.

On the large scale, if we don't know why history exists, the end toward which it is moving, and whose purposes it is serving, then none of our formulas for interpreting it will be right. For example, how do we determine what is important enough from the vast data of six billion lives to record in a single day for consideration in tomorrow's newspaper—or a hundred (or a million) years from now?

Of course, if history has an author—or a playwright—who brought the world's stage and its players into being and will decide when the drama is over, then we can make meaningful judgments about scenes large and small. Apart from this revelation, no person, of however great an education, will ever get history right. Lewis did not mean that secular historians are worthless in finding cause-and-effect relationships—links between events. This, he would have said, is the job of a real historian. His concern lay with those who claim to find an inner meaning from the historical data itself. These he called "historicists."

We must be humble in our approach to history. Vast tracts of the past are forever beyond our reach. Of the teeming world outside ourselves at any one moment, we can know only an infinitesimal part. Of the future, we know nothing that is not revealed from beyond time. In God's judgment, how many of the world's "greats," as recorded in history books, will be great to him? In the book of Revelation, the faithful martyrs are more important than kings and emperors. History is God's story. He gets to interpret it.

1 *Every great man is partly of his own age and partly for all time. What matters . . . is always that which transcends his age, not that which he shared with a thousand forgotten contemporaries.*

"THE WORLD'S LAST NIGHT," P. 95

Throughout the course of human civilization, many individuals have made deep impact that far outlasted the eras in which they lived. You could probably name a dozen or so without breaking a sweat. Many people have followed their philosophies, using these heroes as patterns for their lives. But after centuries or millennia pass, certain views seem archaic or even false. Some views do fall victim to shortsightedness—but not all. No one other than Jesus is wholly relevant for all time.

Here, in his discussion of people's reluctance to believe in the Second Coming, Lewis is quoting the modernist point of view. If we, like the modernist, believe that Jesus was merely a product of his time—a poor man from first-century Palestine who happened to be a good teacher—then we might discount the impact or relevance of his words. *That was fine for people back then to believe in him. It gave a conquered people hope in their day-to-day struggles,* the modernist might think. Jesus' words would seem gracious and even noble, but not transcendent. Or the modernist, having heard of others claiming to be the Messiah, might discount Jesus' words as those of another crackpot. But Lewis cautioned against either limited viewpoint. His belief was that Jesus is all he claimed to be (the Son of God and therefore equal to God) and that his words are for all time, not just for one age.

Jesus warned his disciples against the deceptions of false messiahs. In the passage below, note Jesus' caution that *many* would be deceived. Was that just a caution for their era? We have only to recall the last hundred years. Many *have* claimed to be the promised Messiah and founded their own movements. Some who have not gone so far as to claim to be Jesus have claimed to speak "truth" about his return and been discredited. So, whom do we believe? You can believe the one whose promises have all come true, the one *about* whom prophecies concerning his birth and life all came to pass: Jesus.

Jesus told them, "Don't let anyone mislead you, for many will come in my name, claiming, 'I am the Messiah.' They will deceive many." MATTHEW 24:4-5

2   *It is our attempt to guess the plot of a drama in which we are the characters. But how can the characters in a play guess the plot?*

"THE WORLD'S LAST NIGHT," P. 104

Luigi Pirandello's classic play *Six Characters in Search of an Author* describes the sudden appearance of six people who interrupt a play rehearsal. The six turn out to be characters who are—you guessed it—in search of an author to write the ending of their story. But when the stage manager tries to stage their story using actors, the characters continually argue with him and with one another over how the play should be handled. Tragedy results.

In Lewis's essay on the Second Coming, he discussed Darwin's theories of evolution and used the analogy of people as actors on a stage of life that God has created. By coming up with our own theories concerning the plot, we overstep our roles as actors, Lewis asserts. It is the province of the playwright to come up with the plot. Our job is to play the parts we have been assigned. However, if we lack faith in the playwright, as the six characters lacked faith in the manager, we might rebel.

Rather than dispute Darwin's theories, Lewis discussed them to show Darwin's response to the myths—that is, the beliefs—surrounding the development of human civilization. In a way, Darwin himself was a character in a play who was trying to make sense of its plot.

Of course, in some ways we are all guilty of trying to control and predict our lives. We have our pet theories about how life "should" be. We have our career plans, five-year plans, and retirement plans, as if we can perfectly predict what the outcomes will be. In the book of Jeremiah, God used the analogy of a potter to describe how he shapes his people. Whether potter or playwright, he reserves the right to do with us as he wills. And we have two responses to this notion: we can balk, or we can bow in obedience.

The LORD gave me this message: "O Israel, can I not do to you as this potter has done to his clay? As the clay is in the potter's hand, so are you in my hand."

JEREMIAH 18:5-6

3   *What is important is not that we should always fear (or hope) about the*
   End but that we should always remember, always take it into account.

"THE WORLD'S LAST NIGHT," P. 110

It should be clear by now that Lewis had a way with words. He created poignant word pictures that helped the reader to grasp the simplest yet most profound concepts. In this essay, he says that half the battle of living life in expectation of the return of Jesus is to simply remember and take into account that the Lord is returning. He goes on to compare this awareness to that of a man of seventy who should prepare for the end of his life by making a will and keeping in mind what kinds of projects to embark upon, with the idea that he may not have twenty more years before him.

In the same way, we are not to be living life as if temporal things such as eating, drinking, and frantically trying to meet the demands of the world are the only things that count in life. Rather, we are to live as stewards given tasks that will need to be accounted for when our employer returns. This is hard to do in our *now*-oriented society, where everything has to happen in an instant. We can't stand to wait. Yet we've been waiting two thousand years for Jesus to return. Indeed, to look in the clouds for a returning Jesus is usually the last thing on our minds—yet the Bible says we will see him. He will be revealed. And remembering this should make this world's demands seem a little less insistent, a little less overwhelming in their immediacy. Someday the daily demands will be as if they never existed; something else will take precedence when the Lord returns!

We should live in this evil world with wisdom, righteousness, and devotion to God, while we look forward with hope to that wonderful day when the glory of our great God and Savior, Jesus Christ, will be revealed.   TITUS 2:12-13

4 *Frantic administration of panaceas to the world is certainly discouraged by the reflection that "this present" might be "the world's last night"; sober work for the future, within the limits of ordinary morality and prudence, is not.* "THE WORLD'S LAST NIGHT," P. 111

It is interesting that Lewis used the word *panaceas* here. *Panacea* is defined as "a universal remedy or cure-all." He went on to talk about how people are always jumping on pet doctrines, such as the Second Coming, and overemphasizing them like a drunk man climbing up on a horse and falling off the other side.

It is easy for us as Christians, after discovering a long-neglected truth, to suddenly construct a panacea of our own. We're tempted to decipher the signs of the times and create a rigid set of standards by which we may "cure" other sinners of their tendencies to love the world more than God. We then give them a stamp of approval if they meet the standards. The world is seen as the enemy and we are here just hanging on and doing our duty till Jesus comes. By contrast, Lewis suggested that working soberly at the vocation to which we were called and being faithful are the best preparations we can make for the return of the Lord.

Though this present world will one day end, there is a new reality pending. If we want to make a difference here, it is better to simply love the people in the world rather than trying to force them to accept our cure-all ideas. After all, Jesus said that the most important commandment is to love (see Matthew 22:37-40). This, more than anything else, can help people sense a reality beyond the commonplace. We can also recall that we didn't free ourselves from the misconceptions to which others have fallen prey. As Paul said, Christ is the one who set us free, but not free to judge others.

You have died with Christ, and he has set you free from the spiritual powers of this world. COLOSSIANS 2:20

5 *[H]appy are those whom it [the final judgment] finds laboring in their vocations, whether they were merely going out to feed the pigs or laying good plans to deliver humanity a hundred years hence.*

"THE WORLD'S LAST NIGHT," P. III

Judgment. We can hardly grasp such a word. Not only are we uncomfortable with its starkness, its moralistic implications, but we find it offensive to our right to live our lives as we choose. And yet here Lewis laid it on the line. There will be a judgment, and this knowledge should add a dimension to our lives that will be either a showcase of glory for the person who faithfully did the best possible job with what was given or else the dismal failure of a person who abused what was given. It doesn't matter if the job was great or significant in the world's eyes; what matters is the work being what the master ordered.

One interesting aspect of this verse is the idea that we will be judged according to our responsibility. One who has been given great responsibility will be judged on a greater scale. The one who has been given less responsibility will be judged based on how much was given.

If we are faithful with the little we have, we will receive a reward equal to those who were given much. This is why we are not to pass judgment— that is the sole duty of the employer who created the job description and dispersed the resources for the job.

A faithful, sensible servant is one to whom the master can give the responsibility of managing his other household servants and feeding them. If the master returns and finds that the servant has done a good job, there will be a reward. I tell you the truth, the master will put that servant in charge of all he owns.

MATTHEW 24:45-47

6 *We shall not only believe, we shall know, know beyond doubt in every fibre of our appalled or delighted being, that as the Judge has said, so we are: neither more nor less nor other.*

"THE WORLD'S LAST NIGHT," P. 113

Who are we? We can label ourselves in many different ways. By our current jobs, for instance. Or by our personality traits: outgoing, reserved, funny. But Lewis went a bit deeper here, referring to that uncomfortable moment when we will stand before the Judge naked and vulnerable, stripped of all the titles and veneers, with all our thoughts, motives, and true selves laid before him. Then we will know who we really are, for what he decides will show the whole sum of our beings. Character descriptions such as *faithful*, *honest*, and *true* will become the gems on our crowns and will shine with the splendor of the one who brought all things into being. Words such as *false*, *petty*, and *selfish* will sear us to the core, exposing the terrible truth of decisions we made and thoughts we had that we hoped no one else knew about.

God disciplines his children because he sees what they are becoming. He knows that there will be a judgment, and he cares enough to prepare his people for that event. We can choose to respond positively to his correction and his efforts to shape us according to his good purposes.

The Lord is coming with countless thousands of his holy ones to execute judgment on the people of the world. He will convict every person of all the ungodly things they have done and for all the insults that ungodly sinners have spoken against him. JUDE 1:14-15

7   *We cannot always be excited. We can, perhaps train ourselves to*
ask . . . how the thing which we are saying or doing . . . will look
when the irresistible light streams in upon it.

"THE WORLD'S LAST NIGHT," P. 113

At the time of the final judgment, what things will be judged? Lewis suggested we will be judged by the things we do. These activities—what we say and do—will be subjected to a fire that will burn away all activities that are not eternal. Lewis went even further, using the analogy of a dress: a woman tries it on and sees that it looks nice in the soft light of the store, but when subjected to the relentless brightness of day, the dress looks gaudy or drab. Often we can see our actions and words only in the blurry haze we cast over them with either justifications or self-condemnation. But if we subject ourselves to the severe mercy of God and let his light shine upon our actions—asking him to show them for what they really are—the truth can set us free.

One way to know whether we are really on the right path, in fact, is to hold up to that light whatever course we are on. As Jesus says in John 3:21, if you do what's right, you need not fear the light or shrink back from it in shame. Anything in your life that you would rather die than let others know about may be an area of darkness that God is trying to expose. Better to expose it now, confessing to God and perhaps even a trusted brother or sister, than to wait till "the irresistible light" shines upon it before the whole world.

Those who do what is right come to the light so others can see that they are doing
what God wants.   JOHN 3:21

8 *We must guard against the emotional overtones of a phrase like "the judgment of history." It might lure us into . . . idolizing . . . the goddess History.* "HISTORICISM," P.102

Lewis was not opposed to the study of history. After all, he wrote an entire classic study in The Oxford History of English Literature series. But in his important essay called "Historicism," Lewis distinguished history from what he termed *historicism*. Legitimate history shows what we think happened from the available evidence and even proposes explanations for causes and effects. Historicism, on the other hand, is an attempt to see an overall pattern in human history or to interpret the meaning of history from the inside—with no more than the events to go on. However, historical events do not tell us what is important and why. That is the role of revelation.

The overall meaning of history can come only from someone who knows the whole story from beginning to end and all its details. Without God's revelation, we would know neither beginning nor end. Further, we have only a very few of the innumerable details from the flood of time, and even if we knew by some miracle everything that happened, we would have no template for interpreting it. We bring an outside standard even to the selection of what we include for discussion. When, apart from revelation, we assume that pain or the collapse of civilizations or military conquest is a judgment for or against, we enthrone the goddess History.

Lewis's targets—the ones he named in the essay—are the numerous pagan interpretations, Hegel and Marx in the modern era, and Christian historicists who make irresponsible time lines. Though Lewis gives specific examples, the caution is timeless. The simple fact that something happens or that we like it or dislike it, that we find it convenient or burdensome, is no more an accurate measure for meaning in our personal histories than for the larger sweeps of time. As Lewis showed, this is a tendency we must guard against.

The wisdom of this world is foolishness to God. As the Scriptures say, "He traps the wise in the snare of their own cleverness." I CORINTHIANS 3:19

9 *We have no notion what stage in the journey we have reached.*
. . . We must freely admit that most—that nearly all—history . . . is,
and will remain, wholly unknown to us. "HISTORICISM," PP. 106–107

Do you remember—*really* remember—everything you have ever seen, thought about, said, and done? It simply isn't possible. Every moment that passes is crammed with teeming sensations and events, all becoming a part of history, mostly with no remaining evidence and mostly forgotten. This was Lewis's point. History is really based on a collection of fragments— a parchment here, a painting there, a manuscript of the bits and pieces that people have found—and through these fragments we attempt to construct an idea of history based on a time line. In his published inaugural Cambridge lecture, "De Descriptione Temporum," Lewis described his philosophy of history as being less like a botanist who categorizes a vast collection of events in a systematic manner and more like a woman arranging cut flowers. There is so much that is unknown, he said, that we cannot even begin to really understand the forest of the past.

Let's take this one step further and even venture to say that we are equally limited in our concept of God's work in our lives (never mind the world). We often base our view of God and his work on fragments of memory or information from multiple, partially remembered sources. We try to make time lines and, fitting our age into that time line, guess what God is doing and what stage we have reached in human history. The fact is, we don't know. God is much more vast and complex than our minds can comprehend.

Even though we grow older and learn more, we may end up truly knowing less, because we make erroneous conclusions based on a wrong set of fragments. Since we can't know the whole pattern of history from within its events, we must place our own fragments within what God has chosen to reveal in his Word. We must also come to God as a child with an attitude of humility and ask to be taught, and when we cannot understand, obey. God knows how the fragments of our lives are supposed to fit the big picture.

We don't remember what happened in the past, and in future generations, no one will remember what we are doing now. ECCLESIASTES 1:11

10 *God is every moment "revealed in history," that is, in what MacDonald called "the holy present." Where, except in the present, can the Eternal be met?* "HISTORICISM," P. 113

What does it mean to live in the holy present? According to Lewis, that is where we find God. In many of Lewis's writings, such as his essay "The Weight of Glory," we can see this view of the holy present, which is glimpsing the glory of God in his creation, especially his human creation. It means that we refuse to hold the moment hostage to the past or the future. We have only the present moment in which to worship and obey.

We can learn this lesson from children. They are often totally immersed in the present experience—transfixed by awe of a kitten they have found or crying angrily over the hurt they have just received, only to be playing happily moments later with the same child who hurt them. To be a child is to be totally present in the now of life.

Unfortunately, sometimes the more experience or the more education we have, the more we try to predict the outcome of our circumstances. We try to budget our time to ensure its being spent toward future goals to the extent that we habitually trade living in the real present for living in the imaginary future. Or, we start to think how much better it was in the good old days, instead of seeing the glory of God present in the things he has given us now.

We may take the history of the past and impose it upon our view of the present, and when it doesn't match up, discard the experience instead of being open to the fresh understanding we might gain from it. This is our challenge: to live, aware and clearheaded, looking at things through eyes that seek for fresh perspectives on the Creator and his creation with child-like awe. We cannot live in the past, and the future is neither guaranteed nor any more accessible. We only meet God and do the work he has given us in the present moment.

I saw that there is nothing better for people than to be happy in their work. That is why we are here! No one will bring us back from death to enjoy life after we die.
ECCLESIASTES 3:22

CHAPTER 24

The Last Battle

THIS NOBLE BOOK, 1956 WINNER of the prestigious Carnegie Medal, is a worthy ending to the Chronicles of Narnia. Lewis stated that *The Last Battle* portrays the Antichrist and the second coming of Jesus, both prophesied in the Bible. The themes of faith and doubt have much in common with *Prince Caspian*, which turns on the characters' belief in the old stories about Narnia. In *The Last Battle*, the outcome hinges on belief regarding the stories about Narnia's future. The main antagonist, Shift the Ape, manipulates the gullible donkey, Puzzle, into putting on a lion skin and pretending to be Aslan, hidden away in a stable, emerging only at night to be glimpsed. The equally gullible populace believes the ruse and follows Shift's command for ever-higher taxes, death to the Narnian trees, and slavery for the Narnian animals.

Shift succeeds in bringing Narnia under the heel of its enemy, Calormen. Under such suffering even the good Narnians, such as the young King Tirian, begin to wonder if Aslan's not being tame means that he is also cruel. To maintain his power over the people, Shift claims supernatural authority. He deliberately associates Aslan with Tash, the false god of the Calormenes, calling the combination Tashlan. Thinking only to fool the people, Shift calls on Tash to come. Tash not only comes but claims Shift for his own.

One after another of the good Narnians and the evil forces against them are thrown into the stable (or enter of their own will). Though the human battle seems lost, Aslan has never lost control. In the stable, with its incarnational symbolism, all must look Aslan in the face. Those who do not love him—they seem almost to judge themselves—go to Tash (Satan). Those belonging to Aslan enter the new and real Narnia, of which the old was a mere shadow.

Waiting in the new Narnia for Eustace, Jill, Tirian, and the Narnians in this story are all the characters we have grown to love from the other books. Aslan makes a door separating the old from the new. The sun goes out in the old Narnia, and Aslan closes the door on it forever. But there is no loss—only gain. The newfound strength, energy, and sheer aliveness of the characters are joined to the beauty of the landscape. They have entered a world where nothing is forbidden, because all is goodness and all are pure. A holiday spirit prevails in joyous celebration beyond the power of paraphrase.

Roonwit . . . gave me this message to your Majesty: to remember that all worlds draw to an end and that noble death is a treasure which no one is too poor to buy. CHAP. 1, P. 91

Farsight the Eagle has the sad task of telling Prince Tirian that Roonwit the Centaur has given his life trying to bring a message to Cair Paravel. Just before that message was delivered, in a conversation with Jewel the Unicorn, Lucy had reflected on how wonderful it would be if Narnia would never come to an end. Jewel's response was that all worlds come to an end, except for Aslan's country. Here now is the confirmation of Jewel's words, tragic though it seems.

It may have appeared that Roonwit's message was unsuccessful and his death in vain, but even as he lay dying, he saw a glimpse of the glory that would arise from his sacrifice. His hope rested not on the world he was fighting for but on the world to come.

We're reminded of the long list of saints mentioned in Hebrews who were tortured for their faith and did not get to see on earth the hope for which they were fighting. But they saw it "all from a distance and welcomed it." It is said that there have been more martyrs dying for their faith around the world in this century and the last one than there have been in all of history. We can only imagine that this is because God has given his Spirit to these precious people to be able to see from a distance the heavenly country and the heavenly Kingdom for which they are fighting. Though our struggle may seem minor in comparison, we are fighting the same battle: to remember that all worlds come at last to an end. May we finish well.

All these people died still believing what God had promised them. They did not receive what was promised, but they saw it all from a distance and welcomed it. They agreed that they were foreigners and nomads here on earth.

HEBREWS 11:13

2   *I was going to say I wished we'd never come. But I don't. . . . Even if we are killed. I'd rather be killed fighting for Narnia than grow old and stupid at home.*   CHAP. 9, P. 96

This is Jill's response to Eustace's question as to whether they would die in Narnia. Her words reveal an attitude of profound understanding of the joy of living a life to its fullest and being willing to lay down one's life for a worthy cause, rather than protecting it and clinging to memories of the past. It is this attitude that Jesus commends in the passage about losing one's life only to find it again. Because we as humans dislike pain and suffering, we often cling to things that we think will give us comfort, only to find that in the end they don't comfort us anymore.

How can we testify to this truth in our own lives? Maybe if we think back to our younger days, we can remember when we felt most alive. Did those times involve just surviving from day to day, or did they involve taking risks and doing something we really believed in? Isn't that what makes the great stories great—when the heroes are being put through terrible situations they eventually conquer?

By contrast, the more comfortable life is and the more we cling to our possessions and our routines, the more dull life becomes. We tend to complain more and find less for which to be thankful. Why is this? Perhaps it is because in our clinging to temporal things, they lose their capacity to give satisfaction. Letting them go infuses them with new and deeper meaning.

Let's challenge ourselves to remember afresh the joy of living dangerously in some activity that brings forth God's Kingdom, rather than focusing on living comfortably in a kingdom based on temporal possessions that we will in the end come to despise anyway.

Those who love their life in this world will lose it. Those who care nothing for their life in this world will keep it for eternity.   JOHN 12:25

3
"[W]e shall all, one by one, pass through that dark door before morning." . . .

[Jewel said,] "It may be for us the door to Aslan's country and we shall sup at his table tonight." CHAP. 12, P. 128

The dark door here refers to the door of the stable where at first Puzzle the donkey was housed, but which is now home to something far more horrible—or so everyone believes. So far the Narnians have seen a blinding light come out of the stable and consume Shift, the ape. When Eustace is thrown in as well, the dwarf, Poggin, comments that he would rather die a hundred horrible deaths than pass through the door. Jewel's response above is ironic, for though it seems here that he is speaking figuratively of dying, he doesn't realize how true that statement is. It turns out to be not just a trite, comforting statement to allay their dread, but rather a true hope and, soon afterward, a reality.

In some ways this kind of poignant reality of the nearness of heaven is enviable. Many elderly people, others who are in chronic pain, and those for whom the world has lost its appeal understand and live with a constant desire for heaven. Younger people, who seem to have their whole lives before them, might pity those longing to escape this world. They have a hard time identifying with this longing, because they're under the illusion that their deepest longings can be fulfilled in this life. But that is a fallacy.

As Lewis explained in other writings, we often do not recognize our longing as a longing for heaven, because we do not realize that *nothing on this earth* can really satisfy that part of us. We have learned to label our desires as something else indefinable and may strive to attain that desire through all different means; in the end, the desire remains unfulfilled because we were made to live in heaven in the first place.

They were looking for a better place, a heavenly homeland. That is why God is not ashamed to be called their God, for he has prepared a city for them.
HEBREWS 11:16

4 *She wasted all her school time wanting to . . . race on to the silliest time of one's life as quick as she can and then stop there as long as she can.*
CHAP. 12, P. 135

These words are spoken of Susan, who unfortunately is not able to come back to Narnia because she stopped believing in Aslan. She is stuck in an adolescent stage of an illusion of freedom and vanity in which all she cares about is being beautiful and popular and enjoying herself.

It's so sad to think that the same Susan who wept for Aslan and saw him rise from the dead should trade that knowledge for a life of vanity. Things might have been so different if Susan had only remembered that she was a queen meant to rule a kingdom—if she had not traded her birthright for some baubles of modern society.

If you look at our society, you'll see the same pervasive sickness dominating our culture. Everyone wants to act and look young or live the easy life but still reap the benefits of sensible hard work and sacrifice. Many feel cheated when they don't get what they want, even after spending a lot of money trying to achieve their goals. Half the battle is to realize that this is not the way we were meant to live. The best way to combat this type of thinking is to remember the world to which we were called. It may not be Narnia, but all that Narnia represents. It would be good to learn the hard lesson here from Susan's life and keep our sights set on Jesus and not ourselves.

Think about the things of heaven, not the things of earth. For you died to this life, and your real life is hidden with Christ in God. COLOSSIANS 3:2-3

5 *The sweet air grew suddenly sweeter. A brightness flashed behind them. All turned. . . . There stood his [Tirian's] heart's desire, huge and real, the golden Lion, Aslan himself.* CHAP. 13, P. 146

In this scene, the children and Tirian, the last king of Narnia, have been thrown into the dreaded stable along with the dwarfs and are waiting for something terrible to happen to them. Instead, they find the fulfillment of all their desires in Aslan himself. Though sometimes they doubted, they had tried to stay true to him through all the deceptions and battles, even when they thought that perhaps he had become cruel. It was one thing to hope for him, but another altogether to see him face-to-face, especially for Tirian, who had never met him before.

This image of the fulfillment of our desires is such a comforting one, especially when we consider how long we have waited or the fact that we've been disillusioned or brokenhearted yet still clung to what we believed about God. Sometimes as we wait, we sense his Spirit in a moment in a church service or lingering in a beautiful song, a moment when we sense the air growing sweeter.

John took this meeting one step further when he wrote that when we see Jesus, "We will be like him, for we will see him as he really is." John was not talking just about a change that happens when we throw off the shell of our human bodies and become heavenly beings. There seems to be another change simply from seeing Jesus. When the children see Aslan in Narnia, he breathes on them and strengthens them; when we see Jesus as he is in heaven, there will be such a profound change that we will actually *be* like him. We will become mirrors that reflect his glory the moment we meet.

Dear friends, we are already God's children, but he has not yet shown us what we will be like when Christ appears. But we do know that we will be like him, for we will see him as he really is. I JOHN 3:2

6 *They have chosen cunning instead of belief. Their prison is only in their own minds, yet they are in that prison; and so afraid of being taken in that they cannot be taken out.* CHAP. 13, P. 148

The dwarfs are so tired of being taken in by the lies of the enemy that they decide not to believe in anything except themselves. As a result, when the real Aslan appears, they cannot enjoy the new things Aslan creates. As Aslan explains to Lucy, they are in a prison of their own making.

This is a very sobering thought. Don't we sometimes find ourselves falling into the same trap? We believe a lie about God or our lives only to find that we have been deceived. Our reaction then is to swing all the way to the opposite direction and decide that we will believe nothing we hear ever again.

All of us must on some level fight to believe the true God, instead of the false images of him passed on to us by people who have hurt us in God's name. It is all too easy to be wounded and then build up barriers to protect ourselves from being wounded again by refusing to believe anything at all. This is a form of darkness that can be very subtle. It also is a form of pride—pride in the fact that we must be smart, tough, and independent.

In *The Last Battle*, there were some who believed for a while in the false Aslan yet did not then shut out the real one just because they had been deceived. They, unlike the dwarfs, were able to enter into the new Narnia because they chose to believe again. The same choice lies before us.

Their minds are full of darkness; they wander far from the life God gives because they have closed their minds and hardened their hearts against him.

EPHESIANS 4:18

7 *The ladies do well to weep. See, I do so myself. . . . What world but Narnia have I ever known? It were no virtue, but great discourtesy, if we did not mourn.* CHAP. 14, P. 158

We have so many good things on this earth; heaven seems a bit esoteric compared to the very tangible joys of this world. When we have to leave them behind, we might mourn. Likewise, as the old Narnia passes away, Jill and Lucy weep to see all the beautiful things connected with their beautiful memories die and darken.

When Jesus walked on this earth, he also experienced what we experience and knew what it was like to love it and its people. Did he feel in his human body a twinge of sadness in spite of knowing what the newness of his resurrected body would be like and the new kind of relationship he would have with his disciples?

While the Resurrection was wonderful, the disciples had to be sad, knowing that their relationship with Jesus would be changed forever. He would leave earth and return to heaven. Although he promised to send the Holy Spirit, they would no longer talk with or travel the roads with Jesus. Maybe the breakfast at the seashore (see John 21) was to commemorate those times. It's no wonder Peter leaped out of the boat to see Jesus. He must have missed him.

It is often the case that after we pray and God leads us into a new venture, whether a career or ministry, we head in a new direction with not only excitement but also sadness at leaving the old. After all, the verse that declares God will wipe away all tears from our eyes (see Revelation 21:4) is probably not because of the sadness we will feel at seeing the passing away of all the old things we loved on this earth.

The one sitting on the throne said, "Look, I am making everything new!"
REVELATION 21:5

8 *Beloved, said the Glorious One, unless thy desire had been for me thou wouldst not have sought so long and so truly. For all find what they truly seek.* CHAP. 15, P. 165

God promises over and over in Scripture that those who seek him with a whole heart will find him. So it is with Emeth, who was seeking truth though he was a devoted follower of Tash. Aslan sees that Emeth isn't just interested in his gods for what he thinks they could give him but is interested and persistent in seeking the truth. Because of his desire to understand, in the end he finds in Aslan what he has sought. Lewis chose the name *Emeth*, a word that means "truth" in Turkish, for the character of a man who seeks truth all his life. In his acceptance of Emeth we see the heart of Aslan, who knows and judges everyone's heart.

Emeth is like Cornelius the centurion in Acts 10. This man is described as a person who feared God and gave generously to the poor. We don't know much about him, whether or not he was like the people in Acts 17 who worshiped an unknown God, but the biblical account states that his actions and prayers came before God, who led him to Peter. He had always feared God but didn't know Jesus or the message of salvation. As Aslan does with Emeth, God finally revealed himself to Cornelius and led him to the truth.

How sad that we sometimes confine God to the realm of our own understanding of how he works. When we do so, we might easily judge someone else's spiritual journey, believing that if he or she does not come to God in the way we're used to, then he or she cannot possibly find God. But all who truly seek him find him.

"If you look for me wholeheartedly, you will find me. I will be found by you," says the LORD. JEREMIAH 29:13-14

9

This is my real country! I belong here. . . . The reason why we loved the old Narnia is that it sometimes looked a little like this. Bree-hee-hee! Come further up, come further in! CHAP. 15, P. 171

"Further up and further in" is the constant refrain in the last chapters of *The Last Battle*. With all the amazing sights and sounds that Lucy, Digory, and the others see at every turn, you would think that they would linger and really admire the wonders of the new world. But in this declaration, made by the unicorn, we see why they do not linger: this is the real country. A sense of ownership is conveyed here. They are not merely to be spectators or tourists in the new world but instead have come home. They have always belonged here. The old world had only hints of the true sense of ownership that now overwhelms them. They want to go farther, to take possession of it, to discover the things they had longed for their whole lives but of which they had caught only glimpses.

With the descriptions of heaven as a city of gold with jeweled gates, perhaps it seems unreachable or one to which we find it difficult to relate. But as Lewis describes "the real country," we start to understand that heaven is really only the continuation of a journey started here on earth.

It is tempting to find a comfortable spot here on earth and just camp out. Yet as with Abraham, there is a call compelling us to go further up and further into our relationship with God. When we are given gifts, even items for which we have long prayed, maybe the call is to surrender them, taking them further up and further into the Kingdom that is coming. We are to stretch and grow, to reach forward to the Kingdom that will be ours.

It was by faith that Abraham obeyed when God called him to leave home and go to another land that God would give him as his inheritance. He went without knowing where he was going. . . . Abraham was confidently looking forward to a city with eternal foundations, a city designed and built by God.

HEBREWS 11:8, 10

10 *The term is over: the holidays have begun. The dream is ended: this is the morning.* CHAP. 16, P. 183

"The dream is ended." What an interesting way Lewis put this as Aslan speaks to the children. The chapter this quote comes from is titled "Farewell to Shadowlands." This is one of Lewis's favorite analogies to the world we live in compared to the reality of God's Kingdom. He refers to Plato's vision of chained prisoners in a cave who saw reality only as shadows created from firelight. The world they lived in was really the dream world, but when they dared to climb up to the sunlight, they also found the sun unbearable and would have to climb back down and be content with trying to describe what they saw above.

At this point in the story, Lucy, Peter, and Edmund learn that they died in a railway accident and can remain forever with Aslan. They never have to journey through a wardrobe again. They are home at last.

Our time on this earth is in some way a state of dream existence. We are fettered to the chains of our earthly nature and cannot see much beyond what is reflected to us in our culture. But once in a while, when we get a glimpse of the true sunlight, we remember that we were created to someday be completely content and able to walk in the glorious reality of heaven. This was God's original intent for us; this is the state for which we are being prepared. In his Kingdom, there are no more tears of sorrow; we will never be returned to the grind of cave life. For that is when the true holidays will begin, the holidays that have no end.

He will wipe every tear from their eyes, and there will be no more death or sorrow or crying or pain. All these things are gone forever. REVELATION 21:4

Conclusion

T. S. ELIOT WROTE that "to make an end is to make a beginning" and "the end is where we start from."[1] Our hope is that these reflections have given you a new starting point for thinking and meditating on God, his creation, and the life he has given us. As Lewis saw, there is much to relish in what is and what is to come, even in the midst of suffering. Reading of this kind is not escapist. It is a preparation for re-engagement of life at a deeper level and with renewed purpose.

These reflections should also be the prelude to reading all over again. Lewis defined good books as those worth reading many times and good readers as those who read books more than once. If this volume serves as an appetizer to a banquet of reading in Lewis and, further, in the Bible itself, we have met one major goal. There are many other subjects in Lewis that are only hinted at in this collection of meditations. If you have received encouragement to embrace a pilgrimage—that is, a process—toward Christlikeness, if you have journeyed a little deeper into the Christian faith, if you have caught a better look at some of the many facets of the Christian life, we rejoice with you because the reading and the writing have done that for us. We have also found that a great author like C. S. Lewis, with broad interests and deep reading, can take us many other places as we follow his lead in our reading discipline.

In these meditations, the focus has been varied. It has ranged from the comfortable and familiar favorites to a few representing Lewis's professional and scholarly interests. But in each chapter, the aim is to send us back to our everyday world and see it with new eyes. Most readers will have read the Narnia books and seen some of the movies based on them. The gift of these books, perhaps especially for adult readers, is to re-enchant both the physical and the spiritual world we live in. As the poet Shelley (echoing Coleridge) said of inspired writing, it can strip "the veil of familiarity from the world" to awaken "sleeping beauty."[2]

As Lewis knew, the desire to make meaning of what we see and experience is part of being human. We organize study groups, read and write, compose music and art—all to reach for understanding and expression. We hope that some of these reflections have deepened the connections between Lewis's stories and the broader reality they connect to, particularly biblical truths. We have also journeyed into the imaginative world beyond the Shadowlands, as Lewis calls this world. We have glimpsed eternal destinies and been challenged to choose between them. We have seen that our day-to-day lives are pregnant with eternity and that the folks next door and on the job are not so ordinary after all. We have learned, as Lewis asserts in "Christianity and Culture," that there is no neutral place in the cosmos and no unimportant time.[3] To return to Eliot,

> We shall not cease from exploration
> And the end of all our exploring
> Will be to arrive where we started
> And know the place for the first time.[4]

We have also journeyed further into ourselves. We have seen our worst (and how much worse we could get) and discovered that we are still not beyond hope or redemption or God's love. We have journeyed into the possibilities of holiness and found it the last thing from dull. Holiness and goodness are at the center of human history as guided by unfailing Providence and what will be preserved in the "new Narnia." Even Jadis, Shift, and Frost and Wither—yes, and Screwtape—play their parts under the omniscient eye and omnipotent hand of God. All will play their part in the drama that reveals God's glory, whether as sons and daughters or inadvertent servants. When Christ returns—or, in Narnian terms, when Aslan roars for the last time—it will be the "world's last night" and the beginning of eternity. Every knee will bow, all will know who they really are, and we will see the pattern from the top side of the tapestry. When we are face-to-face with Wisdom himself, we will know that to obey is better than to understand, that love engulfs duty. In helping us to glimpse that wisdom now, Lewis has given us a great and enduring gift.

And this is only the beginning. Many of us have followed an interest in something Lewis wrote about and pursued it with a growing passion for the learning that is evident everywhere in his writing. After you finish reading everything Lewis wrote, you can set out to read everything Lewis read—and that's a life's work! Above all, may you be encouraged by this journey to read and so to draw strength from the Word of God, which is the very backbone of the books Lewis wrote and the life he lived. But the ultimate goal is not even to be a better reader of the Bible: it is to be a better follower of Jesus. Lewis did not want disciples. He would say of Christ as John the Baptist did, "He must become greater and greater, and I must become less and less" (John 3:30).

Bibliography

All C. S. Lewis works cited are listed below; endnote sources and permissions information follow.

ALPHABETICAL LISTING OF WORKS CITED

The Abolition of Man: Or, Reflections on Education with Special Reference to the Teaching of English in the Upper Forms of Schools (San Francisco: Harper Collins, 1947, 2001).

The Discarded Image: An Introduction to Medieval and Renaissance Literature (Cambridge: Cambridge University Press, 1964, 1974).

Dymer in Narrative Poems, Walter Hooper, ed. (San Diego: Harvest/Harcourt Brace Jovanovich, 1979).

An Experiment in Criticism (Cambridge: Cambridge University Press, 1961).

From the introduction: "Fairy Stories" in *Of Other Worlds* (London: Geoffrey Bles, 1966), p. 37.

The Great Divorce in *The Best of C. S. Lewis*, *Christianity Today* Edition (New York: The Iversen Associates/Macmillan, 1945, 1969).

A Grief Observed, with an introduction by Walter Hooper (New York: HarperCollins Publishers, 1961, 1966).

"Historicism," in *The Collected Works of C. S Lewis* (New York: Inspirational Press, 1950, 1996).

The Horse and His Boy (New York: HarperCollins Publishers, 1954, 1982).

The Last Battle (New York: Macmillan Publishing Company, Inc., 1956).

Letters to Malcolm: Chiefly on Prayer (London: Geoffrey Bles Ltd., 1964, 1991).

The Lion, the Witch and the Wardrobe (New York: Collier Books, 1950, 1970, 1978).

The Magician's Nephew (New York: HarperCollins Publishers, 1955, 1983).

Out of the Silent Planet (New York: Scribner/Simon & Schuster, 1938).

Perelandra (New York: Scribner/Simon & Schuster, 2003); copyright renewed 1972 by Alfred Cecil Harwood and Arthur Owen Barfield as executors of C. S. Lewis.

The Pilgrim's Regress: An Allegorical Apology for Christianity Reason and Romanticism (Grand Rapids, MI: William B. Eerdmans, 1933, 1943, 1981).

A Preface to Paradise Lost, Being the Ballard Matthews Lectures Delivered at University College, North Wales, 1941, revised and enlarged (London: Oxford University Press, 1942, 1961).

Prince Caspian (New York: HarperCollins Publishers, 1951).

The Screwtape Letters (New York: Bantam Books, 1982).

The Silver Chair (New York: Macmillan Publishing Company, Inc., 1953).

Studies in Words (Cambridge: Cambridge University Press, 1960, 1967).

Surprised by Joy: The Shape of My Early Life (New York: Harcourt Brace, 1956).

That Hideous Strength: A Modern Fairy-tale for Grown-ups, reprint (New York: Scribner/Simon and Schuster, 1945, 1946, 1973, 1974, 2003).

Till We Have Faces: A Myth Retold (San Diego: Harvest/Harcourt Brace, 1957, 1984).

The Voyage of the Dawn Treader (New York: Macmillan Publishing Company, 1952).

The Weight of Glory and Other Addresses, with an introduction by Walter Hooper (New York: Simon & Schuster/Touchstone, 1962, 1965, 1975, 1980).

"The World's Last Night" in *The Essential C. S. Lewis*, Lyle W. Dorsett, ed. (New York: Simon & Schuster, 1988); "The World's Last Night" from *The World's Last Night and Other Essays* (New York: Harcourt Brace and Company, 1952).

Notes

CHAPTER 1

1. *Letters from Baron Friedrich von Hügel to a Niece*, edited with an introduction by Gwendolyn Greene (London: J. M. Dent, 1932), p. 74.
2. Guy Boas, *Tennyson and Browning* (London: Thomas Nelson & Sons, 1938), p. 230.
3. Augustine, *Confessions*, Book I, Section 3, The Great Books of the Western World (Chicago: Encyclopedia Britannica, Robert Maynard Hutchins, Editor in Chief, 1952), vol. 18, p. 2.
4. See book of Acts, chapters 6 and 7.
5. G. K. Chesterton, *Orthodoxy* (Colorado Springs: Harold Shaw Publishers, 1994, 2001), p. 64.
6. From "Meditation XVII," *Devotions upon Emergent Occasions* (John Donne, 1624).

CHAPTER 2

1. *Letters from Baron Friedrich von Hügel to a Niece*, edited with an introduction by Gwendolyn Greene (London: J. M. Dent, 1932), p. 74.
2. Blaise Pascal, *Pensées*, W. F. Trotter, trans. (New York: Dover Philosophical Classics, 2003), no. 484, p. 134.

CHAPTER 3

1. *George Macdonald Anthology*, with an Introduction by C. S. Lewis (London: Geoffrey Bles, 1946).
2. *Institues of the Christian Religion* (John Calvin), Book I.

CHAPTER 4

1. From "Meditation XVII," *Devotions upon Emergent Occasions* (John Donne, 1624).

CHAPTER 5

1. Frederick Buechner, *Wishful Thinking: A Seeker's ABC* (San Francisco: HarperOne, 1993), p. 20.

CHAPTER 6

1. Michael Ward, *Planet Narnia* (Oxford University Press USA, 2008), p. 132.

CHAPTER 8

1. Carroll Kilpatrick, "Nixon Tells Editors, 'I'm Not a Crook,'" *Washington Post*, 18 November 1973.

CHAPTER 14

1. James Boswell, *The Life of Samuel Johnson*, quoted in *Samuel Johnson* by Walter Jackson Bate (New York: Harcourt Brace Jovanovich, 1977), p. 535.

GOING DEEPER INTRO

1. Euripides, *Alcesti* in *The Plays of Euripides*, Edward Philip Coleridge & Frederick Apthorp Paley, trans. (New York: Macmillan, 1906), p. 149.

CONCLUSION

1. T. S. Eliot, *The Four Quartets*, "Little Gidding" (lines 215–216), quoted in Stephen Greenblatt, ed. *The Norton Anthology of English Literature*, eighth ed., *The Major Authors* (New York: Norton, 2006), p. 2638.
2. Percy Bysshe Shelley in "A Defence of Poetry," Donald Reiman and Neil Fraistat, eds. *Shelley's Poetry and Prose*, second ed. (New York: Norton, 2002), p. 533.
3. C. S. Lewis, "Christianity and Culture," *Christian Reflections*, Walter Hooper, ed. (Grand Rapids, MI: Eerdmans, 1980), p. 33.
4. Eliot, "Little Gidding," lines X–X.

Permissions

The extracts in this book that were written by C. S. Lewis have been used by permission.

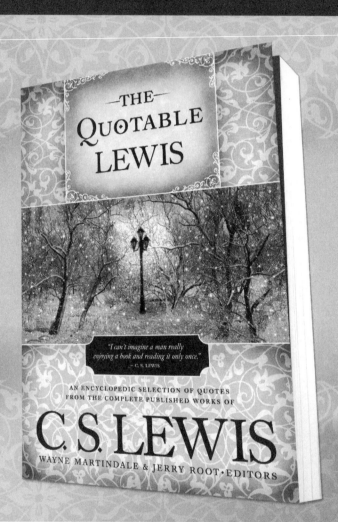